The Women's Movement Agenda for the '80s

Timely Reports to Keep
Journalists, Scholars and the Public
Abreast of Developing Issues, Events and Trends

Editorial Research Reports
Published by Congressional Quarterly Inc.
1414 22nd Street, N.W.
Washington, D.C. 20037

About the Cover

The cover was designed by Staff Artist Robert Redding

PRINTED IN THE UNITED STATES OF AMERICA
October 1981

Editor, Hoyt Gimlin
Managing Editor, Sandra Stencel
Editorial Assistants, Joseph Kessler, Nancy Blanpied

Production Manager, I. D. Fuller
Assistant Production Manager, Maceo Mayo

Library of Congress Cataloging in Publication Data
Main entry under title:

Editorial research reports on the women's movement, agenda for the '80s.

    Bibliography: p.
    Includes index.

    1. Feminism — United States — Addresses, essays, lectures. 2. Women's rights — United States — Addresses, essays, lectures. I. Editorial Research reports. II. Congressional Quarterly, inc. III. Title: Women's movement, agenda for the '80s.

HQ1426.E363   305.4'2'0973   81-17277
ISBN 0-87187-223-4   AACR2

Contents

Foreword

Over the past two decades, women experienced significant changes in their role and status in the workplace, society and home. Americans became more conscious of problems women face, and government-sponsored affirmative action programs lent support to women's strivings toward equality. Increasing numbers of women entered the labor force, many in higher paying and more responsible positions. With over half of all wives working, men assumed more responsibilities for child care and household chores.

Yet as the 1980s begin, there are signs of a backlash against the victories — and the still unachieved goals — of the women's movement. The nation appears to have turned more conservative and less receptive to social change. Anti-abortion groups have gained increased influence among members of Congress and in the White House. Affirmative action for better jobs and higher pay is increasingly under attack. Perhaps most disconcerting of all to women's rights advocates, the Equal Rights Amendment to the Constitution appears dead in the water. No state has ratified the amendment since Indiana in 1977. With the ratification deadline set for June 30, 1982, approval by state legislatures is likely to top the agenda of feminists during the early months of the year. But other issues will receive attention whether the amendment lives or dies.

Closing the wage gap between the sexes is high on the list. Since the mid-1960s the campaign for pay equity has focused primarily on moving women into non-traditional occupations and encouraging employers to promote women with managerial potential. Now many women believe this is not enough. They are less concerned about moving women out of existing jobs and more concerned with getting traditional women's jobs re-evaluated according to their "real worth." The goal is not just equal pay for equal work but "equal pay for work of comparable value."

With more and more families dependent on the incomes of both spouses, another goal is to convince employers to adopt policies that would make it easier for working parents to care for their children. These include flexible work schedules, more part-time employment opportunities, sick leave for parents when children are ill, and paternity as well as maternity leave.

Women 65 and older are the fastest growing segment of the population — they are also the poorest. Tackling the economic problems of older women will be a major goal of the women's movement in the years ahead. Among the issues to be addressed are employment discrimination against older women and inequities in the Social Security system relating to widows, homemakers and working women.

The 10 reports included in this book discuss these and other issues that will affect the direction of the women's movement in the 1980s.

October 1981
Washington, D.C.

Sandra Stencel
Managing Editor

EQUAL PAY FIGHT

by

Sandra Stencel

Mar. 20
1 9 8 1

Editor's Note: A June 8, 1981, ruling by the U.S. Supreme Court paved the way for new lawsuits by women facing pay discrimination. The court ruled in the case of *Washington County, Ore. v. Gunther*, discussed on p. 16, that women may file suit under the 1964 Civil Rights Act without having to prove they were denied "equal pay for equal work" as forbidden by the 1963 Equal Pay Act. All that is necessary, the court indicated, is for a woman to show that her sex was used against her in the determination of her pay scale. The justices specifically declined to address the argument, discussed on p. 8, that women are entitled to the same pay as men when their jobs, however different, are of "comparable worth" to society. That question was not raised by the Gunther case, the court majority said.

Persistent discrimination and not free market forces alone account for much of the pay differentials between men and women, according to a report released Sept. 1, 1981, by the National Research Council of the National Academy of Sciences. The report said that the concept of comparable worth "merits consideration" by companies seeking to eliminate such discrimination by revising job-evaluation systems *(see p. 17)*.

Comparable worth was a crucial issue in a nine-day public employee strike in San Jose, Calif. The strike ended July 14, 1981, with an agreement to bring women's pay up to men's pay for comparable work. A two-year, $5 million contract agreed upon by the city and striking employees contained $1.5 million to correct the pay disparities.

EQUAL PAY FIGHT

GREEN and white buttons marked "59¢" have been much in evidence at women's-rights gatherings in recent years. The buttons are part of a campaign begun by the National Organization for Women (NOW) to call attention to the fact that a woman, on average, makes only 59 cents for every dollar earned by a man. Women working full time, year-round in 1979, the latest year for which statistics are available, had median annual earnings of $10,168 compared to $17,062 for full-time male workers. The difference between men's and women's pay is actually wider today than it was in 1963 — the year the federal Equal Pay Act was enacted *(see p. 13)*. Women earn substantially less than men at the same level of education. In fact, the average woman college graduate earns less than the average male high school dropout.

Many factors are cited to explain the persistent wage gap between the sexes. The significant rise in the number and proportion of women who work *(see chart, p. 5)* has meant more women in entry-level jobs. Because of their family responsibilities many women prefer jobs that require little or no overtime. In addition, women generally have fewer years of work experience than men. But by far the most important factor in women's lower earnings is their continued concentration in low-paying, low-status jobs.

Although women now comprise 42 percent of the nation's labor force, nearly 80 percent of them are employed in clerical, sales, service, factory or plant jobs. More than a third of all women workers hold clerical jobs, which pay on average less than $10,000 a year.[1] Only 16 percent of the women are classified as professionals and most of them are elementary and secondary school teachers, nurses, health technicians or librarians. Of the 40.4 million women workers in 1979, only 6.4 percent were managers. Of the 56.5 million men employed that year, 14 percent were managers.[2]

A substantial number of women have made inroads into nontraditional, higher-status fields. In 1970, 60 percent of all female professional-technical workers were registered nurses or non-college teachers; by 1979 this proportion had dropped to about

---

[1] According to figures released by the U.S. Census Bureau in the summer of 1980 the average female clerical worker earned $9,158 in 1978.
[2] See "Women in the Executive Suite," *E.R.R.*, 1980 Vol. II, pp. 485-504.

52 percent. During the same period the percentage of all lawyers and judges who were women jumped from 4.7 to 12.4. Nearly 11 percent of all physicians in 1979 were women, up from 8.9 percent in 1970.[3]

But for every woman who moved into a traditionally male-dominated profession, there were thousands who remained in occupations in which more than two-thirds of the work force were female. In 1979, according to the Bureau of Labor Statistics[4], 80.3 percent of all clerical workers were women, as were 70.8 percent of all non-college teachers, 80.9 percent of librarians, 96.8 percent of nurses and 69.5 percent of health technologists and technicians.

Recent news stories have focused attention on men who work in professions long dominated by women *(see box, p. 16)*. But in most cases, the extent of occupational segregation has changed only slightly since the early 1960s, as the following table illustrates:

	Female in 1979	Female in 1975	Female in 1962
Registered nurses	96.8%	97.0%	98.5%
Elementary school teachers	84.3	85.4	86.5
Typists	96.7	96.6	94.8
Telephone operators	91.7	93.3	96.3
Secretaries	99.1	99.1	98.5
Hairdressers	89.2	90.5	88.1
Waiters and waitresses	89.4	91.1	88.1

"Despite recent changes in the structure of the labor force, and women's increasing attachment to their jobs, historical patterns concerning 'men's jobs' and 'women's jobs' still persist," declared a report issued in 1979 by the Women's Bureau of the Department of Labor. "Although this pattern has become less rigid in recent years, such sex stereotyping still seems to restrict or discourage women, especially older women, from entering higher-paying traditionally male occupations."[5]

Influences on Female Employment Choices

Occupational segregation stems from many sources — discrimination, cultural conditioning and the personal desires of women themselves. The jobs women traditionally have held are frequently related to the work they performed in the home —

[3] See U.S. Department of Labor, Bureau of Labor Statistics, "Perspectives on Working Women: A Databook," October 1980, pp. 1, 10.

[4] U.S. Department of Labor, Bureau of Labor Statistics, "Employment and Earnings," January 1980, Vol. 27, No. 1.

[5] Women's Bureau, U.S. Department of Labor, "The Earnings Gap Between Women and Men," 1979, p. 2.

Women in the Work Force

Year	Number (add 000)	Percentage of Adult Female Population*
1947	16,683	31.8
1951	19,054	34.7
1956	21,495	36.9
1961	23,838	38.1
1966	27,333	40.3
1971	32,132	43.4
1976	38,520	47.4
1977	39,952	48.4
1978	41,878	50.0
1979	43,391	51.0
1980	44,574	51.6

*Ages 16 and older

Source: U.S. Department of Labor

teaching children and young adults, nursing the sick, preparing food. According to Dr. Nancy Smith Barrett, an economics professor at American University in Washington, D.C., women have been conditioned to believe that these are the only "proper" jobs.[6]

Until the late 1960s, a significant factor in the male-female segregation of jobs was related to state laws that regulated what women could or could not do in the workplace. Paradoxically, many of those state laws were enacted originally to protect women in such matters as long hours, night work and physically difficult work. State laws protecting women workers were held unlawful under the sex-discrimination ban in Title VII of the Civil Rights Act of 1964 (see p. 14).

During the period in which women were entering the job market in large numbers, jobs in retail sales and the service industries — including health care, teaching, and food service[7] — were opening up faster than in other occupations. According to Department of Labor figures, services and retail trade provided more than 70 percent of all new jobs created between 1973 and the summer of 1980.[8]

Not surprisingly, many women entering the job market in the 1970s were drawn to these jobs. While women accounted for 41 percent of the labor force in 1979, they held 56 percent of the

[6] See Nancy S. Barrett, *The Theory of Discrimination Revisited* (1975), p. 17.
[7] See "Fast Food: U.S. Growth Industry," *E.R.R.*, 1978 Vol. II, pp. 905-924.
[8] For a further account of women's fast entry into those fields, see Emma Rothschild, "Reagan and the Real America," *The New York Review of Books*, Feb. 5, 1981, p. 12.

jobs in eating and drinking places, 43 percent in business services and 81 percent in health services. Another factor contributing to the concentration of women in these occupations is that part-time employment is more obtainable there than elsewhere. About 28.2 percent of all working women held part-time jobs in 1980, according to the Department of Labor.

The movement of women into higher paying jobs continues to be hindered by their educational backgrounds. In 1979, for the first time, there were more women than men enrolled in American colleges and universities. But according to a recent study, most degrees awarded to women are in six fields where their interest has long been concentrated — education, English and journalism, fine and applied arts, foreign languages and literature, nursing, and library science. The study, conducted by Pearl M. Kamer, the chief economist for the Long Island Regional Planning Board, concludes that if women "continue to cling to traditional, female-intensive professions," the gap between their earnings and those of male college graduates will remain wide. What is needed, she said, is a "major push to guide women into faster-growing 'non-traditional' professions such as mathematics, economics, business and the physical sciences."[9]

The pay gap does not disappear when women go into predominantly male professions. Overall, women in managerial and administrative jobs earn only 60 percent as much as their male colleagues do. For women engineers the figure is 86 percent, and for full-time women college professors it is 71 percent. Women earn less than men even in traditionally female occupations. Among high school and elementary teachers, it is 81 percent. And for clerical jobs the ratio drops to 60 percent.

Family Responsibilities and Women's Jobs

Some observers have argued that women earn less money because they are apt to leave the labor force. Employers may reason that men merit higher salaries or preference in hiring because they will not quit for marriage and child rearing; that men can give more time and effort to the job because they have fewer domestic responsibilities; that they are more valuable as employees because of their greater mobility; or that they need more money to support their families. Because they see women as temporary fixtures in the labor force many employers tend to shuttle women into jobs where there is little opportunity for advancement.

"The threat of discontinuity in a woman's work life is perhaps the greatest single barrier to higher wages for young women," Juanita Kreps wrote a decade ago, before she became secretary of commerce. She added:

9 Quoted in *The New York Times,* May 11, 1980.

The period of heaviest domestic responsibility occurs fairly early in a woman's work life, when she is likely to be forced to make some quite long-range decisions: whether to acquire further job training, or additional formal education; how many children she will have; whether to continue working, at least part-time, during the child-bearing period. . . . Her immediate job choice is dictated in large measure by the time constraint imposed in the short-run, and this choice in turn directs her subsequent career development.[10]

The relationship between women's earnings and their domestic responsibilities was discussed in a recent article by Lester C. Thurow, author of the widely publicized book *Zero-Sum Society* (1980). Thurow points out that "the decade between [ages] 25 and 35 is when . . . lawyers become partners in the good firms, when business managers make it onto the 'fast track,' when academics get tenure at good universities, and when blue-collar workers find the job opportunities that will lead to training opportunities and the skills that will generate high earnings." But it "is precisely the decade when women are most apt to leave the labor force or become part-time workers to have children." Thurow proposes two solutions:

Families where women wish to have successful careers, compete with men, and achieve the same earnings should alter their family plans and have their children either before 25 or after 35. Or society can attempt to alter the existing promotion system so that there is a longer time period in which both men and women can attempt to successfully enter the labor force.

"Without some combination of these two factors," he concludes, "a substantial fraction of the male-female earnings differentials are apt to persist for the next 40 years, even if discrimination against women is eliminated."[11]

Length and continuity of work experience certainly explain a large part of the wage gap. But many studies have indicated that large differences persist even when years of service, job classification, years of school completed and other variables are held constant. One explanation was offered by Patricia Cayo Sexton in her Department of Labor monograph on "Women and Work." "Women's earnings suffer because they remain committed, steady, able workers, even when wage and promotional incentives are low. . . ," she wrote. "The problem, then, is not that women are less committed workers than men, but that they may be too committed and undemanding, and therefore less able to increase their compensation."[12]

---

[10] Juanita Kreps, *Sex in the Marketplace: American Women at Work* (1971), pp. 43-44.

[11] Writing in *The New York Times*, March 8, 1981. Thurow is professor of economics and management at Massachusetts Institute of Technology.

[12] Department of Labor, "Women and Work," 1977 reprint, pp. 66-67.

Demand for Pay Equity

S INCE the mid-1960s the campaign to end sex segregation on the job has focused primarily on moving women into non-traditional occupations and encouraging employers to promote women with managerial potential. Attempts to open up employment opportunities for women are still considered important. But many women now believe that this affirmative action approach is not enough. They say women do not necessarily gravitate toward dead-end jobs, but rather that these positions are considered low-status and are usually low-paying because they are held primarily by women.

Those who support this view are less concerned about getting women out of the jobs they currently hold and more concerned with getting traditional women's jobs re-evaluated according to their "real worth." What they want is not just equal pay for equal work, as is mandated by the 1963 law, but "equal pay for work of comparable value."

"The jobs that women do are often complicated and highly skilled," said Eleanor Smeal, president of the National Organization for Women. "A secretary needs training on business machines, a command of the English language, discretion, the ability to make decisions. We have to ask why she is paid on the lower end of the scale. . . . Most bus drivers . . . get paid more than a licensed practical nurse. Yet they are both jobs with physical labor, life-and-death decisions, and both take special training."[13]

Eleanor Holmes Norton, who resigned Feb. 21 as head of the Equal Employment Opportunity Commission, has said that the practice of paying women less than men for jobs that require similar skill, responsibility and effort is "comparable to the separate-but-equal laws that used to apply to blacks." Addressing the first national "Conference on Pay Equity," held Oct. 24, 1979, in Washington, D.C., Norton said comparable pay for comparable work would be the "issue of the Eighties for women in the labor force."[14]

So far supporters have had only limited success in winning acceptance for the comparable worth principle in the courts. The labor movement has been more receptive. The Coalition of Labor Union Women, which was founded in 1974 and now has

[13] Quoted by Ellen Goodman in a column in *The Washington Post*, May 21, 1977.
[14] The conference was sponsored by the Committee on Pay Equity, a national coalition of labor, women's, public interest, legal, government and education organizations founded in June 1979. The conference proceedings are contained in the "Manual on Pay Equity," edited by Joy Ann Grune and published in May 1980 by the Conference on Alternative State and Local Policies, 2000 Florida Ave., N.W., Washington, D.C. 20009. Norton has accepted a position as a senior fellow at the Urban Institute in Washington, D.C.

8

more than 8,000 members representing 65 international unions, has made comparable worth "a top priority." The AFL-CIO endorsed the principle at its November 1979 convention and urged individual unions to adopt the concept "in organizing and in negotiating collective bargaining agreements." The International Union of Electrical, Radio and Machine Workers, an AFL-CIO affiliate, has been a pioneer in trying to force employers to upgrade the pay of women's jobs *(see p. 16)*. According to the union's general counsel, Winn Newman, the IUE has been filing comparable worth lawsuits on behalf of its women members since at least 1969.[15]

Opposition From the Business Community

Although many people still have not heard of the comparable worth concept, the business community takes the issue very seriously. *Business Week* magazine said, "Comparable worth may be the civil rights issue of the 1980s and it could cost employers billions in payroll dollars." An earlier article in *Fortune* magazine, by Lee Smith, said the concept "has ominous implications for all employers, many employees and even the future course of the U.S. economy." It said that equal pay for work of equal value is a "fallacious notion that apples are equal to oranges and that prices for both should be the same, even if that means overriding the law of supply and demand."[16]

Opponents of the comparable worth concept argue that raising salaries to comparable levels would be inflationary and that the free marketplace should determine the level of wages. They contend that the generally lower wage rates paid to women in certain jobs stem from social, cultural and economic forces beyond the control of particular employers, and, as such, are beyond the intended reach of federal anti-discrimination laws. They also argue that there is no existing method by which the worth or value of dissimilar jobs can be compared with legal certainty.

Leading the opposition is a Washington, D.C., lobbying group called the Equal Employment Advisory Council, which was formed in 1976 to represent the employer position in equal employment opportunity issues. In addition to filing friend-of-the-court briefs and commenting on proposed regulations and legislation, the council recently published a book on the subject, *Comparable Worth: Issues and Alternatives* (1980). The book features articles by seven job evaluation experts who argue that the issue is ill-defined, that the wage gap has little to do with

[15] More than a million women are employed in the electrical equipment manufacturing industry in the United States, representing 40 percent of the industry's work force. For a summary of IUE activities in the comparable worth area, see "Manual on Pay Equity," pp. 79-86 and 156-164.

[16] Lee Smith, "The EEOC's Bold Foray Into Job Evaluation," *Fortune,* Sept. 11, 1978, p. 58. The *Business Week* article appeared in the issue of Nov. 10, 1980, p. 102.

The Wage Gap, 1955-1979

Year	Median earnings* Women	Men	Earnings gap in dollars	Women's earnings as % of men's
1979	$10,168	$17,062	$6,894	59.5
1978	9,350	15,730	6,380	59.4
1977	8,618	14,626	6,008	58.9
1976	8,099	13,455	5,356	60.2
1975	7,504	12,758	5,254	58.8
1970	5,323	8,966	3,643	59.4
1965	3,823	6,375	2,552	60.0
1960	3,293	5,417	2,124	60.8
1955	2,719	4,252	1,533	63.9

* Of full-time, year-round workers

Source: U.S. Department of Labor, Women's Bureau

discrimination and that the answer is not arbitrary realignment of pay but "the increased upward mobility of women."[17]

Opponents stress the economic consequences that the application of the comparable worth concept would have on the economy. U.S. District Court Judge Fred Winner, who in April 1978 upheld the right of the city and county of Denver to pay tree trimmers, sign painters and other maintenance personnel more than hospital nurses *(see p. 17)*, said the comparable worth concept was "pregnant with the possibility of disrupting the entire economic system of the United States." The article in *Fortune* estimated the cost of equalizing the pay for men and women at $150 billion a year.

Supporters of the comparable worth theory admit that the economic ramifications would be enormous. But according to Eleanor Holmes Norton, "the economic issue is used as a scare tactic. I can't imagine that we would effect a remedy that all at once would change the wage system." Rather, she said, the impact probably would be more gradual.[18]

Responding to "market forces arguments," a consultant to the Equal Employment Opportunity Commission pointed out that "the influence of discrimination on wage structures is well-recognized by virtually all modern economists." Ruth Blumrosen, the consultant, said: "They have concluded that the classical economic model, which assumed that the market reflected only 'pure' competitive factors, is simply inadequate to explain the wage setting process." She said community wage rates, on which employers frequently base their pay schedules,

---

[17] The book was financed by a grant from The Business Roundtable; its members are the chief executive officers of 200 large corporations.

[18] Quoted in *The Washington Post*, Nov. 13, 1979.

are a product in part of discriminatory practices by other employers.[19]

Attempts to Organize Clerical Workers

In the recent movie "Nine to Five" three oppressed office workers — played by Jane Fonda, Lily Tomlin and Dolly Parton — kidnap their ogre of a boss and rebuild their office into a model workplace (with day care services, job sharing, flexible hours, etc.) while maintaining the illusion that their boss is still at his desk. Real life office workers have found a simpler way to improve their work environment and their wages. They are organizing unions or more informal employee associations to bargain with employers for better working conditions and higher salaries.

The movement to organize clerical workers is part of a large campaign to organize women workers. Currently only 17.2 percent of all working women belong to unions or employee associations. According to Nancy D. Perlman, executive director of the Center for Women in Government, and Bruce J. Ennis, legal director of the American Civil Liberties Union, unionization is "the most successful pay equity strategy to date." They report that organized women workers earn 20-26 percent more than non-union women in white-collar jobs and 20-46 percent more in blue-collar jobs.[20]

Until recently most attempts to organize clerical workers came from outside the traditional union framework. Groups with names like "Women Employed" and "9-to-5" organized drives to upgrade salaries and promotion opportunities in banks, insurance companies, law firms, publishing houses, brokerage houses and universities. Working Women, which has chapters in 13 cities and some 10,000 members across the country, was responsible for winning over $1 million in back pay for women and minority employees in Boston's publishing industry and has instigated legal action to get back-pay awards from four Cleveland banks. The group also has helped office workers win cost-of-living pay increases, job posting requirements, promotions and access to training programs from some 50 companies. Its efforts to increase respect for office workers through its annual National Secretaries Week activities have gained national attention.

The possibilities of enlisting the aid of independent women's groups, which can reach many women who might initially be

---

[19] Writing in *The Michigan Journal of Law Reform*, spring 1979, quoted in "Manual on Pay Equity," p. 39.
[20] Nancy D. Perlman and Bruce J. Ennis, "Preliminary Memorandum on Pay Equity: Achieving Equal Pay for Work of Comparable Value," Center for Women in Government, April 1980, p. 22.

turned off by a traditional union, have recently been recognized by union officials. On March 3, the 650,000-member Service Employees International Union, the seventh largest in the AFL-CIO, announced that it was joining forces with Working Women in a nationwide campaign to organize clerical workers. Secretarial and office workers will be organized for membership in a new national local union called District 925 — a play on "9-to-5." Karen Nussbaum, executive director of Working Women, will serve as an acting president of District 925, which will be an affiliate of the service employees union.

A separate recruitment effort for female clerical workers was announced recently by the AFL-CIO's Industrial Union Department and the Coalition of Labor Union Women. The two groups are developing a program to be tried in some medium-sized U.S. city where a significant portion of plant and hospital workers are women. So far, the United Steel Workers and the Amalgamated Clothing Workers have agreed to participate in the organizing drive. The Coalition of Labor Union Women has been in the vanguard of the movement to organize working women and to get more women into union leadership positions.

Government Initiatives

F EDERAL efforts to end the traditional low-wage status of women can be traced back at least to World War II. As millions of men went into uniform, the government embarked on an all-out effort to encourage women to enter the labor force.[21] "The War Manpower Commission itself attempted to facilitate the process by issuing guidelines designed to end sex discrimination," historian William Henry Chafe has recounted. Employers were told to hire and train women "on a basis of equality with men," to "remove all barriers to the employment of women in any occupation for which they are or can be fitted," and to use "every method available" to ensure women's complete acceptance.[22]

Those who supported a uniform pay scale for men and women were given a boost in September 1942 when the National War Labor Board (NWLB) endorsed the principle of equal pay "for female employees who in comparable jobs produce work of the same quantity and quality as that performed by men." The nation had an obligation, the board declared, "to provide the

---

[21] During the war years women went into industry as never before, accounting for 36 percent of the nation's labor force in 1945, up from 25 percent in 1940.
[22] William Henry Chafe, *The American Woman: Her Changing Social, Economic and Political Roles, 1920-1970* (1972), pp. 147-148.

utmost assurance that women will not be subject to discriminatory treatment in their compensation." But according to
Chafe, the board "in a series of subsequent decisions . . . gave
employers a series of loopholes through which they could continue to discriminate in their wage scales."

"The worst form of discrimination against female workers"
was the rate paid for "women's" jobs, Chafe wrote. "At the root
of the disparity was the pervasive assumption that any job
historically filled by women had less intrinsic value than a
comparable position held by men. The premise prevailed even
where 'objective' evaluations showed a woman's occupation to
require more skill than a man's. . . . [I]t was presumed that
women deserved less pay than men."

Employers justified the existence of separate job categories for
women and the differential in wages paid to men and women by
pointing to long-held assumptions about women's work patterns. For example, a 1939 Westinghouse wage manual in-
structed plant officials to pay women less than men "because of
the more transient character of the service of the former, the
relative shortness of their activity in industry, the differences in
environment required, the extra services that must be provided,
overtime limitations, extra help needed for the occasional heavy
work, and the general sociological factors not requiring discus-
sion herein."

Long Struggle for Equal Pay Legislation

Congressional legislation incorporating the equal-pay-for-
equal-work concept was considered several times in the postwar
era and won the backing of the Truman, Eisenhower and Kennedy administrations. The equal pay bills usually specified that
the wage scale should be adjusted upward for women rather
than downward for men.

These bills were consistently backed by organized labor,
which saw in them a way to prevent business from undermining
general wage scales by hiring low-wage women workers. Almost
the only opposition was voiced by business organizations, nota-
bly the National Association of Manufacturers and the U.S.
Chamber of Commerce. Those organizations approved the equal
pay principle but opposed action by Congress to require its
observance. They contended that an army of bureaucrats would
descend upon business. Some business groups also complained
of the cost involved.

Despite business opposition, Congress in 1963 passed the federal Equal Pay Act. It required all employers subject to the Fair
Labor Standards Act to provide equal pay for men and women
performing similar work. Differences in wages based on senior-

ity, merit and piecework were permitted. Employers were forbidden to reduce the wages of any employee in order to comply. In 1972, coverage of this act was extended to executives, administrators and professionals, including all employees of private and public educational institutions.[23]

The courts have held that jobs do not have to be identical, only "substantially equal," for the Equal Pay Act to apply. In a well-publicized case involving the Corning Glass Works, the U.S. Supreme Court ruled in 1974 that shift differences (with men working at night and women working during the day) did not make the working conditions of the men and women dissimilar and thus would not justify a higher wage for the men.[24]

Title VII, the EEOC and Eleanor Norton

A milestone in equal employment opportunity for women was reached with the passage of the Civil Rights Act of 1964. Title VII of that act prohibited discrimination based on sex — as well as race, religion and national origin — in hiring or firing, wages and salaries, promotions or any terms, conditions or privileges of employment. Exceptions were permitted only when sex was a bona fide occupational qualification, as in the case of an actor or a wet nurse.

Title VII is administered by the Equal Employment Opportunity Commission, whose five members are appointed by the president. Initially, the powers of the EEOC were limited largely to investigation and conciliation, but Congress amended the act in 1972 to let the agency go directly to court to enforce the law. The 1972 amendments also provided that discrimination charges could be filed by organizations on behalf of aggrieved individuals, as well as by employees and job applicants themselves. In July 1979 the EEOC took on the added tasks of enforcing the Equal Pay Act and the Age Discrimination Act.

Eleanor Holmes Norton, who was named head of the commission in 1977, frequently spoke out on the issue of equal pay for work of comparable value. "Issues as large as this need government participation and more government leadership if they are to have a prayer of succeeding," she told the October 1979 Conference on Pay Equity. In addition to filing friend-of-the-court briefs in several comparable worth cases, the commission in September 1977 asked the National Academy of Sciences to "determine whether appropriate job measurement procedures exist or can be developed to assess the worth of jobs."

[23] The Fair Labor Standards Act of 1938 established a minimum wage for individuals engaged in interstate commerce or the production of goods for commerce. The law has been amended from time to time to increase the minimum rate and to extend coverage to new groups of employees.
[24] *Corning Glass Works v. Brennan,* 417 U.S. 188 (1974).

In April 1980 the EEOC sponsored hearings in Washington, D.C., on the link between job segregation and wage discrimination. "Because of the magnitude, complexity and stage of development of the issue involved," Norton said in her opening remarks, "these are the most important hearings this commission has had in a decade. Wage discrimination is likely to be one of the central legal and industrial relations issues of the 1980s."

The Department of Labor also has been involved in the comparable worth issue. The department's Women's Bureau is a member of the Committee on Pay Equity and has collected and distributed information on the issue. Donald Elisburg, assistant secretary of labor for employment standards under President Carter, reviewed the department's position on comparable worth in a speech Feb. 4, 1980, before the District of Columbia Bar Association. "We are taking the view that the law does reach the pay equity concept and are studying the possible applications to our compliance effort," he said. The department's Office of Federal Contract Compliance Program is charged with enforcement of executive orders requiring federal contractors to take "affirmative action" to prevent racial or sexual discrimination.[25]

Future of Pay Equity Issue

M ANY believe that the validity of the comparable worth concept ultimately will be decided by the Supreme Court. Because coverage of the Equal Pay Act is limited to equal pay for substantially equal work, most litigation to achieve pay equity between jobs of comparable value has been brought under Title VII of the 1964 Civil Rights Act. "Thus far, litigation has not resulted in recognition of a constitutional right to pay equity and the courts have divided on whether Title VII . . . provides a statutory right to pay equity."[26]

One section of Title VII, commonly known as the Bennett Amendment,[27] exempts compensation claims from Title VII's

[25] In September 1966 President Johnson issued Executive Order 11246 requiring federal contractors "to take affirmative action to ensure applicants are employed, and that employees are treated during employment, without regard to their race, creed, color or national origin." Executive Order 11246 was amended in 1967 to apply also to sexual discrimination.

[26] Nancy D. Perlman and Bruce J. Ennis, *op. cit.*, p. 4.

[27] The Bennett Amendment states: "It shall not be an unlawful employment practice under [Title VII] for any employer to differentiate upon the basis of sex in determining the amount of wages or compensation paid or to be paid to employees of such employer if such differentiation is authorized by the provisions of [the Equal Pay Act]." The amendment was introduced by Sen. Wallace F. Bennett, R-Utah.

> ## Typecasting
>
> A male secretary probably still draws a few stares but — like women executives — it is a sight that is becoming less rare. An Urban Institute study estimates that the number of male secretaries rose 24 percent to 31,000 in 1978, up from 25,000 in 1972. The number of male telephone operators increased 38 percent, while the number of male nurses nearly doubled.
>
> The study attributed the increases to the tightness of the job market. June O'Neill, an official at the institute, also observed that younger men with less rigid views on what constitutes male and female work "may not feel there's such a stigma to working in a female-dominated field."

coverage if the employer's compensation system is "authorized" by the Equal Pay Act. Opponents of the comparable worth concept take the position that unless the situation challenged fits within the narrow Equal Pay Act framework, that is, where a woman is doing virtually the same work as a man for less pay, Title VII does not apply. Supporters take the position that Title VII is much broader than the Equal Pay Act, and covers any form of sex discrimination in wages or compensation.

The Supreme Court on Nov. 3, 1980, agreed to hear a case that could decide the question of whether Title VII is broad enough to cover comparable worth situations. The case, *Gunther v. County of Washington,* stems from a charge brought by matrons at a county jail in Oregon who had been paid less than male guards with similar duties. A federal district judge ruled against them, holding that their claim did not meet the test imposed in the Equal Pay Act and therefore could not be grounds for a Title VII suit.

But the U.S. Court of Appeals for the Ninth Circuit, in San Francisco, took a broader view. In a decision handed down Aug. 16, 1979, the appeals court said that while the suit brought by the matrons did not meet the Equal Pay Act criteria, this did not preclude an opportunity to prove to the satisfaction of a court that pay differentials were the result of sex discrimination.

A similar position was taken last year by the Third Circuit Court of Appeals, in Philadelphia, in the case of *International Union of Electrical, Radio and Machine Workers (IUE) v. Westinghouse Electric Corp.* The IUE brought that case on behalf of women workers at a Westinghouse factory in Trenton, N.J., where, the union contends, a lower wage structure for women was the outgrowth of a blatant double standard of job evaluation dating from 1939 *(see p. 13).* In a 2-1 decision the appeals court reversed the district court and said that the women should have an opportunity to prove in court that they

16

were discriminated against even if the circumstances did not fall within the confines of the Equal Pay Act. The Supreme Court has not yet decided whether to review the Westinghouse case.[28] On Oct. 6, 1980, the court denied review in *Lemons v. City and County of Denver,* the case involving the Denver nurses.

Many women believe that the legal battle to end sex-based discrimination in employment would be helped by ratification of the Equal Rights Amendment.[29] "The current piecemeal approach without a basic and nationwide commitment to eliminating sex discrimination clearly is not workable," NOW President Eleanor Smeal told the Senate Committee on Labor and Human Resources, Jan. 28, 1981. "Ratification of the Equal Rights Amendment is essential to end discriminatory governmental programs and procedures and to close loopholes in existing legislation and regulations. Equally important . . . [it] would require a stricter standard of review for discrimination suits and thereby would provide the climate necessary for more vigorous enforcement of laws, policies and regulations concerning sex discrimination."

Assessments of Job Evaluation Systems

The belief that pay equity can be achieved assumes that a bias-free job evaluation system can be developed to measure the comparable worth of dissimilar jobs. Helen Remick, director of the office of affirmative action at the University of Washington, has done extensive studies of existing job-rating systems, many of which award points for certain skills or responsibilities that are required for a job. She believes that most of these systems are inherently discriminatory — that they tend to award an excessive number of points for work characteristics, such as physical strength, in which men are likely to outperform women.

Many traditionally female jobs require a high degree of motor control, rapid movement with low error rate and responsibilities for human life, as in teaching or nursing. But according to Remick, these assets are generally given few points or ignored altogether.[30] David Thomsen, director of the Compensation Institute in Los Angeles, shares Remick's view. "Job evaluation is the single most effective device by which organizations retain and create discriminatory pay practices," he told the Equal Employment Opportunity Commission last April.

---

[28] A request for review was filed on Nov. 14, 1980. See *The United States Law Week,* Jan. 20, 1981, p. 3519.

[29] No state has ratified the amendment since 1977, when Indiana became the 35th state to do so. With time for ratification running out, and three more states needed, Congress in 1978 extended the ratification deadline to June 30, 1982. See "Equal Rights Fight," *E.R.R.,* 1978 Vol. II, pp. 925-944.

[30] Quoted by Linda Stern in "Equal Pay For Work of Equal Value," *Working Woman* magazine, April 1979, p. 21.

Even those who criticize existing job evaluation systems believe that they can be useful tools in documenting the extent of
wage depression for women. The first study deliberately designed to test for unequal compensation rates between sex segregated jobs was conducted by the state of Washington in 1973-
74. A management consulting firm evaluated 121 state job
classifications according to knowledge and skills required, mental demands, accountability and working conditions. The results
showed that among jobs having the same evaluation points, pay
rates for female-dominated jobs averaged about 80 percent of
those dominated by males. By the time a follow-up study was
released in 1976, women's wages had slipped to 75 percent.[31]

Study by National Academy of Sciences

Opponents of the comparable worth concept maintain that it
is virtually impossible to develop bias-free evaluation systems.
"Developing the perfect, universal job-evaluation system is
somewhat like trying to find all the links on the Great Chain of
Being from archangels to the meanest of creatures, an exercise
that preoccupied ancient and medieval philosophers for centuries," Lee Smith wrote in *Fortune*. According to Harvard
Professor E. Robert Livernash, "there is simply no known technique by which job 'worth' in any intrinsic sense can be
measured."[32]

In 1977 the Equal Employment Opportunity Commission
asked the National Academy of Sciences to study whether objective, bias-free job evaluations exist or can be developed. The
academy's final report and recommendations are not likely to be
published before the fall of 1981. An interim paper published in
June 1979 discussed some features of formal job evaluation
"that render problematic their utility for job worth assessment. . . ." But it said more study was needed before the academy could decide whether "the utility of these procedures . . .
outweighs any shortcomings."[33]

It is still too soon to tell what position the Reagan administration will take on the issue of comparable worth. For one thing, as
of March 18, Reagan still had not named a successor to Eleanor
Holmes Norton as head of the Equal Employment Opportunity
Commission. "It's a little hard to say right now what the Reagan

---

[31] A second follow-up study is scheduled to be released this year. So far, a uniform pay
structure has not been implemented. See Michelle Celarier, "The Paycheck Challenge of
the Eighties — Comparing Job Worth," *Ms.*, March 1981, p. 38, and "Manual on Pay
Equity," pp. 106-108.

[32] E. Robert Livernash, "An Overview," in *Comparable Worth: Issues and Alternatives*,
p. 3.

[33] National Academy of Sciences, "Job Evaluation: An Analytic Review," Interim Report
to the Equal Employment Opportunity Commission, June 1979.

administration will do because a lot will depend on what the Supreme Court does [in the Gunther case]," said July Schup, legislative director of the National Federation of Business and Professional Women in Washington, D.C.[34] The government recently filed a friend-of-the-court brief in the Gunther case which supports the position that Title VII is broader than the Equal Pay Act and asks the court to affirm the appeals court ruling to that effect.

Defenders and critics of the comparable worth concept agree that it is a complex issue deeply rooted in tradition. Eve Johnson, coordinator of women's activities for the American Federation of State, County and Municipal Employees, tells this story: A few summers ago, her teen-age daughter took a full-time baby-sitting job, while her teen-age son mowed lawns. He was paid $6 an hour and spent afternoons at the beach. Her daughter made breakfast, cleaned the kitchen, dressed the kids, fed them lunch, took them to Little League games or ran errands, made dinner and put the kids to sleep. For this she was paid less than $2 an hour. "Most people would consider their kids more important than their lawn," Johnson said. "But at age 13, my daughter understood her value in the marketplace in relation to her brother."

---

[34] Interview March 11, 1981.

Selected Bibliography

Books

Blaxall, Martha, ed., *Women and the Workplace: The Implications of Occupational Segregation,* University of Chicago Press, 1976.

Chafe, William Henry, *The American Woman: Her Changing Social, Economic and Political Roles, 1920-1970,* Oxford University Press, 1972.

Howe, Louise Kapp, *Pink Collar Workers: Inside the World of Women's Work,* Avon, 1977.

Kreps, Juanita, *Sex in the Marketplace: American Women at Work,* The Johns Hopkins University Press, 1971.

Livernash, E. Robert, ed., *Comparable Worth: Issues and Alternatives,* Equal Employment Advisory Council, 1980.

Articles

"A Business Group Fights 'Comparable Worth,' " *Business Week,* Nov. 10, 1980.

Celarier, Michelle, "The Paycheck Challenge of the Eighties — Comparing Job Worth," *Ms.,* March 1981.

Curran, Ann, "Interview With Eleanor Holmes Norton," *Working Woman,* March 1980.

Dimos, Helen, "Getting Mad," *Ms.,* May 1980.

Killingsworth, Vivienne, "Labor: What's A Job Worth," *Atlantic,* February 1981.

Smith, Lee, "The EEOC's Bold Foray into Job Evaluation," *Fortune,* Sept. 11, 1978.

Stern, Linda, "Equal Pay For Work of Equal Value," *Working Woman,* April 1979.

"The New Pay Push for Women," *Business Week,* Dec. 17, 1979.

Reports and Studies

Committee on Pay Equity, "Manual on Pay Equity: Raising Wages for Women's Work," Conference on Alternative State and Local Policies, May 1980.

Editorial Research Reports: "Women in the Work Force," 1977 Vol. I, p. 121; "Affirmative Action Under Attack," 1979 Vol. I, p. 225; "Two-Income Families," 1979 Vol. II, p. 501; "Women in the Executive Suite," 1980 Vol. II, p. 485.

Equal Employment Opportunity Commission, "Hearings on Job Segregation and Wage Discrimination," U.S. Government Printing Office, 1980.

Perlman, Nancy D. and Bruce J. Ennis, eds., "Preliminary Memorandum on Pay Equity: Achieving Equal Pay For Work of Comparable Value," Center for Women in Government, April 1980.

National Academy of Sciences, "Job Evaluation: An Analytic Review," June 1979.

Sexton, Patricia Cayo, "Women and Work," U.S. Department of Labor, 1977 reprint.

U.S. Department of Labor: "The Earnings Gap Between Men and Women," 1979; "Perspectives on Working Women: A Databook," October 1980.

AFFIRMATIVE ACTION RECONSIDERED

by

Marc Leepson

**July 31
1 9 8 1**

Editor's Note: The Reagan administration's proposed changes in affirmative action guidelines for federal contractors, mentioned on p. 28, were published in the *Federal Register* on Aug. 25, 1981.

A Justice Department spokesman told the House Subcommittee on Employment Opportunities Sept. 23, 1981, that the administration will no longer resolve employment discrimination complaints by imposing mandatory race and sex hiring goals without regard to whether those given preferential hiring treatment were themselves victims of discrimination. William Bradford Reynolds, who heads the department's civil rights division, said that the administration would instead emphasize (1) specific relief for individual victims of proven discriminatory practices, (2) increased recruitment efforts directed at the group or groups previously disadvantaged, and (3) injunctive relief requiring color-blind and sex-neutral non-discriminatory employment practices in the future.

AFFIRMATIVE ACTION RECONSIDERED

A FFIRMATIVE ACTION to overcome or prevent racial and sexual discrimination in employment and education has been extremely controversial since the first program was started in 1964. The business community has been particularly critical, saying that affirmative action requires time-consuming personnel work and often results in discrimination of another sort: hiring women or minority applicants who are less qualified than competing white males. Many political conservatives go further, saying that it is nothing more than an unconstitutional government-mandated quota system.

Affirmative action still has a legion of defenders who argue that it is a necessary corrective to centuries of job restrictions, but they feel more embattled than ever. It is no surprise that affirmative action has come under fire from the Reagan administration. Today there is an "all-out attack against affirmative action mounted by the administration, the Congress and the business community," said a recent report by Working Women, a national organization of office workers.[1] President Reagan expressed skepticism about affirmative action in his first news conference after assuming office. "I think we've made great progress in the civil rights field," the president said Jan. 29 at the White House. "I think there are some things, however, that ... may not be as useful as they once were, or that may even be distorted in the practice, such as some affirmative action programs becoming quota systems. ... I'm old enough to remember when quotas existed in the United States for the purpose of discrimination. And I don't want to see that happen again."

Attorney General William French Smith announced May 22 that the Department of Justice had begun a "re-evaluation" of affirmative action programs. Smith, speaking further about the re-evaluation before the American Law Institute in Philadelphia, said: "For a quarter of a century we have devoted considerable governmental resources to the task of fashioning remedies to assist members of minority groups that have historically been the victims of discrimination. Too often, some of those remedies have proved ineffective.... [W]e must begin to take a more practical and effective approach to the problem

---

[1] Working Women, "In Defense of Affirmative Action: Taking the Profit Out of Discrimination," June 18, 1981, p. 1.

23

of equal education and occupational opportunity." Fred Barbash of *The Washington Post* observed that the "re-evaluation" amounted to a "major departure from two decades of civil rights policy."[2]

Smith pledged that the Department of Justice would "vigorously enforce" the nation's civil rights laws, but he left unclear how the re-evaluation would reshape the government's approach to ending discrimination. When asked if the administration remained committed to the "general goals of affirmative action," Smith replied: "What we're committed to is to eliminate segregation, and to provide equal rights for all citizens, and we intend to do what is necessary to accomplish that result. Our approach ... will be different, and we think the time now is ripe for reviewing on a very objective basis what has been done in the past, and the best steps to be taken in the future."[3]

Congressional Attempts to Bar Quotas

Sen. Orrin G. Hatch, R-Utah, is the leader of congressional opposition to affirmative action. As chairman of the Senate Judiciary Subcommittee on the Constitution, Hatch has conducted a series of hearings[4] to examine the constitutionality of affirmative action, which he characterized in a Senate speech last Sept. 3 as "an assault upon America, conceived in lies and fostered with an irresponsibility so extreme as to verge upon the malign." "It may take years, even decades, to redress this wrong," he added, "but the time to start is now." Hatch has proposed a constitutional amendment — the Equal Protection Amendment — to prohibit quotas and timetables for achieving employment equality and to bar any laws that make distinctions based on race, color or national origin. Hatch also wants the Department of Labor to ease its enforcement of affirmative action programs involving federal contracts.

Rep. Robert S. Walker, R-Pa., shares Hatch's distaste for affirmative action. He has introduced a bill — the Equal Opportunity Act of 1981 — to amend Title VII of the 1964 Civil Rights Act to eliminate government-mandated quotas in employment and school admissions. Walker said at a news conference in Washington on May 6 that his bill would also permit federal contractors to practice affirmative action without "fear of sanctions for failure to meet artificial, federally imposed numerical quotas." A quota system, he said, defied the Civil Rights Act "by judging a person solely on the basis of his race or

---

[2] *The Washington Post*, May 23, 1981.
[3] Smith was questioned by correspondent Charlayne Hunter-Gault on the PBS-TV show "The MacNeil/Lehrer Report," broadcast May 25, 1981.
[4] The subcommittee's first hearing was on May 4, 1981, and subsequent hearings were held June 11, 18 and July 16. Further hearings are scheduled for Sept. 10, 24, Oct. 15 and Nov. 12.

What is Affirmative Action?

Today's sometimes emotional debate over the future of affirmative action has clouded the precise definition of the term. Some argue that affirmative action sets up quota systems. Others say these plans mean hiring or promoting unqualified persons. Others contend that affirmative action plans simply set up remedies for discrimination against minorities and women.

One reason for the differing interpretations is that affirmative action programs take different forms, even though their overall aims are the same. The general aims are to prevent or overcome racial and sexual discrimination in the workplace, including admission to job programs and colleges.

In making up for past discriminatory practices, the concept goes beyond simply ordering a firm that has never had a black employee to hire ten blacks. Affirmative action might entail such steps as setting up recruiting programs to seek out minority applicants or posting job vacancy notices so that current employees can ask to be considered for advanced positions.

"Affirmative action includes all programs that help to achieve a qualified work force that is reflective of the nation's diversity," said Warren A. Hemphill, an equal employment officer who heads the Federal Equal Employment Opportunity Coalition of Small Agencies. "It means making a serious effort to locate qualified persons to fill jobs and administering the selection process equitably so that qualified persons — regardless of their minority group, ethnic group or gender — are hired and promoted."

Vilma S. Martinez, president and general counsel of the Mexican American Defense and Educational Fund, defined affirmative action as "a collection of race and sex-conscious remedies designed to ensure that otherwise fully qualified minorities are allowed to participate in those institutions in our society which have historically been closed to them."

sex." The bill, referred to the House Committee on Education and Labor, has not been acted on so far.

Liberal Voices in a Conservative Chorus

Conservative opponents of affirmative action have been joined by some liberals, including representatives of several Jewish groups. Morris B. Abram, a human rights activist and civil rights lawyer who is a former president of the American Jewish Committee, wrote recently that he believes affirmative action programs are not being implemented in the correct fashion. "The laudable purpose of affirmative action has been skewed into a program of quotas, goals and timetables used not to test quality of opportunity, but rather to enforce equality of result. Affirmative action has been turned into preferential treatment."[5]

[5] Writing in *The New York Times,* June 7, 1981.

These sentiments were echoed by Nathan Z. Dershowitz, testifying June 11 on behalf of the American Jewish Congress before Sen. Hatch's subcommittee. "We continue to believe that the affirmative steps are a necessary part of the national commitment to quality," Dershowitz said. But, he added, the American Jewish Congress believes "there is a need for a fundamental re-evaluation of what is meant by 'affirmative action.' For that concept, which originally called for going beyond mere non-discrimination, has been perverted into a new form of discrimination."

Author John Hart Ely has written that Jewish groups oppose laws that single out any ethnic group because Jews have had restrictive quotas imposed upon them. Ely maintained that there is a fear by some Jewish groups that quotas and preferential college admissions for blacks will work against Jews, and that "most of these 'black places' will be taken from Jews." Ely wrote: "Anti-Semitism is a danger — one that should ... be combated by every available tool ... — but the danger is independent of a decision to extend preferences to blacks."[6]

Among other liberals who have attacked affirmative action is Professor William Van Alstyne of Duke University, a former civil rights attorney in the Department of Justice who has served on the national board of directors of the American Civil Liberties Union. Van Alstyne told the Hatch subcommittee on May 4 that even though he supports civil rights programs, he believes Congress should enact a law "forbidding any form of racial discrimination by the government of the United States" — a law that would bar the designation of any minority or ethnic group to receive favorable or unfavorable treatment. Van Alstyne said that affirmative action programs have been "stamping" women and minorities with an "empirical badge of inferiority" because of the widespread perception that they were given jobs or promotions solely because of their sex or race.

Civil Rights and Feminist Group Support

Civil rights and feminist organizations remain committed to the concept of affirmative action. It "is a necessary and effective means of changing the ingrained patterns of discrimination which still plague our nation," the Working Women report said. "Its benefits — to women and minorities, to other employees, and to society at large — are many. Its costs have been exaggerated."

The report cited examples of several successful affirmative action programs in businesses in which women have long been underrepresented and underpaid. Among banks, the report said,

---

[6] John Hart Ely, *Democracy and Distrust* (1980), p. 171.

those that "received the greatest government attention made the greatest progress in certain employment areas." The First National Bank of Boston, it said, gave employees their first cost-of-living raise in four years and began the practice of posting job vacancy notices — something affirmative action supporters push for as an equalizing factor for employee advancement — after being investigated in an affirmative action review.

In a three-year period during which hiring and promotion at five large Cleveland banks were being reviewed by the Department of Labor, the number of female officials and managers rose 20 percent, the report added. And the number of minority employees of those banks rose from 14.5 to 20.4 percent. To cite another example in the Working Women report, there was not one woman employed in the nation's coal mines until 1972. By last December there were some 3,300.

"The available statistical data indicate that the job situation for women and minorities has improved with the aggressive aid of affirmative action enforcement," the report concluded. This has been true as well in government and in education.

In 1941, there were only four blacks among the 500 first-year students at the Harvard Law School. Today, following implementation of affirmative action programs, the student body is composed of about 10 percent minority students. "I know the tremendous opportunity that my Harvard Law School training provided me," testified former Secretary of Transportation William T. Coleman Jr., one of the four black students in 1941, "and I believe it is genuine progress to be able to say that ten times as many members of minority groups today have the advantage of that opportunity."[7]

Coleman gave details about the gains made by blacks and other minorities in the Department of Transportation after it

---

[7] Testimony before the Hatch subcommittee, June 11, 1981. Coleman, who served as secretary of transportation during the Ford administration, is chairman of the board of the National Association for the Advancement of Colored People's Legal Defense and Educational Fund.

implemented an affirmative action program. At Coleman's direction, the department made affirmative action an "essential prerequisite" for private companies doing work under department contract. This resulted, Coleman said, in "substantial progress" in several areas. For the first time it hired accounting firms with black accountants, and blacks were recruited and hired as air traffic controllers, where very few worked before.

Many large-city police departments point to increased minority hiring as a result of affirmative action programs. In Louisville, Ky., after a 1974 lawsuit by a black policeman, a judge ordered that one of every three police officers hired be black until blacks make up 15 percent of the police force. It was then 94 percent white, and had no black sergeants or lieutenants, although the city's population was 24 percent black. By 1980 blacks made up 10 percent of the department. Among other cities that have numerical hiring requirements for police and fire departments are Cleveland, Detroit, Los Angeles, San Francisco, Memphis and New York. "Quotas are an unfortunate necessity in cases where voluntary compliance is not adhered to," said Frederick D. Hobby, Louisville's affirmative action director.[8]

Changes in Government Contract Rules

Executive Order 11246 has become extremely controversial. The order, signed by President Johnson in September 1964, requires that businesses employing at least 50 persons and receiving federal contracts of $50,000 or more have affirmative action programs that meet government standards. The programs must include goals and timetables for the employment of minorities, women, members of religious and ethnic groups, handicapped persons and Vietnam-era veterans. The program is monitored and enforced by the Department of Labor's Office of Federal Contract Compliance Programs (OFCCP). Among its powers, OFCCP can grant back pay and retroactive seniority.

The Reagan administration is now considering a new set of rules which would apply only to companies with at least 250 workers and contracts of $1 million or more. The administration would shift OFCCP's monitoring procedures to concentrate on future actions rather than on past infractions. This would cut down the number of back-pay awards. The proposed new rules[9]

---

[8] Quoted in *U.S. News & World Report*, July 7, 1980, p. 46.
[9] The Carter administration had revised the rules last Dec. 30, and the changes were due to take effect Jan. 29. But the Reagan administration delayed the effective date until April 29 to enable the Department of Labor to review all of OFCCP's affirmative action regulations. The administration then proposed new changes, due to be published in the *Federal Register*, July 15. That date was later changed to Aug. 26. The public has until Sept. 14 to comment on the changes, which will not go into effect until the Department of Labor reviews the public comments. Comments should be sent to James W. Cisco, acting director, Division of Program Policy, Office of Federal Contract Compliance Programs, Room C-3324, U.S. Department of Labor, Washington, D.C. 20210.

would require less reporting and would give greater leeway to the requirement that employers hire minorities and women in the same proportion as they are available in the work force. Observers say that the agency is doing very little to promote affirmative action while the new guidelines are being considered. Ellen M. Shong, who was appointed OFCCP director in June, said recently that the agency is currently going through a "period of transition."[10]

Civil rights and feminist groups are deeply concerned about the proposed changes. "It's very apparent to us that they really just want to eliminate affirmative action from employers' consideration," said Janice Blood, director of public information for Working Women.[11] "Under the smokescreen of such buzzwords as 'overregulation' and 'paperwork burdens,' the administration is substantially withdrawing the federal government from its longstanding commitment to equal opportunity for women and minorities," said Eleanor Smeal, president of the National Organization for Women.[12] A number of groups have said they will bring court action to reinstate the current affirmative action rules if the changes go into effect.

Development of Affirmative Action

S ENATOR HATCH finds it "remarkable" that affirmative action began "to take root within our system almost totally in the absence of legislative sanction ... solely through judicial and executive branch decisions." It is true that most of the government's affirmative action programs stem from presidential executive orders and have been upheld by Supreme Court decisions. But others are direct offshoots of legislation.

The first significant federal effort to promote equal employment opportunity came in June 1941, when President Roosevelt — faced with the threat of a march on Washington the next month by blacks protesting discrimination in the nation's new defense industries — issued an executive order to "implement a national policy of non-discriminatory employment and training."[13] It applied to all governmental agencies, as well as to private companies receiving federal contracts.

---

[10] Quoted in *The New York Times*, July 15, 1981.
[11] Interview, July 9, 1981.
[12] Testifying before the House Education and Labor Subcommittee on Employment Opportunities, July 15, 1981.
[13] See "Negro Employment," *E.R.R.*, 1959 Vol. II, pp. 581-583.

In September 1942 the National War Labor Board (NWLB) endorsed the principle of equal pay "for female employees who in comparable jobs produce work of the same quantity and quality as that performed by men."[14] This ruling came during World War II when millions of American women entered the labor force to replace men who went to war. Although the board said the nation had an obligation "to provide the utmost assurance that women will not be subject to discriminatory treatment in their compensation," it also allowed many exceptions. In the end, many women did not receive equal pay. It was not until 1963 that Congress passed a law, the Equal Pay Act, that required all employers subject to the Fair Labor Standards Act to provide equal pay for men and women performing similar work.

Significance of the 1964 Civil Rights Act

It was a law, the landmark Civil Rights Act of 1964, that gave birth to the affirmative action concept. Congress passed the law under the prodding of President Johnson in an attempt to halt centuries of discrimination, especially against black Americans who had recently taken their protests to the streets. Title VII of the act prohibited discrimination based on race, religion, sex or national origin in hiring or firing, wages and salaries, promotions or any terms, conditions or privileges of employment.

When Congress passed the Civil Rights Act, it was generally believed that discrimination took place primarily through conscious, overt actions against individuals, such as the denial of employment because of race or sex. But it soon became apparent that the processes of discrimination were much more subtle and complex than originally envisioned. In addition to the obvious, overt actions, seemingly neutral policies such as seniority, aptitude, personnel tests, high school diploma requirements and college admission tests could perpetuate the effects of past discrimination. This realization is what led to the development of the concept of affirmative action.

In a commencement address at Howard University on June 4, 1965, President Johnson spelled out the need for affirmative action to begin to redress past actions by the federal government that infringed on the rights of minorities. "You do not wipe out scars of centuries by saying 'now you're free to go where you want and do as you desire,' " Johnson said. "You do not take a person who for years has been hobbled by chains and liberate him, bringing him up to the starting line of a race and then say 'you're free to compete,' and justly believe that you have been completely fair."

---

[14] See "Equal Pay Fight," *E.R.R.*, 1981 Vol. I, pp. 209-228.

Johnson issued Executive Order 11246 on Sept. 24, 1964. The order required federal contractors to "take affirmative action to ensure that applicants are employed and that employees are treated during employment without regard to their race, creed, color or national origin." (The order was amended in 1967 to apply also to sexual discrimination.) Contractors governed by the order were required to submit written affirmative action compliance programs which are monitored by the Department of Labor's Office of Federal Contract Compliance — the office that today is the target of proposed rules changes.

". . . [T]ake affirmative action to ensure that applicants are employed and that employees are treated during employment without regard to their race, creed, color or national origin."

George P. Schultz, President Nixon's secretary of labor, issued guidelines in January 1970 for the affirmative action plan, as required by the executive order. The guidelines, revised in December 1971, stated that affirmative action was "results oriented." This meant that if the government found that a contractor had too few women or minority employees, the contractor was made to establish goals for each job classification by sex and race, as well as timetables to specify the date when the situation would be corrected. This "results oriented" concept of setting goals and timetables has become the focal point of today's opposition to affirmative action programs.

The Department of Labor had meanwhile — on June 29, 1969 — announced a plan to increase minority employment in the construction trades in Philadelphia. This was the "Philadelphia Plan," which set goals for the number of blacks and other minority workers to be hired on construction projects financed with federal funds. Comptroller General Elmer B. Staats created a controversy when he said in a report to Congress on Aug. 5 that the plan violated the 1964 Civil Rights Act by requiring racial hiring quotas.

Staats was overruled by Attorney General John Mitchell, who said that while the 1964 act forbade employers to make race a factor in hiring, "it is now well recognized in judicial opinions that the obligation of non-discrimination . . . does not require, and, in some circumstances, may not permit obliviousness or indifference to the racial consequences of alternative courses of action. . . ."

With Mitchell's approval, the Department of Labor put the Philadelphia Plan into effect on Sept. 23, 1969, and soon afterward announced that similar plans would become effective in other large cities. The AFL-CIO and the building trades actively opposed all the plans, and lobbied to have them overturned by Congress. When this failed, they turned to the courts, but in 1971 the plans were upheld in federal appeals court.[15]

Divided Court in *DeFunis, Bakke* Cases

The Supreme Court has been a prime shaper of the affirmative action concept through a series of decisions handed down in the last seven years. The last three decisions — in the *Bakke, Weber* and *Fullilove* cases — tended to back the concept of affirmative action. All three were extremely controversial, though. The court itself was badly divided, and suffused with dissenting opinions.

In the 1974 *DeFunis* case[16] the justices avoided ruling on the issue of reverse discrimination by finding the case moot. The plaintiff, Marco DeFunis, a white Phi Beta Kappa graduate of the University of Washington, had charged that in 1971 he was denied admission to the university's law school in order that the school might accept a less-qualified minority student. The law school, which had received 1,600 applicants for 150 openings, acknowledged that minority applicants had been judged separately and that 36 minority students were admitted with grades and law school test scores lower than DeFunis'. The court voted 5-4 to refuse to decide the case because DeFunis had been permitted to attend the law school while the case was being decided.

The court did not rule on the issue of reverse discrimination until the 1978 *Bakke* case.[17] Allen Bakke, who is white, had applied to 13 medical schools in 1972 and 1973. He was turned down by all of them. Bakke applied to the University of California at Davis for the second time in 1974, and again was rejected. On both occasions, 16 minority applicants were admitted to Davis under affirmative action programs. Bakke sued the university, saying his grades and test scores were better than those of most of the minority applicants who were admitted.

In the *Bakke* case, the Supreme Court, in another 5-4 vote, held that state universities may not set aside a fixed quota of

---

[15] *Contractors Association of Eastern Pennsylvania v. Secretary of Labor*, 442 F 2d 159 (3d Cir. 1971).

[16] *DeFunis v. Odegaard*, 416 U.S. 312 (1974).

[17] *University of California Regents v. Bakke*, 438 U.S. 265 at 412, 418 (1978).

seats in each class for minority-group members, denying white applicants the opportunity to compete for those places. But at the same time, the court — in yet another 5-4 vote but with a different five-justice majority — held that it is constitutionally permissible for admissions officers to consider race as one of the many factors that determine which applicants are accepted.

The two decisions put a cloud on the meaning of the *Bakke* case, which observers had predicted would be the most important civil rights decision since 1954 when *Brown v. Board of Education* struck down "separate but equal" segregation laws. The *Bakke* decision (in which six separate opinions were issued by the justices) was characterized by one observer as "the Court's complex and muddled series of opinions effectively ordering Bakke's admission to the Davis Medical School with the one hand while giving rhetorical support to covert racial quotas on the other."[18] A report by the U.S. Commission of Civil Rights said: "Despite its ambiguities and its focus on illegal discrimination, ... the result arrived at by the nine justices permits professional schools to take those steps necessary to identify and dismantle the process of discrimination as it affects professional education."[19]

Impact of *Weber* and *Fullilove* Decisions

The court faced another decision the next year in the *Weber* case[20], which also was billed by some as the most important civil rights case since 1954. It stemmed from joint action by Kaiser Aluminum and the United Steelworkers of America reserving half of all in-plant craft-training slots for minorities. The agreement, a voluntary one, was intended to increase the number of minority participants holding skilled jobs in the aluminum industry. Brian Weber, a white man, applied in 1974 for a training program at the Kaiser plant in Gramercy, La., where he worked. Weber was rejected, even though he had more seniority than most blacks accepted for the program. He sued, claiming he was a victim of reverse discrimination, and the case eventually wound up before the Supreme Court.

By a 5-2 vote, the court held that Title VII of the 1964 Civil Rights Act did not bar the Kaiser-United Steelworkers program. The majority, in reversing a lower court verdict, said that in passing Title VII, Congress could not have intended to prohibit private employers from voluntarily instituting affirmative action plans to open opportunities to blacks in job areas traditionally closed to them.

---

[18] Michael J. Phillips, assistant professor of business law at the Indiana University School of Business, writing in *Business Horizons*, August 1980, p. 41.

[19] U.S. Commission on Civil Rights, "Affirmative Action in the 1980s: Dismantling the Process of Discrimination," January 1981, p. 28.

[20] *United Steelworkers of America v. Weber, Kaiser Aluminum and Chemical Corp. v. Weber, United States v. Weber*, 443 U.S. 193 (1979).

The court said that such programs were constitutional provided they met certain criteria. To be legal, affirmative action plans should not "unnecessarily trammel the interests" of white employees, nor force the discharge of white workers to be replaced by blacks, nor "create an absolute bar" to the career advancement of whites. The plans should be "temporary" and should be set up not only to "maintain racial balance" but also to eliminate "manifest racial imbalance." These guidelines, Professors David E. Robertson and Ronald D. Johnson wrote, "while still leaving some questions unanswered, have clearly helped to clarify the legal status of race-conscious employee selection procedures."[21]

The Supreme Court's latest ruling on affirmative action came on July 2, 1980. It held in a 6-3 decision in the *Fullilove* case[22] that when Congress spends federal funds, the lawmakers may impose racial quotas to remedy past discrimination. The court concluded that Congress did not violate the constitutional guarantee of equal protection when it set aside 10 percent of federal funds for local public works projects to be awarded, if possible, to qualified minority businesses.[23] For most of the 1979-80 term, the court had deliberated on that challenge to a provision of the 1977 Public Works Employment Act. Chief Justice Warren E. Burger, writing for the court, said that the use of racial and ethnic criteria to remedy past discrimination was permissible.

Although some white-owned businesses might lose income, Burger wrote, such a limited effect is acceptable. The chief justice described the situation as "sharing the burden." In dissent, Justices Potter Stewart, William H. Rehnquist and John Paul Stevens argued that Congress should act in a wholly "color-blind" fashion and should not single out blacks or other minorities by name in law.

Liberals applauded the *Fullilove* decision; conservatives criticized it. "The importance of the Fullilove decision cannot be overestimated," said an editorial in *The Nation*. "Despite ambiguities, qualifiers and the lack of a majority opinion (there were five opinions in the case, none of which commanded more than three votes), it is now clear that seven of the nine justices think that race-conscious programs to overcome the effects of past discrimination are constitutional.... If Burger and Lewis Powell stick to their opinions, there are six justices who will uphold almost any congressionally mandated affirmative action program, so long as there is some factual basis for the legislative

---

[21] Writing in the *Labor Law Journal*, November 1980, p. 699. Robertson is associate professor of management at Northeast Louisiana University and Johnson is visiting associate professor at the University of Wisconsin.
[22] *Fullilove v. Klutznick*, 448 U.S. 448 (1980).
[23] See Congressional Quarterly's *Weekly Report*, July 5, 1980, p. 1853.

action."[24] Sen. Hatch called the *Fullilove* decision "disgraceful" and "a shattering blow for tyranny, discrimination and arbitrary government."[25]

Dealing With Job Discrimination

NEARLY ALL who oppose affirmative action nevertheless agree that racial and sexual discrimination remain significant problems. But others say that affirmative action is not needed because discrimination has been eliminated. George Gilder, the author who is program director of the International Center for Economic Policy Studies, wrote recently of the "possibility" that "discrimination has already been effectively abolished in this country."[26]

The last three decades, Gilder argued, have seen "a relentless and thoroughly successful advance against the old prejudices" of racism and sexism. Gilder maintained that gaps in income "between truly comparable blacks and whites have nearly closed." He conceded that problems remain, "but it would seem genuinely difficult to sustain the idea that America is still oppressive and discriminatory.... In fact, bigotry of the traditional kind no longer plays a significant role in the market for jobs."

Gilder said "widespread misconceptions" lead people to believe that discrimination is alive and well. One of these misconceptions is income comparisons between black and white families, which always show large gaps in favor of whites. "Much of the difference between black and white incomes," Gilder claimed, "simply reflects the fact that the average age of the black population is around 22, about seven years less than the white average, and that half of the blacks live in the South, the nation's poorest region in income."

Gilder's thesis is disputed by civil rights and feminist organizations. The U.S. Commission on Civil Rights, an independent federal government agency, for example, in a January 1981 report, found evidence of "continued inequalities [that] compel the conclusion that our history of racism and sexism continues to affect the present."[27] The commission wrote of a "steady flow of data" that "shows unmistakably that most of the historic

---

[24] *The Nation,* July 19, 1980, p. 67.
[25] Senate speech, Sept. 3, 1980.
[26] Writing in *National Review,* Nov. 14, 1980, p. 1381. Gilder's book *Wealth and Poverty,* published early this year, was much admired and quoted by Reagan administration officials. One chapter is titled "The Myth of Discrimination."
[27] U.S. Commission on Civil Rights, *op. cit.,* p. 4.

victims of discrimination are still being victimized and that more recently arrived groups have also become victims of on-going discriminatory attitudes and processes. Social indicators reveal persistent and widespread gaps throughout our society between the status of white males and the rest of the population."

Pay Differences Between Sexes, Races

A 1978 commission report comparing the social conditions of minorities and females to white males[28] said minorities and women are less likely to have as many years of schooling as white males. Minorities and women, the report added, also tend to be educationally overqualified for the work they do and earn less than comparably educated white males. The report also said that women and minorities are more likely to be un-employed and to have less "prestigious occupations" than white males.

According to the Census Bureau's latest findings, for 1979, black families had a median income of $16,896 — half of all black families earned less and half earned more. For Hispanics the figure was $16,604. This is compared to the white family median income of $21,841. There is a similar earnings gap between men and women *(see box)*. The Bureau of Labor Statistics reported that the median weekly earnings of full-time wage and salary women workers in 1980 was $204; for men the figure was $322. The median weekly salary for blacks last year was $219, compared to $273 for whites. The lowest category of weekly income was for Hispanic females, $177 in 1980, com-pared to $329 for white males.

Gilder maintains such statistics do not reflect reality. "Most of the differences in pay between men and women ... derive from the fact that women between the ages of 25 and 59 are 11 times more likely than men to leave work voluntarily, and the average woman spends only eight months on a job compared to almost three years for a man," he wrote. "Everyone seems to want indoor work with no heavy lifting, but only women nearly always get it, thus driving down their pay."

As for blacks, Gilder wrote, differences in pay "relate chiefly not to discrimination against them but to earlier discrimination against their parents and to government induced dependency and female-headed families.... There are many examples of American black groups that earn essentially the same incomes as comparable whites." These include doctoral scientists, en-gineers and college professors.

[28] U.S. Commission on Civil Rights, "Social Indicators of Equality for Minorities and Women," 1978.

Median Weekly Earnings*

Males vs. Females

	1970	1974	1975	1976	1977	1978	1979	1980
All workers	$130	$169	$185	$197	$212	$227	$244	$266
Males	151	204	221	234	253	272	298	322
Females	94	124	137	145	156	166	186	204

Whites vs. Blacks and Hispanics

	1970	1974	1975	1976	1977	1978	1979	1980
Whites	$134	$173	$190	$202	$217	$232	$249	$273
Blacks**	99	140	156	162	171	186	204	219
Hispanics	—	—	—	—	—	—	197	214
White Males	157	209	225	239	259	279	306	329
Black Males**	113	160	173	187	201	218	233	247
Hispanic Males	—	—	—	—	—	—	226	238
White Females	95	125	138	147	157	167	187	206
Black Females**	81	117	130	138	147	158	174	190
Hispanic Females	—	—	—	—	—	—	156	177

*For full-time wage and salary workers. In current dollars. Data for 1979 and 1980 represent annual averages and are not strictly comparable with earlier years.
**Hispanics included with blacks 1970-78.

Source: Bureau of Labor Statistics

There may be disagreement over the validity of the earnings statistics, but even government officials opposed to affirmative action say they remain committed to ending discrimination. President Reagan, in his June 29 speech before the National Association for the Advancement of Colored People in Denver, pledged a "national commitment to battle against discrimination." William French Smith, the attorney general, said in a May 25 appearance on "The MacNeil/Lehrer Report" television program that while the Justice Department is "re-evaluating" government affirmative action programs, "this administration is committed, and the Department of Justice is committed, to fully and vigorously enforcing the civil rights laws."

Those laws, Smith continued, "have accomplished a good deal in this country, and nothing that we intend to do will in any way lessen that effort." Vice President George Bush, in a speech at the annual convention of the National Urban League in Washington on July 20, said the Reagan administration shares "a commitment to the principle of equal rights and opportunity for all Americans regardless of race, creed and sex."

The two agencies that do the bulk of the government's civil rights work are the Office of Federal Contract Compliance (see p. 28) and the Equal Employment Opportunity Commission.

The EEOC was created to administer Title VII of the 1964 Civil Rights Act. Initially the powers of the EEOC — whose five commissioners are appointed by the president and confirmed by the Senate for five-year terms — were limited to investigation and conciliation. But Congress amended the act in 1972 to enable the commission to go directly to court to enforce the law. The 1972 amendments also provided that discrimination charges could be filed by organizations on behalf of aggrieved individuals, as well as by employees and job applicants themselves.

EEOC won a series of significant judgments in the early 1970s. These included a 1971 ruling ordering Anaconda Aluminum Co. to pay $190,000 in back wages and court costs to 276 women who had charged that the company maintained sex-segregated job classifications. In one of the most far-reaching of all affirmative action settlements, the American Telephone & Telegraph Co. agreed in January 1973 to pay $15 million in back wages for past discrimination.

Eleanor Holmes Norton, who headed the EEOC during the Carter administration, earned a reputation for streamlining the agency's procedures and reducing a backlog of unsettled cases with aggressive pursuit of anti-discriminatory policies. Norton resigned in February, and the Reagan administration has yet to appoint a permanent chairman. J. Clay Smith Jr., an attorney who had been an EEOC commissioner since 1978, was named acting chairman March 3.

Fate of Equal Employment Commission

The administration is studying the recommendations of an EEOC transition team headed by Jay Parker, the head of the Lincoln Institute for Research in Institutions, a conservative think tank. The Parker transition team was severely critical of the EEOC and the concept of affirmative action. Its report to the president said that the agency has "created a new racism in America" by using affirmative action programs with quotas, thus violating the "spirit" of the 1964 Civil Rights Act. The report recommended, among other things, that the administration cut the agency's budget, institute no new lawsuits or guidelines for 12 months, shift the burden of proof from employers to accusers in equal opportunity suits, and make the guidelines subject to review by the Office of Management and Budget.

The agency's supporters reacted strongly to the proposals. EEOC Vice Chairman Daniel Leach said that, if adopted, the report's recommendations "would probably set the civil rights movement back 25 or 30 years." Judith Lichtman, executive director of the Women's Legal Defense Fund, added: "I think the report is total garbage and filled with a lot of mistakes."[29] Leach said the transition team report disregarded the Supreme Court decisions in the *Bakke*, *Weber* and *Fullilove* cases, and contained many "inadequacies and inaccuracies." Leach questioned whether the report's drafters had "read the statutes or any relevant case law."

Even though the administration has not yet acted on the transiton team's report, there have been budgetary and personnel changes at EEOC. For fiscal year 1982, which begins this Oct. 1, the agency's budget is expected to be about the same as this year's, $140 million. The Office of Management and Budget has proposed, though, that the budget be pared in the next four fiscal years to:

1983	$135.9 million	1985	$130.5 million
1984	$133.2 million	1986	$127.9 million

And, in keeping with the administration's cutting of the federal bureaucracy, the EEOC will reduce its staff by 85 by Aug. 15. Currently it has fewer than 3,500 employees.

Howell Raines of *The New York Times* characterized the EEOC today as marked by a "virtual paralysis of activity."[30] But Acting Chairman Smith maintains that "decisions are being made and the commission will remain alive and well." Smith said in a speech July 13[31] that the agency "will aggressively continue to review and revise its regulations and guidelines with a consistent view toward reducing burdensome or inappropriate requirements...." Smith pledged, however, that "discrimination will result in swift, effective litigation."

Doing away with "burdensome" and "inappropriate" regulations fits in well with the Reagan administration's less-is-more regulatory philosophy. It seems probable that the EEOC and the other government agencies involved in affirmative action will continue their slow pace in the coming months. It seems certain that civil rights and feminist organizations will closely monitor any change of direction, and lobby intently to keep all anti-discrimination programs intact.

If the administration decides to scrap all affirmative action programs, there is sure to be a loud outcry from blacks, women's groups and liberals. But the conservative groups that helped Reagan get elected probably will see the step as the fulfillment of presidential campaign promises to cut back government regulation.

---

[29] Leach and Lichtman were quoted in *The Wall Street Journal*, Jan. 30, 1981.
[30] *The New York Times*, July 16, 1981.
[31] Before the EEOC's district directors, regional attorneys and senior staff in Washington.

Selected Bibliography

Books

Ely, John Hart, *Democracy and Distrust: A Theory of Judicial Review,* Harvard University Press, 1980.
Gilder, George, *Wealth and Poverty,* Basic Books, 1980.
Glazer, Nathan, *Affirmative Discrimination: Ethnic Inequality and Public Policy,* Basic Books, 1975.
Jongeward, Dorothy and Dru Scott, *Affirmative Action for Women,* Addison-Wesley, 1975.

Articles

Appleson, Gail, "Labor Department, Congressmen Take Aim," *American Bar Association Journal,* June 1981.
Fry, Fred L., "Affirmative Action: How it Affects Small Business," *American Journal of Small Business,* October-December 1980.
Gilder, George, "The Myths of Racial and Sexual Discrimination," *National Review,* Nov. 14, 1980.
Hatch, Orrin G., "Loading the Economy," *Policy Review,* spring 1980.
Lamb, Charles M., "Legal Foundations of Civil Rights and Pluralism in America," *The Annals of the American Academy of Political and Social Science,* March 1981.
Phillips, Michael J., "Paradox of Equal Opportunity: 'Voluntary' Racial Preferences and the Weber Case," *Business Horizons,* August 1980.
Reed, Leonard, "What's Wrong with Affirmative Action," *The Washington Monthly,* January 1981.
"Rewriting the Job-Bias Rules," *Business Week,* April 13, 1981.
Robertson, David E. and Ronald D. Johnson, "Reverse Discrimination: Did Weber Decide the Issue?" *Labor Law Journal,* November 1980.

Reports and Studies

Editorial Research Reports: "Equal Pay Fight," 1981 Vol. I, p. 209; "Affirmative Action Under Attack," 1979 Vol. I, p. 225; "Women in the Work Force," 1977 Vol. I, p. 121; "Reverse Discrimination," 1976 Vol. II, p. 561.
National Urban League, "Affirmative Action, 1981," July 21, 1981.
Sowell, Thomas, "Affirmative Action Reconsidered: Was it Necessary in Academia?" American Enterprise Institute, 1975.
U.S. Commission on Civil Rights, "Affirmative Action in the 1980s: Dismantling the Process of Discrimination," January 1981.
——"Social Indicators of Equality for Minorities and Women," 1978.
Working Women, "In Defense of Affirmative Action: Taking the Profit Out of Discrimination," June 18, 1981.

Cover art by George Rehb; photo on p. 559
courtesy of the U.S. Department of Labor

Women in the Executive Suite

by

Sandra Stencel

July 4
1980

Editor's Note: Jane Cahill Pfeiffer, mentioned on p. 48, formally resigned as chairman of the National Broadcasting Corp. on July 10, 1980. She reportedly had major disagreements with Edgar H. Griffiths, chairman of RCA, NBC's parent corporation.

Over 2.85 million women were employed in managerial and administrative jobs in 1980, according to the Bureau of Labor Statistics. Women accounted for 26.1 percent of all workers in this occupational group that year. According to bureau statistics, about 544,000 women earned $25,000 or more in 1979, the latest year for which figures are available. Of these women, about 30 percent were managers or administrators, while 41 percent were professional or technical workers.

WOMEN IN THE EXECUTIVE SUITE

A FTER more than a decade of affirmative action legislation, pressure from the women's movement and some significant victories in the courts by women alleging job-related sex discrimination, U.S. corporations are opening their managerial ranks to women as never before. The number of women in high-level, high-paying corporate jobs still is quite small and it is likely to be at least several decades before women come anywhere near parity of representation in the executive suite. But, according to a recent report published by The Conference Board, an independent business research organization, "a change process leading in that direction is now clearly under way and it has already had, an important effect on at least some very large U.S. corporations."[1]

Women are such recent entrants in the race up the corporate ladder that up-to-date statistics are difficult to find; the numbers are changing too rapidly. Between 1970 and 1975, The Conference Board reported, the overall representation of women in the corporate sector increased from 31 percent to 32 percent.[2] During that period the number of women managers and administrators in U.S. corporations increased from 13 percent to 17 percent, while the number of women professional and technical workers rose from 13 percent to 15 percent.

The Bureau of Labor Statistics reports that in 1979 nearly 2.6 million women were employed in managerial and administrative jobs in both private industry and government. Women accounted for nearly a quarter (24.6 percent) of all workers in this occupational group last year, up from 16.6 percent in 1970, 14.4 percent in 1960 and 13.8 percent in 1950. Put another way, 6.4 percent of the 40.4 million women employed in 1979 were managers. Of the 56.5 million men employed last year, 14 percent were managers.

Although women managers are no longer oddities, they still face many problems in the male-dominated business world.

---

[1] Ruth Gilbert Shaeffer and Edith F. Lynton, "Corporate Experiences in Improving Women's Job Opportunities," The Conference Board, 1979, p. 15.
[2] This compares with an increase from 38 percent in 1970 to 40 percent in 1975 in the representation of women in the labor force throughout the economy. As of April 1980, women comprised 42.5 percent of the U.S. labor force, according to the Bureau of Labor Statistics.

"Many managers are perplexed about women's changing roles," said managment consultant Barbara Susin. "They appear uncertain about how to act, speak, criticize, praise, and encourage their women subordinates in management and non-management positions. They also appear uncertain about how to relate to women managers who are their peers and superiors."[3]

Many of the problems faced by women managers can be traced to lingering male chauvinism. Some companies still spend more time justifying why they cannot find qualified women to promote than they do in recruiting and training women with managerial potential. Unlike her male counterpart, whose competence generally is assumed until proven otherwise, the managerial woman must prove herself over and over again. This is especially true if there is any concern among her co-workers that her promotion was the result of government pressure to comply with fair employment requirements.

Women managers carry another burden not shared by their male colleagues. Because so few women have made it to the upper reaches of the corporate ladder, those who have made it to the top frequently believe that their performance will influence other women's promotions and job opportunities. "Women at the top are under constant scrutiny," said Lynne Finney, the first woman director at the Federal Home Loan Bank Board. "If a woman makes a mistake, somehow all women are stuck with that failure. If a man fails, you don't say, 'Now isn't that just like a man.' "[4]

Federal Pressure and Corporate Response

Most experts agree that the recent influx of women into managerial jobs would not have occurred, at least to the extent that it has, without government pressure. As late as 1970 — six years after the passage of the Civil Rights Act of 1964, which banned discrimination based on sex as well as race and national origin — "most major U.S. employers still had not thought very much about how to broaden and improve job opportunities for women," The Conference Board reported. "Many were not even aware that there was a problem."

Several developments in the early 1970s changed all that. Federal contractors had been required since 1967 to take "affirmative action" to prevent racial or sexual discrimination.[5] In 1971 the government issued guidelines which stated that affirmative action was to be "results oriented." A contractor who was considered to have too few women or minority employees

---

[3] Barbara Susin, "Managers Seek Truce in the Battle of the Sexes," *MBA Executive,* November-December 1979, p. 5. *MBA Executive* is the newsletter of the New York-based Association of MBA Executives.
[4] Quoted in *The Washingtonian* magazine, December 1979, p. 173.
[5] By Executive Orders 11246 and 11375.

Drawing by Frascino © 1973 The New Yorker Magazine, Inc.

"I want you to know, gentlemen, that at this moment I feel I have realized my full potential as a woman."

Another sign of women's rising status in corporate America is the growing number of women serving on boards of directors. At least 425 companies of the top 1,300 listed by *Fortune* magazine have at least one woman serving on their boards. Since some of these women serve on more than one board, they may number no more than 300, in contrast to possibly 15,000 men.

To help corporations find more women directors, the Financial Women's Association of New York set up The Directors Resource Bank. They maintain dossiers on accomplished FWA members who are interested in board service. A similar service — the Corporate Board Resource — was started by Catalyst, a New York career counseling organization. "Corporations can no longer keep going back to those 30 to 50 highly visible women already serving on boards," Catalyst president Felice Schwartz told *Savvy* magazine. "Those women are overcommitted now ... Corporations will have to start looking for equally competent but less visible women."

had to establish goals for each job classification, by sex and race, and timetables specifying the date when the situation would be corrected.

The campaign to wipe out sex discrimination was given further impetus by court decisions and out-of-court settlements costing employers hundreds of millions of dollars in back pay and other benefits. Particularly significant was a 1971 U.S. Supreme Court ruling that discrimination need not be intentional to be unlawful.[6] Perhaps the most important out-of-court settlements were the two that the Equal Employment Opportunity Commission[7] arranged with American Telephone & Telegraph Co.

---

[6] *Griggs et al. v. Duke Power Co.*, 401 U.S. 424 (1971).

[7] The Equal Employment Opportunity Commission was established to administer Title VII of the 1964 Civil Rights Act, which prohibited discrimination in hiring or firing, wages and salaries, promotions or any terms, conditions or privileges of employment. Initially, the powers of the EEOC were limited largely to investigation and conciliation, but Congress amended the act in 1972 to let the agency go directly to court to enforce the law.

The first, signed January 1973, applied mostly to women and also to minority-group males who had been denied equal pay and promotion opportunities in non-management jobs. The agency ordered AT&T to award them $15 million in back pay and up to $23 million in pay increases. The second settlement, filed in May 1974, provided similar awards to management employees who were victims of illegal sex discrimination in pay. "The AT&T decision was important for symbolic reasons," said Isabel Sawhill, a labor-market economist at the Urban Institute in Washington. "It established that companies have to look at their patterns of employment."[8]

Put on notice that the government was closely monitoring their efforts to improve and expand job opportunities for women, the nation's corporations responded to the challenge. Many set up special education and "self-development" programs for their women employees and stepped up their efforts to recruit women with management potential. In many companies change did not come easily. Outside consultants frequently were called in to help companies cope with the social and psychological problems created by affirmative action requirements. The result was the development of a whole new industry that, as one executive put it, "is recruiting women managers, training them, promoting them, sensitizing them and preparing men for their arrival."[9]

Firms specializing in recruitment of professional and managerial women have sprung up across the country. Most operate like traditional male executive search firms. Among the oldest is the New York-based Management Woman, Inc., set up in 1974. "Until there are a greater number of executive women in the work force," said co-founder Anne Hyde, "firms will need a specialist to spend time ferreting out women."[10]

Women aiming for managerial jobs quickly realized that they would have to take steps to prepare themselves. The discovery that women were willing to pay to learn how to advance their careers led to a burgeoning of seminars on everything from assertiveness training and corporate "gamesmanship" to how to dress for success. While such seminars undoubtedly increase women's confidence, some experts have mixed feelings about them. "The problems with these seminars and talk about clothes," said Jan Orloff, director of administration at Stanford University's Graduate School of Business, "is that they tend

[8] Quoted in *Newsweek*, Dec. 16, 1976, p. 69. Other big sex-discrimination cases involved the Bank of America and the brokerage firm of Merrill Lynch, Pierce, Fenner & Smith.
[9] Quoted in *Business Week*, Nov. 24, 1975, p. 58.
[10] Quoted by Beth Rosenthal in "Headhunters (Women's Division)," *Across the Board*, August 1977, p. 21. *Across the Board* is published by The Conference Board.

to deflect women from thinking about the hard, substantive skills they need to make an impact professionally."[11]

It did not take the publishing industry long to respond to the growing interest in executive women. Articles directed at women interested in advancing their careers have appeared in virtually every issue of *Working Woman* magazine, which began publication in 1976. Last year *Working Woman* was joined by a new publication, *Savvy,* which calls itself "the magazine for executive women." Even traditional business magazines have taken note of the trend. *Business Week* began publishing its Corporate Woman department in November 1975. *Fortune* profiled the top women in big business in April 1973 and again in July 1978.[12] In August 1978 *Fortune* devoted eight pages to an article on the growing number of women getting graduate degrees in business administration *(see p. 50).*[13]

The presence of women in the executive suite also has been a hot topic with book publishers. Since the mid-1970s dozens of books on the subject have appeared. Among the best-known are John T. Molloy's *The Woman's Dress for Success Book* (1977), Margaret Hennig and Ann Jardim's *The Managerial Women* (1976), Rosabeth Moss Kanter's *Men and Women of the Corporation* (1977), Betty Lehan Harragan's *Games Mother Never Taught You: Corporate Gamesmanship for Women* (1977) and Jane Adams' *Women on Top: Success Patterns and Personal Growth* (1979).

Scarcity of Women in the Highest Positions

The influx of women into managerial jobs, and the attention it has received, have tended to overshadow another fact — the continued concentration of women in relatively low-skilled, low-paying jobs. Only 365,000 women earned $25,000 or more in 1978, according to the Bureau of Labor Statistics. Of those, 87,000 or 24 percent were managers or administrators, while 49 percent were professional or technical workers. "Sex polarization and sex segregation of occupations is a fact of the American work world," wrote Rosabeth Moss Kanter. "Women are to clerical labor what men are to management — in almost the same proportions."[14] Statistics compiled by The Conference Board support Kanter's observation. Over three-fourths (76 percent) of those employed by U.S. corporations as clerical

---

[11] Quoted in *The Washingtonian,* December 1979, p. 189.
[12] See Wyndham Robertson, "The Ten Highest-Ranking Women in Big Business," *Fortune,* April 1973, pp. 81-89 and "The Top Women in Big Business," *Fortune,* July 17, 1978, pp. 58-63.
[13] Wyndham Robertson, "Women M.B.A.'s, Harvard '73 — How They're Doing," *Fortune,* Aug. 28, 1978, pp. 50-66.
[14] Rosabeth Moss Kanter, *Men and Women of the Corporation* (1977), pp. 16,17.

or office workers in 1975 were women, up from 71 percent in 1970, the board reported.

Although women clearly have expanded their occupational horizons in recent years, very few have made it to the top echelons of management. *Business Week* reported in November 1975 that women totaled 15 percent of entry-level management, 5 percent of middle management and 1 percent of top management. Three years later the magazine asked 43 corporations, "chosen for their preeminence in 13 major industries," to identify their top-ranking women. "Only seven," *Business Week* reported, "named women who by any stretch of business definition could be called top management."[15]

A recent survey conducted by Heidrick and Struggles, Inc., an international management-consulting and executive-search firm, found that in 1979 there were only 485 women officers in the nation's largest business organizations.[16] In 1978 *Fortune* magazine surveyed the companies in its directory of the nation's 1,300 largest corporations. The companies were required by law to file proxy statements with the Securities and Exchange Commission that included the names and salaries of the three highest-paid officers and any director earning more than $40,000. Of some 6,400 officers and directors whose names were listed, only 10 were women. Only one woman on the list — Katharine Graham of the Washington Post Co. — was designated as chief executive of her company.[17] No woman was listed in *Forbes* magazine's 1980 annual survey of the 801 chief executive officers of the largest U.S. corporations.[18]

Of those women who have made it to the top, many have inherited family businesses. Marion O. Sandler, vice chairman of the Golden West Financial Corp., Olive Ann Beech, chairman of the Beech Aircraft Corp., and Katharine Graham are among them. Other women make it to the top by starting their own businesses. This list includes advertising ace Mary Wells, Mary Kay Ash of Mary Kay Cosmetics and Paula K. Meehan of Redken Laboratories. Of those women who have worked their way up the corporate ladder, perhaps the best known is Jane Cahill Pfeiffer, a former vice president of International Business Machines (IBM) who is now chairman of the board of the National Broadcasting Co. She was recently described as "the most powerful woman in corporate America."[19]

---

[15] *Business Week,* Nov. 24, 1975, p. 58 and June 5, 1978, p. 99.
[16] Heidrick and Struggles, Inc., "Profile of a Woman Officer, 1979." There were 416 women officers in 1978 and 325 in 1977.
[17] See Wyndham Robertson, "The Top Women in Big Business," *Fortune,* July 17, 1978, p. 58. A similar survey conducted by *Fortune* in 1973 showed 11 women in top positions. See April 1973 issue, p. 81.
[18] "It Ain't Hay, But Is It Clover?" *Forbes,* June 9, 1980, pp. 116-148.
[19] Michael VerMeulin, "The Corporate Face of Jane Cahill Pfeiffer," *Savvy,* May 1980, p. 24.

Women At The Top

Name	Position	Annual Earnings*
Lilyan H. Affinito	President, Simplicity Pattern Co.	$143,500
Mary Kay Ash	Chairman, Mary Kay Cosmetics, Inc.	120,000
Olive Ann Beech	Chairman, Beech Aircraft Corp.	220,000
Carol M. Conklin	Corporate secretary, General Motors	87,000
Alma Cunningham	Vice president, Simplicity Pattern Co.	55,833
Katharine Graham	Chairman, Washington Post Co.	375,000**
Royle G. Lasky	President and chairman Revell Inc.	117,782
Joan Manley	Chairman, Time/Life Books and Group vice president, Time Inc.	203,000***
Paula K. Meehan	Chairman, Redken Labs	97,656****
Juliette M. Moran	Vice president, GAF Corp.	195,000
Jane Cahill Pfeiffer	Chairman, NBC and director, RCA Corp.	425,000
Marion O. Sandler	Vice-chairman, Golden West Financial Corp., World Savings and Loan Association	156,467
Rosemarie Sena	Senior vice president, Shearson Hayden Stone Inc.	300,000+

* All 1979 figures (including bonuses and director's fees, but excluding personal benefits) unless otherwise noted.
** 1978 salary.
*** 1977 salary.
**** excludes bonuses.

Source: *Savvy magazine,* January 1980.

Why aren't more women in high-level management jobs? For one thing, there are very few jobs at the top — and a large number of mid-level executives, male and female, eager to fill them. Furthermore, there is a long gestation period for developing top executive talent. Most of the women who have entered management in recent years are too far down the "management pipeline" to qualify for the top jobs.

According to the experts, most top corporate executives come up through the operating or line departments — those branches concerned either with producing or selling whatever goods or services the company deals in. Because of their educational backgrounds and interests, many women work in staff or support departments, such as personnel, accounting, data processing, advertising and public relations. This, the experts say, limits their advancement. "Without some profit-and-loss responsibility, a job where results are measured in dollars and cents, it's impossible to reach the top," explained Max Ulrich, president of a leading executive search firm.[20]

Another reason for the shortage of women in top management positions is that until recently few women had the necessary educational qualifications. Harvard did not even accept women into its master's program in business administration until the fall of 1963. The class of 1973 was the first to have as many as 5 percent women. In 1972, nationwide, only 4 percent of the persons receiving MBAs were women. But by 1978 the figure was 18 percent. Today women account for 24 to 27 percent of those enrolled in MBA programs, according to Barbara Nelson of the Association of MBA executives. At New York University's Graduate School of Business the female enrollment is over 40 percent, up from just 9 percent five years ago.

Pay Differences Between Men and Women

For many women, job discrimination does not end once they make it to the top. On average, women in managerial and administrative jobs earn only 60 percent of what their male colleagues make, according to the 1980 salary survey conducted by *Working Women* magazine.[21] This is particularly true for managers with long years of service. Among young managers pay discrepancies are starting to disappear.

Salary differences exist even among men and women who have earned master's degrees in business. A study conducted by Harvard Professor Anne Harlan found that among men and women who had graduated from Harvard Business School between 1970 and 1975, the men earned an average of $6,000 to $12,000 a year more than the women did and were twice as likely to hold upper-level managerial positions and be involved in setting organizational policy.[22]

Similar findings emerged from a recent study conducted by the Association of MBA Executives and Egon Zehnder International Inc., an international executive search firm. Several factors account for the salary differences. Some 13 percent

---

[20] Quoted by William Flanagan in "High Salaries Now Open to Women in Top Management Posts," *Vogue*, August 1979, p. 91.
[21] *Working Women*, February 1980, p. 33.
[22] The study was based on information from 1976. See *Fortune*, Aug. 28, 1978, p. 54 and *Working Woman*, December 1979, p. 41.

Women Managers in Selected Industries		
Industry	1970	1975
Durable goods manufacturing	5%	6%
Non-durable goods manufacturing	9	10
Transportation	9	11
Communications	15	27
Electric and gas utilities	4	3
Retail Trade	21	24
Banking	19	29
Insurance	17	18
Overall	13	17

Sources: U.S. Bureau of the Census.

of the women had interrupted their careers to have children. The study also found that the women were in positions of less authority than their male counterparts; while 8 percent of the men were chief executives, presidents or managing partners of their companies, only 4 percent of the women held those positions. Another factor that could account for these salary differences, said Roderic C. Hodgins, director of the Office of Career Development at Harvard Business School, is the shortage of women with technical backgrounds. "Until recently there were no women with technical backgrounds going for MBAs, and engineers tend to earn a premium," he said.[23]

Women themselves play a role in their underpayment, according to Drs. Anne Jardim and Margaret Hennig, co-directors of the Graduate Program in Management at Simmons College in Boston and co-authors of *The Managerial Woman* (1977). Women executives frequently underestimate their own achievements and attribute their success to luck. Male executives assume they are competent and try to make sure somebody important realizes it. Women generally play it safe, wait to be recognized and blame themselves if they are not rewarded with a promotion or a raise.

Some observers point out that women as a group seem to place as much importance on the "psychic rewards" of a job as on financial remuneration. "Women still have other options," said Anne Hyde of Management Women Inc. "Emotionally, they're not as tied up with what they make. They can still afford to look for fulfillment."[24] Women's emphasis on the qualitative rather than the quantitative "is exactly the reason why

---

[23] The survey of 5,000 MBA's was published in the association's monthly newsletter, *MBA Executive,* September 1979. It found that in the youngest age group (25-29) women's salaries trailed those of the entire group (both men and women) by about $2,500. In the oldest group surveyed (35-39) the pay difference had widened to about $12,500.

[24] Quoted in *Savvy,* January 1980, p. 83.

they have difficulty moving ahead," according to Betty Lehan Harragan, author of *Games Mother Never Taught You: Corporate Gamesmanship for Women.* "Women must come to terms with money — as the medium of exchange and as the source of power," she declared. "Money also has a lot to do with the quality of life, but women tend to put the cart before the horse."

Psychic Barriers to Advancement

PERHAPS in another decade the role of manager and boss will seem as natural to women as the role of homemaker and mother has been. But today many women still encounter hostility when they enter the executive suite. Both men and women frequently believe that women will be less effective bosses than men. Outdated ideas are often at the root of the problem, according to Professor Eli Ginzberg of Columbia University's Graduate School of Business. "Not everyone has gotten over the idea that women were not supposed to be bosses," he said, adding that there still is an assumption among some men that a female boss "makes for just one additional problem in what is already a complicated relationship."[25]

Clinical psychologist Lynn Kahn maintains that women managers evoke a special hostility that male bosses do not. The hostility stems from "the conflict between the stereotypical view that the woman is going to be nurturant and caretaking and the reality that she [the boss] isn't," Kahn said recently. "It stirs up all the anxiety people feel when they're not sure where their emotional support is coming from."[26]

Women managers are caught in another bind. Traits that are generally perceived as required for success in the business world — competitiveness, ambition, toughness, objectivity, aggressiveness — are looked on with disfavor in women. "Lots of times, behavior patterns which are considered appropriate in men are interpreted as vindictiveness, emotionalism and super ambition in women," explained Dr. Judith Bardwick, an associate dean and professor of psychology at the University of Michigan.[27]

Rosabeth Moss Kanter pointed out that many of the char-

---

[25] Quoted in "How Men Adjust to a Female Boss," *Business Week,* Sept. 5, 1977, p. 90.
[26] Quoted in *The Washingtonian,* December 1979, pp. 175-176.
[27] Quoted in *Parade,* April 27, 1980, p. 13.

acteristics frequently attributed to women supervisors — bossiness, a tendency to take things too personally, emotionalism, excessive concern with efficiency and routine details, an inability to delegate authority — are linked to women's relatively low status in the corporate managerial hierarchy. The stereotype of the "mean and bossy" woman manager "is a perfect picture of people who are powerless," she wrote. "Furthermore, people who feel vulnerable and unsure of themselves, who are plunged into jobs without sufficient training . . . are more likely to first adopt authoritarian-controlling leadership styles. The behavior attributed to women supervisors is likely to be characteristic of new and insecure supervisors generally."

Problems Attributed to Early Conditioning

Some of the problems women face as managers appear to be rooted in the conditioning that they get in childhood. Psychologists say working women are frequently handicapped by a weak self-image and lack of confidence. In a classic study in 1968, psychologist Matina Horner, now president of Radcliffe College, concluded that as a result of their childhood training and various social pressures, many women are hobbled by a "fear of success" — an acquired fear that the risks of succeeding are "loss of femininity."

The reasons for the shortage of women in top management positions go beyond the "fear of success" syndrome, according to Margaret Hennig and Anne Jardim. They found that women's attitudes toward work are totally different from men's and that this impedes women's progress in the male-dominated corporate world. Men, they said, tend to have long-term career goals, while women are likelier to focus on short-term planning, largely because they have been brought up to think of careers conditionally — as an alternative to marriage. This ambiguity causes women to make their career decisions later than men, who generally build the foundations of their careers while they are still in their twenties.

Another reason women tend to be less successful than men at corporate strategy lies in the way they respond to risk. Hennig and Jardim theorize that men tend to view risk as offering potential for loss or gain while women tend to think only of loss. Consequently men are more willing to gamble in order to achieve some later career goal. Women are further hindered by their lack of exposure to the informal factors that govern a man's world. "In most organizations," the two authors wrote in their book *The Managerial Woman,* "the informal system of relationships finds both its origins and present function in the male culture and in the male experience. Its forms, its rules of behavior, its style of communication and its mode of relationships grow directly out of the male developmental experience." As a result, women enter the corporate world as outsiders unaware of the subliminal rules of the game.

Hennig and Jardim place a great deal of emphasis on women's limited exposure to team sports. "As team members," they wrote, "men have already learned the ground rules for relationships among their mostly male colleagues in management." Consequently, "in the competition for career advancement in the ranks of today's corporate management, men have a clear advantage over women," they concluded.

Insecurities Arising From Token Status

Rosabeth Moss Kanter agrees that women managers have a tough time, but she insists it is not because they never played team sports. "The notion that women aren't successful in the workplace because we didn't play football when we were 12 has a hidden 'blame the victim' message," she said in an interview with *Ms.* magazine in October 1979. "It's not that we don't know how to play on teams. It's just very hard to play on a team that doesn't want you on it."

Kanter believes that most of the problems women managers face in fitting in and gaining peer acceptance are directly related to the fact that there are so few of them. Their token status gives managerial women a certain advantage — high visibility in a system where success is tied to becoming known. But at the same time, this heightened visibility increases the pressures on them to perform well, since it's almost impossible for them to hide their mistakes. Token status also creates another kind of performance pressure.

> Tokenism sets up a dynamic [Kanter wrote] that can make tokens afraid of being too outstanding in performance on group events and tasks. When a token does well enough to 'show up' a dominant, it cannot be kept a secret, since all eyes are upon the token, and therefore, it is more difficult to avoid the public humiliation of a dominant.

> Thus, paradoxically, while the token women felt they had to do better than anyone else in order to be seen as competent and allowed to continue, they also felt, in some cases, that their successes would not be rewarded and should be kept to themselves. They needed to toe the fine line between doing just well enough and too well.

Even if women managers succeed at their jobs, Kanter concluded, the pressures created by their token status "take their toll in psychological stress" — an observation shared by Tobias W. Brocher, director of the Center for Applied Behavior Science of the Menninger Foundation. However, Brocher believes that tokenism and the stresses it produces will soon be a thing of the past. "Once women executives survive the current highly stressful period of being conspicuous exceptions in unfamiliar roles, they will probably stand the gaff better than men," he said. "They will find safety in numbers, which is a great aid to mental and physical health."[28]

Stresses of Job, Home and Family Roles

There is one problem that women executives share with all working women — the constant pressure to balance home, family and work. Although men are doing more of the child-rearing and housework these days, the women still bear the brunt of it. "A woman who feels that she must take primary responsibility for her marriage and family as well as manage a career — a Superwoman — is setting herself up for failure in one or another of these spheres," said Dr. Ruth Weeks, a psychiatrist at the University of Virginia Medical Center. "Disappointment, lowered self-esteem and depression are going to be the result."[29]

Because of the added burdens created by their dual responsibilities — at home and at work — some worry that women supervisors will be even more vulnerable than men to the so-called executive diseases, such as hypertension, heart attacks and ulcers. But so far there is no conclusive medical evidence to support this. In fact, a recent study indicated that professional women are less likely to develop heart disease than are women clerical workers, including secretaries, bookkeepers, bank cashiers and sales clerks. The study also found that women as a group continue to enjoy lower rates of coronary heart disease than men and that going to work only slightly increases that risk for women.[30]

According to Chicago psychiatrist Irvin H. Gracer, women "are not as likely to suffer stress-related illnesses as men in similar jobs because they find it easier to vent their emotions and verbalize their frustration." But, he added, "if women executives attempt to emulate the emotional patterns of their male peers and restrain their tendencies to be open and candid about how they feel, they also may pay the penalty that men pay."[31]

---

[28] Quoted by Jane Adams in *Women on Top* (1979), p. 171.
[29] Quoted in *Working Woman*, January 1980, p. 51.
[30] The results of the study were published in the February 1980 issue of the *American Journal of Public Health*. The study was conducted by Drs. Suzanne G. Haynes and Manning Feinleib of the Heart, Lung and Blood Institute of the National Institutes of Health. The clerical workers at greatest risk, the study found, were those who had a non-supportive boss, suffered suppressed anger, had children at home, had little opportunity to change jobs, and had to work for economic reasons.
[31] Quoted by Adams, *op cit.*, p. 173.

Outlook for Managerial Women

ONE WAY successful women are coping with the "alone at the top" syndrome is by joining with other women to organize professional networks. Network members meet on a regular or informal basis to exchange information on job openings, make contacts, give each other emotional support and talk over the problems of being professional women in male-dominated institutions. Of course, the idea of using friends and referrals to move ahead is not new. For years women watched men advance up the corporate ladder with the help of contacts built up through clubs and golf games, or "old boy" relationships that often started in college. Women now hope the "new girls' network" can do the same for them.

Some literature on "networking" is beginning to take shape. In addition to dozens of magazine articles, at least one book on the subject has been published this year, Mary Scott Welch's *Networking: The Great New Way To Get Ahead. Working Woman* magazine published a national directory of women's networks in its March 1980 issue. These networks differ considerably. Some are open to anyone interested in joining, while others are open by invitation only. Some are composed of women who work in the same company, others are limited to women in a specific field. Some include everyone from secretaries to corporate vice presidents, while others are restricted to the same occupational level.

In addition, some traditional women's groups are beginning to adopt the technique. "Members of alumnae associations, The Junior League, the League of Women Voters, the AAUW [American Association of University Women], sororities and church groups have always shared information within the context of their major purpose," wrote Mary Scott Welch. "Now the women are consulting each other about the career side of their lives as well." Barbara Stern, whose book *Is Networking For You?* will be published later this year, believes networks can benefit corporations as well as the women who work for them. "If networking improves the women's confidence ... helps them to make better presentations and to communicate more effectively, then in the long run it will also improve the operation and productivity of the corporation."[32]

Drawbacks in Traditional Fields of Study

The movement of women into high-paying, high-status jobs continues to be hindered by their educational backgrounds. Last year, for the first time, there were more women than

[32] Quoted by Jane Wilson in "Networks," *Savvy*, January 1980, p. 21.

Women in the Corporate Sector, 1970-1975

Occupational Category	1970	1972	1975
Managers and administrators	13%	15%	17%
Professional and technical workers	13	13	15
Sales workers	39	42	43
Office and clerical workers	71	74	76
Skilled craft workers	5	3	4
Semiskilled operatives (including transport operatives)	37	38	38
Unskilled laborers	4	4	5
Service workers	52	53	54
Overall	31	31	32

Sources: *U.S. Census of Population,* 1970, and *Current Population Surveys,* 1972 and 1975.

men enrolled in American colleges and universities.[33] But according to a recent study, most college women still are studying for traditional female occupations where jobs are scarce and salaries relatively low. The study, conducted by Pearl M. Kamer, the chief economist for the Long Island Regional Planning Board, concludes that if women "continue to cling to traditional, female-intensive professions," the gap between their earnings and those of male college graduates will remain wide. According to 1978 figures compiled by the U.S. Census Bureau, the average female college graduate working full-time earned 60 percent of the salary of a male college graduate working full-time.

Kamer's study, based primarily on 1976 statistics compiled by the Census Bureau, documents the presence of more and more women in the nation's law, medical and business schools. Between 1950 and 1976, she said, the number of female college graduates increased by almost 400 percent, while the number earning master's degrees and doctorates went up 750 percent and 1,200 percent, respectively. Between 1966 and 1976 the number of women receiving medical degrees increased by 335 percent. In law, the increase was more than 1,200 percent, while in dentistry it was 664 percent.

When women's fields of study were considered generally, a more traditional picture emerged. In 1976, 49 percent of all bachelor's degrees, 72 percent of all master's degrees and 53 percent of all doctorates awarded to women were in six fields where their interest has long been concentrated — in education, English and journalism, fine and applied arts, foreign language

---

[33] Women comprised 50.7 percent of all college students in 1979-80, according to the National Center for Educational Statistics.

and literature, nursing, and library science. Kamer admitted that she was surprised by her findings. "We tend to focus on the exceptional women as role models, but this obscures the fact that most women are not moving into traditionally male fields rapidly," she told *New York Times* reporter Frances Cerra. What is needed, she said, is a "major push to guide women into faster-growing 'non-traditional' professions such as mathematics, economics, business and the physical sciences."[34]

One of the keys to getting more women into supervisory jobs, educators agree, is to help them overcome their "math anxiety." "Most mid- and executive-level management jobs — whether it's running a Seven-Eleven or being executive vice president of General Motors — require an ability to handle figures, work with a budget, set up a system on paper," said Shiela Tobias, author of *Overcoming Math Anxiety* (1978). "The message is clear — if you want to get ahead in your career you need math."

Potential Roadblocks in Faltering Economy

Although the movement of women into the executive suite is likely to continue, some observers see potential problems ahead. "We will see a deepening of discrimination against women and minorities in the 1980s," Eleanor Holmes Norton, head of the Equal Employment Opportunity Commission, said last September. If the recession deepens, she said, the impulse to follow the "last hired, first fired" pattern will be difficult to resist.

Eva M. June, president of Ability Search Inc., a nationwide executive recruiting company in Washington, D.C., believes that as more women get closer to the top they will encounter more competition, from both men and women, and there will be "fewer helping hands." Leslie Wolfe, director of the Women's Educational Equity Action Program in the Department of Education, detects a "great hostility to affirmative action, with people believing that it means hiring unqualified women and minorities."

Management consultant John Thackray expressed concern about "the country's mood of grim conservatism," which he fears will curtail women's progress. "To a considerable extent, the women's movement in the corporation rests upon demographics and vast social changes far more than it rests on any firm moral base," he said. "Unfortunately for the would-be women managers, the corporation has momentous problems of its own right now: its legitimacy, its very survival, its mainte-

---

[34] Quoted in *The New York Times,* May 11, 1980.

nance of traditional values. Thus it is only capable of token gestures to women who need far more."[35]

Rosabeth Moss Kanter described the future of corporate women this way: "For entry-level women the situation is much brighter than it ever was before. Clearly, they have talent. Companies recognize that. They're getting their credentials and they are going to do well. The places we still have problems are at the upper levels of organizations. The executive woman still gets defined as an exception. . . . She'd like to be just another executive and yet everyone is paying attention to her special qualities."

The way to alleviate the pressures on executive women, Kanter said, is for corporations to hire more of them. "Instead of token hiring . . . they should make sure there are enough women around so that the women they have are not unusual," she explained. "Secondly, their managers have to know how to support people in those positions. The trap managers fall into is either to overprotect their [women executives] — put them off in a corner, give them safe jobs, protect them from risk, which keeps them out of power — or they overexpose them — give them harder tasks, more chances to fail. So managers have to know how to treat a woman just like another member of the group."[36]

Manpower experts believe efforts to increase the number of women in management positions are doomed to failure if corporations do not become more responsive to the needs of working parents — men and women. They stress the need for such things as day care facilities, flexible work schedules, more part-time jobs, extension of maternal and paternal leaves and more liberal sick leave. At the same time, they also acknowledge that many companies probably will not accommodate the needs of working parents until more women get into positions of responsibility and authority. This dilemma represents something of a corporate Gordian knot and untying it in a way that satisfies all parties could be one of the principal challenges U.S. businesses and labor face in the 1980s.

---

[35] Quoted in *Management Review,* October 1979, p. 4. *Management Review* is published by American Management Associations.
[36] Interview on "The Today Show" (NBC-TV), June 18, 1980.

Selected Bibliography

Books

Adams, Jane, *Women On Top: Success Patterns and Personal Growth,* Hawthorn Books, 1979.

Greiff, Barrie S. and Preston K. Munter, *Tradeoffs: Executive, Family and Organizational Life,* New American Library, 1980.

Harragan, Betty Lehan, *Games Mother Never Taught You: Corporate Gamesmanship for Women,* Rawson Associates Publishers, 1977.

Hennig, Margaret and Anne Jardim, *The Managerial Woman,* Anchor Press/Doubleday, 1977.

Jongeward, Dorothy and Dru Scott, *Affirmative Action for Women: A Practical Guide for Women and Management,* Addison-Wesley Publishing Co., 1975.

Kanter, Rosabeth Moss, *Men and Women of the Corporation,* Basic Books, 1977.

Molloy, John T., *The Woman's Dress for Success Book,* Follett, 1977.

Tobias, Shiela, *Overcoming Math Anxiety,* Norton, 1978.

Welch, Mary Scott, *Networking: The Great New Way to Get Ahead,* Harcourt Brace Jovanovich, 1980.

Articles

Business Week, selected issues.

Flanagan, William, "High Salaries Now Open To Women in Top Management Posts," *Vogue,* August 1979.

Langway, Lynn, "The Superwoman Squeeze," *Newsweek,* May 19, 1980.

Robertson, Wyndham, "The Ten Highest-Ranking Women in Big Business," *Fortune,* April 1973.

——"The Top Women in Big Business," *Fortune,* July 17, 1978.

——"Women MBA's, Harvard '73 — How They're Doing," *Fortune,* Aug. 28, 1978.

Savvy, selected issues.

Seliger, Susan, "Working Women," *The Washingtonian,* December 1979.

Shah, Diane K., "The New Girls' Network," *Newsweek,* Dec. 4, 1978.

Working Woman, selected issues.

Reports and Studies

Armstrong, Jane M., "Achievement and Participation of Women in Mathematics," Education Commission of the States, March 1980.

Editorial Research Reports: "Child Care," 1972 Vol. II, p. 661; "Reverse Discrimination," 1976 Vol. II, p. 561; "Women in the Work Force," 1977 Vol. I, p. 121; "Affirmative Action Under Attack," 1979 Vol. I, p. 225; "Two-Income Families," 1979 Vol. II, p. 501.

"Improving Job Opportunities for Women, A Chartbook Focusing on the Progress in Business," The Corporate Board, 1978.

Shaeffer, Ruth Gilbert and Edith F. Lynton, "Corporate Experiences in Improving Women's Job Opportunities," The Conference Board, 1979.

Two-INCOME FAMILIES

by

William V. Thomas

July 13
1 9 7 9

Editor's Note: By March 1980, 25 million wives, half of all married women living with their husbands, were working or looking for work, according to a report published in June 1981 by the Washington-based Population Reference Bureau. The report also indicated that 45 percent of married mothers of preschool children under age six were working in 1980. Working women put in an average of two hours and 23 minutes a day on housework in 1980, compared to 25 minutes a day for married men, according to the report.

TWO-INCOME FAMILIES

WITHOUT THEM, the good life would be out of reach for millions of American families. With their help, families that otherwise would be struggling to make ends meet are enjoying $100,000 homes, $12,000 cars and $5,000 European vacations. Expensive department stores and exclusive restaurants count on their business. They are part of the reason for the upsurge in private school enrollment and the boom in real estate investment.[1] Remove them from the picture and a sizable portion of the nation's buying power would disappear.

They are working wives, and today there are over 20 million of them in this country, according to the Bureau of Labor Statistics.[2] Two-income families constitute an increasingly powerful economic group. Working husbands and wives are generally young, well-educated, career-oriented and free-spending. There are 18.7 million working couples nationwide,[3] and nearly one-fourth of them are between the ages of 24 and 34. Families with two wage earners working full- or part-time had an annual median income of $21,064 in 1978, or $6,037 above that of single-earner households.

With 49 percent of all married women now working,[4] wives who stay home soon may become as unusual as women who worked in offices and factories once were. Last year, according to the Bureau of Labor Statistics, 58 perent of the women with school-age children were working; 41 percent of the mothers with children too young to attend school also had jobs.[5] Columbia University sociologist Eli Ginzberg has called the employment of women outside the home the most important social change of the 20th century. "But its long-term implications," he

---

[1] See "Private School Resurgence," *E.R.R.*, 1979 Vol. I, pp. 285-304, and "Housing Restoration and Displacement," *E.R.R.*, 1978 Vol. II, pp. 861-880.

[2] The Bureau of Labor Statistics reported in March 1979 that there were 22.8 million married women in the work force. This includes women who are working and women who are actively looking for work.

[3] The number of working wives exceeds the number of working couples because some husbands are unemployed or unable to work.

[4] The Bureau of Labor Statistics reported in March 1979 that 51 percent of all American women 16 and older held jobs or were looking for work.

[5] Bureau of Labor Statistics figures for March 1978.

Married Women in the Work Force

Year	All Women (add 000)	Married Women (add 000)	Percentage of Working Women Who are Married
1971	32,132	18,530	40.8%
1972	33,320	19,249	41.5
1973	34,561	19,821	42.2
1974	35,892	20,367	43.0
1975	37,087	21,111	44.4
1976	38,520	21,554	45.0
1977	39,374	22,377	46.6
1978	40,971	22,789	47.6

SOURCE: Bureau of Labor Statistics

added, "are absolutely unchartable. It will affect women, men and children, and the cumulative consequences of that will only be revealed in the 21st and 22nd centuries."[6]

The rapid increase in the number of working wives can be traced in part to the fading of the social stigma that used to be attached to married women — especially mothers — who held jobs. Today, a good job is as much a status symbol for a wife as it is for a husband. But an equally compelling factor encouraging wives to work is financial need. The rising cost of living has forced many married women to enter the job market, not simply to earn money for family necessities, but to afford the luxury items middle-class Americans have come to expect.

Keeping Up With the Cost of Inflation

Today's two-income couples can afford a life-style most single-income households cannot. Compared to older affluent couples, they tend to spend money more casually on travel, entertainment and recreation. In fact, spending money itself seems to have become a form of recreation for many young husbands and wives. But rising inflation, some confess, has made it difficult to ever really feel wealthy. "The costs so far outdistance the value," said one young Washington lawyer, "you don't feel at the top of the ladder at all."[7]

Consumer prices spiraled upward at an annual rate of 10.9 percent for the first five months of 1979. Housing, transportation, food and clothing all showed substantial increases. In addition, American budgets have been squeezed by rising Social Security payments and the higher federal income taxes that

---

[6] Eli Ginzberg, quoted by Caroline Bird in *The Two-Paycheck Family* (1979), p. xii-xiii.
[7] Quoted in James Fallows, "Washington: Fat City," *The Atlantic,* July 1979, p. 6.

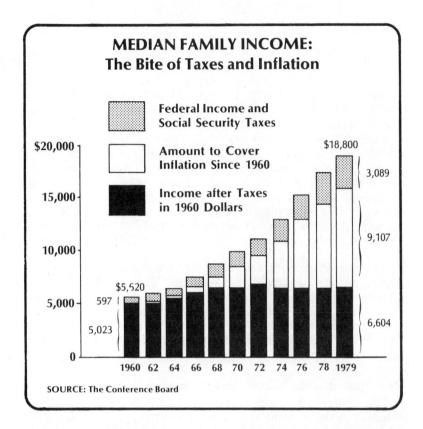

MEDIAN FAMILY INCOME:
The Bite of Taxes and Inflation

Federal Income and
Social Security Taxes

Amount to Cover
Inflation Since 1960

Income after Taxes
in 1960 Dollars

$20,000

15,000

10,000

5,000

0

$18,800

3,089

9,107

$5,520

597

5,023

6,604

1960 62 64 66 68 70 72 74 76 78 1979

SOURCE: The Conference Board

come with rising earnings.[8] The Conference Board, an independent economic research organization, reported in May that the average family now must earn almost double its 1970 pretax income to maintain the same standard of living it had nine years ago. For example, a family of four earning $13,200 in 1970 now requires over $25,000 to equal its 1970 purchasing power. This is up from $23,000 last year.[9]

"The experts and people themselves have said it again and again," Caroline Bird wrote in her new book, *The Two-Paycheck Family*. "When the prices are high, it takes two to get ahead."[10] Women have put themselves to work to defend a standard of living they see threatened. "Most don't have the option of working inside the home or outside the home anymore," said Alexis M. Herman, director of the Women's Bureau of the Labor Department. "Economic needs require that they go out and get a job."[11]

[8] See "Social Security Reassessment," *E.R.R.*, 1979 Vol. I, pp. 461-480.
[9] The Conference Board, "The Two-Way Squeeze, 1979," Economic Road Maps No. 1852-53, April 1979.
[10] Bird, *op. cit.*, p. 8.
[11] Quoted in *The New York Times*, May 7, 1978.

With inflation playing havoc on the finances of lower-income families, many two-salary households occupy a privileged position, free from worry over cutting corners and making hard decisions on what to buy. This holds true for black families as well as white. The U.S. Bureau of the Census released a study in June that indicated that young black working couples have managed to achieve economic equality with their white counterparts. Other blacks, however, continue to suffer disproportionately from unemployment and rising prices. The report noted that 45 percent of young black wives work year round, compared to 33 percent of the white wives in the same age category. Black couples under age 35 in the North and West earned annual median family incomes of $16,715 in 1976. Similar white families earned median incomes of $16,691 that year.[12]

As the cost of living increases, two-income families may become the only ones able to keep up. The Bureau of Labor Statistics reported in July that the median inflation-adjusted purchasing power of two-income households was 23.5 percent greater than that of families with only one wage earner. If the demands of inflation draw more wives into the job market, that gap can be expected to widen.

Real Estate Boom: Shelter for Earnings

The Conference Board estimated in 1977 that four out of five families in the wealthiest fifth of the population — those with combined incomes of $25,000 or more — had two wage earners.[13] With taxes threatening a larger portion of their salaries *(see box, p. 65)*, one of the things these families are doing to protect their earnings is investing in real estate. The U.S. League of Savings Associations reported that 45 percent of all home buyers in 1977 were two-income families.

"Single-income families want the most modern homes, with everything showy," said David Costa, a real estate broker at Swanson Associates in Winchester, Mass. "The double-income couple likes older houses with character."[14] This new interest in older homes is responsible for the revitalization of many inner-city neighborhoods across the country. But it also has contributed to housing inflation at all levels. According to the National Association of Home Builders, the median cost of new homes rose from $23,400 in 1970 to $55,700 in 1978. During that same period, the cost of used homes went up from $23,000 to $48,700.

---

[12] U.S. Bureau of the Census, "The Social and Economic Status of the Black Population in the United States: An Historical View, 1790-1978," June 1979.

[13] Fabian Linden, "The Two- and Three-Income Family," *Across the Board,* May 1977, p. 49-51. *Across the Board* is a monthly publication of the Conference Board.

[14] Quoted in *Time,* Aug. 21, 1978, p. 56.

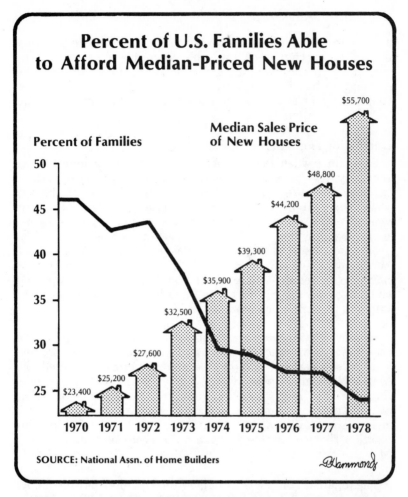

Percent of U.S. Families Able to Afford Median-Priced New Houses

Percent of Families

Median Sales Price of New Houses

$55,700

$48,800

$44,200

$39,300

$35,900

$32,500

$27,600

$25,200

$23,400

50 —
45 —
40 —
35 —
30 —
25 —

1970 1971 1972 1973 1974 1975 1976 1977 1978

SOURCE: National Assn. of Home Builders

Hammond

"Real estate isn't just [a tax] shelter anymore," said David Jensen, a real estate salesman in Farmington Hills, outside Detroit. Young couples with money to spend are "really buying for investment. They're betting on inflation. They keep buying ... because the tax laws encourage it — the government is really paying for all of this — and they've figured out that there's no point in living in a $100,000 house if you can get a mortgage on one for $125,000. The more the house costs, the more money they're making as it keeps appreciating."[15]

As a result of the increasing cost of housing, mortgage debt has nearly doubled over the last five years. New and used homes still appear to be a good investment in most markets. But Alfred L. Malabre, news editor of *The Wall Street Journal*, warned that during an "infationary spiral a point ultimately will arrive when enjoyment turns to misery. . . . If the current inflation,

---

[15] Quoted in *Esquire*, July 3, 1979, p. 8.

already in double digits, is allowed to keep accelerating, history makes clear that jobs and the economy eventually will shrivel."[16] In the event of a drastic economic slowdown, the demand for housing undoubtedly would decline, and the homes couples bought at inflated prices hoping to make money would begin to lose their value.

Decreasing Emphasis on Homemaker Role

At a time when double incomes are seen as a middle-class necessity, the full-time wife and mother is becoming something of an oddity. Working wives often speak wistfully of the day when they might stay home and raise children. But many women today who identify themselves as housewives or home-makers admit they do so with a certain defensiveness. "For every one person telling me I'm doing the right thing staying home and taking care of my child," said a Maryland mother, "I have three people telling me I should go back to work. It shouldn't be a dirty word to say I'm a housewife. But that's the way you're sometimes made to feel."[17]

Women who decide to give up jobs to raise children believe they deserve as much support and encouragement as women who pursue careers. A Virginia-based organization called the Martha Movement was organized in 1976 with that purpose as its goal. The group's founder, suburban housewife Jinx Melia, claims the movement has 6,500 dues-paying members in 75 chapters in all 50 states. "We are a national membership organization that exists solely to meet the needs of homemakers," Melia said.[18]

The organization takes its name from the biblical Martha. As recounted in Luke's Gospel, Martha, the sister of Mary, invites Jesus into her home, and is then distracted by domestic chores while other guests listen to his philosophy. The parable, the Martha Movement suggests, is an apt metaphor for the current lack of importance attached to homemaking. "We feel that most of today's attention is to the Marys, with Martha continuing unrecognized," says one of the group's brochures.

The movement is avowedly non-ideological, a stance that has earned it the opprobrium of some other, more politically ori-ented women's groups. The Marthas have been criticized for not taking a stand on such issues as government-supported child care, the Equal Rights Amendment and abortion. In response,

---

[16] Alfred L. Malabre, writing in *The Wall Street Journal*, June 7, 1979.

[17] Quoted in *The Washington Post*, May 5, 1978.

[18] Quoted in *The New York Times*, Oct. 29, 1977.

members contend the Martha Movement was never meant to address political issues. Its chief function, Melia said, has been to set up a "network of support" through newsletters and meetings for women who have determined that the role of wife and mother is more important than that of a supplementary wage earner. In a society where buying things has become one of the last remaining activities that holds a family together, Melia said, the Marthas are searching for ways "to strengthen our marriages, raise our children and keep our wits."[19]

Wives in the U.S. Work Force

HISTORIANS have traced the "economic liberation" of married women back to the late 19th century when the growth of American industry put an end to the family as the chief economic unit of production. The affluence that accompanied industrialization swelled the ranks of the middle class, making it possible for many women to remain at home. But the expansion of business and industry also created new jobs for women, and thousands moved into positions in offices and factories previously held by men. Among the four million working girls and women counted in the 1890 census, about 500,000 were married.

Despite the growing employment of women, the popular turn-of-the-century notion was that wives should not take jobs. Homemaking was looked upon as a vocation in itself. That attitude waned, however, with America's entry into World War I, when women joined the work force in unprecedented numbers. Feminist leaders in the campaign for women's suffrage were convinced that a new era of equality was dawning. Margaret Drier Robbins told the Women's Trade Union League in 1917: "At last, after centuries of disabilities and discrimination, women are coming into the labor [market] on equal terms with men."[20]

But such optimism was premature. After the war, both employers and male employees tried to force many women to relinquish the new jobs and skills they had acquired. The male-dominated AFL unions led the fight for legislation to exclude women from certain blue-collar occupations. In some areas, women were barred from night work and overtime, effectively

---

[19] *Ibid.*

[20] Quoted by William Henry Chafe in *The American Working Woman: Her Changing Social and Political Roles, 1920-1970* (1972), p. 49.

eliminating them from high-paying jobs in fields like printing and transportation.

Despite these restrictions, more women were working than ever before. By the end of the 1920s, the female labor force had grown to 10.7 million from 8.4 million the previous decade, a 26 percent increase. Women were entering clerical and sales work in increasing numbers. Frederick Lewis Allen noted in *Only Yesterday* (1931), his account of the 1920s, that after passage of the suffrage amendment in 1919, middle-class girls "poured out of schools and colleges into all manner of occupations." But according to Professor William Henry Chafe of Duke University, historians have overstated the amount of economic change which occurred in the decade.

> There is no evidence that a revolution took place in women's economic role after World War I [Chafe wrote], nor can it be said that the 1920s represented a watershed in the history of women at work. . . . Aspiring career women were still limited to positions traditionally set aside for females; the overwhelming majority of American working women continued to toil at menial occupations for inadequate pay; and the drive to abolish economic discrimination enlisted little popular support.[21]

The number of married women entering the labor force grew steadily. By 1940, 17 percent of all women who worked were married. Still many people continued to oppose married women working, particularly during the Depression. A Gallup Poll in 1936 found that 82 percent of the population objected. In the late 1930s, bills were introduced in 26 state legislatures to keep married women from holding jobs. Only one of these passed. This was in Louisiana, and it was later repealed.

World War II and the New Consumer Age

World War II had profound effects on the U.S. economy and the status of working women. The war effort opened millions of new jobs to women, and female workers entered the labor force as never before. They accounted for 36 percent of the nation's jobholders in 1945, up from 25 percent in 1940. Wages rose, the number of working wives doubled and unionization of women quadrupled. In general, employers' attitudes toward women workers remained skeptical, but since women were the only available labor, they were hired.

The war gave women access to more skilled and higher-paying jobs. Previous bans on the employment of married women were discarded; by 1944, married women comprised almost half of the female labor force. Although the war made rapid changes in

---

[21] *Ibid.*, p. 51.

women's economic status, it did not make a lasting or profound difference in the public attitude toward working women, nor did it lead to greater equality between the sexes. Women continued to receive less pay than men, to be denied opportunities for advancement and to work in separate job categories. During the war, concluded William Henry Chafe, "traditional attitudes toward women's place remained largely unchanged."

After the war, women were expected to return to their traditional role of homemaker. Behind the efforts of employers, educators, social workers and the media to persuade women to leave the work force were two important economic considerations, said the editors of *America's Working Women:* "On the one hand, the system could not provide full employment; on the other hand, continued industrial profits required, with the diminution of military spending, an expansion in the consumption of household durable goods. An emphasis on 'homemaking' encouraged women to buy."[22]

This view overlooked the fact that the majority of women were working for economic reasons. A Department of Labor survey in 1945 found that 96 percent of all single women, 98 percent of widowed and divorced women and 57 percent of the married women seriously needed to continue working after the war. Many women were laid off in heavy industries. But for the most part, these women did not return to their kitchens. At the same time the war economy was changing into a consumer economy, significant changes also were occurring in the workplace. The rapid shift from manufacturing to service industries created new technical and office jobs in which brute strength was not a prerequisite and in which women could feel comfortable.

During the postwar baby boom,[23] when large families were the rule, many married women with children started back to work to help meet rising costs. Although the overall proportion of female workers fell to 28 percent after the war, thousands of housewives took full- or part-time jobs to supplement family incomes. Working wives of the 1940s and 1950s, according to Professor Chafe, "provided the indispensable condition for the middle-class life for millions."[24] They went to work, he added, not out of any great desire for self-fulfillment, but to increase their families' buying power in the new consumer age.

---

[22] Rosalyn Baxandall, Linda Gordon and Susan Reverby, eds., *America's Working Women* (1976), pp. 83-84.

[23] The baby boom spans the period from 1946 through 1964. In those 19 years, 76.4 million babies were born in the United States. Annual births rose from 2.9 million in 1945, before the boom began, to a peak of 4.3 million in 1957. From 1954 to 1964, there were more than four million babies born each year.

[24] Quoted in *The New York Times,* Nov. 30, 1978.

During the 1950s, the largest increase in labor force participation was among married women beyond the usual childbearing years (20 to 34). Working wives generally were regarded as "cakewinners" rather than "breadwinners," since their wages often provided extra money to buy luxury items families could not afford on the husband's salary alone. As a result, many married women were shunted into low-paying jobs with little chance for advancement. It was not uncommon for employers to pay them at a lower rate than single women or men doing the same work.

Outlawing Sex Discrimination on the Job

This practice and other forms of sex-related job discrimination have been banned by state and federal laws enacted over the last two decades. The first of these was the federal Equal Pay Act of 1963. It required all employers subject to the Fair Labor Standards Act[25] to provide equal pay for men and women performing similar work.

The following year, Congress passed the Civil Rights Act of 1964. Title VII of that act prohibited discrimination based on sex — as well as race, religion and national origin — in hiring or firing, wages, promotions or any terms or conditions of employment. Exceptions were permitted only when sex was a bona fide occupational qualification, as in the case of an actor or a model. Title VII is administered by the Equal Employment Opportunity Commission, whose five members are appointed by the president. Initially, the powers of the EEOC were limited largely to investigation and conciliation, but Congress amended the act in 1972 to let the agency go directly to court to enforce the law.

Because sex discrimination sometimes takes forms different from race discrimination, the EEOC issued sex-discrimination guidelines. They stated that the refusal to hire an individual cannot be based on assumed employment characteristics of women in general. The guidelines also prohibited hiring based on classification or labeling of "men's jobs" and "women's jobs," or advertising under male and female headings.

The EEOC guidelines declared that state laws that prohibited or limited the employment of women, such as those barring them from work immediately before or after childbirth, discriminate on the basis of sex because they do not take into account individual capacities and preferences. Forms of discrimination against married women, while not specifically

---

[25] The Fair Labor Standards Act of 1938 established a minimum wage for individuals engaged in interstate commerce or the production of goods for commerce. The law has been amended several times to increase the minimum rate and to extend coverage to new groups of employees.

forbidden, are considered by the commission to be in violation of its broader anti-sex bias rules.

In October 1967, President Johnson issued an executive order prohibiting sex discrimination and other forms of bias in hiring by federal contractors. The order required federal contractors to take "affirmative action" to ensure that applicants are employed and that they are treated during employment without regard to their race, color, religion, sex or national origin."[26] Other federal laws, orders and regulations have prohibited employment discrimination in special occupations or industries. For example, Title IX of the Education Amendments of 1972 specifically prohibited sex discrimination in education.

"After World War I. . . , the overwhelming majority of American working women continued to toil at menial occupations for inadequate pay, and the drive to abolish economic discrimination enlisted little popular support."

William Henry Chafe, *The American Working Woman: Her Changing Social and Political Roles* (1972)

The movement to end sex bias in employment and pay "is evidence of how interested women are in work, regardless of their motives in seeking it," *The Wall Street Journal* stated last year.[27] But figures cited in the *Journal* indicated that a majority of women working today hold clerical jobs and on the average earn about $6 for every $10 earned by men. That ratio has not changed greatly since 1955 when the government first began keeping such data.

Pregnancy Pay: Boost for Working Wives

In a sweeping expansion of the rights of working married women, the 95th Congress passed legislation in October 1978 to ban employment discrimination on the basis of pregnancy and require disability and health insurance plans to cover pregnant workers. The law amended Title VII of the 1964 Civil Rights Act to ban discrimination against all pregnant women in any area of employment, including hiring, promotion, seniority rights and job security. It also required employers who offered health insurance and temporary disability plans to extend coverage to women for pregnancy, childbirth and related medical conditions.

---

[26] See "Reverse Discrimination," *E.R.R.*, 1976 Vol. II, pp. 561-580.
[27] *The Wall Street Journal*, Oct. 28, 1978.

The law was intended to reverse a 1976 Supreme Court decision, *General Electric v. Gilbert,* which held that employers need not include pregnancy in their disability pay plans. In 1976, writing for the court's 6-3 majority, Justice William H. Rehnquist said the exclusion was not discriminatory because "there is no risk from which men are protected and women are not...." In dissent, Justice William J. Brennan Jr. wrote: "Surely it offends common sense to suggest . . . that a classification revolving around pregnancy is not, at the minimum, strongly 'sex-related.' "[28]

Supporters of pregnancy disability pay argued that discrimination based on pregnancy was at the root of women's employment problems because employers' views on pregnancy had relegated many women of childbearing age to marginal, low-wage positions. Opponents of the bill, including the U.S. Chamber of Commerce, countered that pregnancy is a voluntary condition that should not be regarded as an illness. They also expressed concern over the high cost of the legislation, citing estimates of $571 million a year for disability payments and $1 billion for health and medical expenses.

Opposition to one of the bill's provisions came from within the ranks of the women's movement. The legislation allows employers to exempt elective abortions from health insurance coverage. Representatives of a number of women's groups argued that the anti-abortion provision was unnecessary, since the legislation by its very nature was "pro-life" and "pro-family." The extension of disability benefits and job security to pregnant workers, they

---

[28] Also dissenting were Justices Thurgood Marshall and John Paul Stevens.

said, would encourage women to carry their babies to term rather than electing to have abortions. In addition, the payment of pregnancy benefits would prompt more women to go back to work after having children.

Impact on Society and Families

THE CHILDREN of the "permissive generation" of the late 1940s and 1950s have become the working husbands and wives of the present "acquisitive generation." The oldest postwar babies are now 33. Over the next ten years, their ranks will swell the typically big-spending 34-to-44 age group from its current 28 million to 40 million. According to Data Resources, a private economic organization, there are now 12.2 million couples in that age bracket. In a decade, there are expected to be 18.2 million.

Because of their growing numbers, the "baby boom" adults are being wooed by merchandisers of all kinds. Married couples are the most avidly courted, since they have more money to spend. As *Time* magazine described them, "baby boomers" were children of inflation, "born with credit cards in their mouths and oriented toward spending rather than saving. They are part of the instant-gratification, self-indulgent Me decade, which has a taste for high-priced gadgets and little interest in self-denial."[29]

Advertising seems to be keeping pace with this generation as it grows older, catering particularly to what is often regarded as its "almost religious" sense of self-esteem. These are the first adults to have been exposed to television all their lives. They are also the first generation to have grown up under the shadow of the Atomic Age. That combination, some social critics theorize, has created in many young adults a kind of "live now" mentality, encouraging them to buy what they want, when they want it — a craving that often requires two incomes to be satisfied.

New Division of Labor Within the Home

Nearly half (48 percent) of those responding to a 1977 *New York Times-CBS News* poll said they believed the most "satisfying" marriages were those in which both husband and wife worked and both shared the housework and child-rearing responsibilities. Some 43 percent favored the traditional marriage in which the husband was the breadwinner and the wife stayed home and took care of the house and children. The poll

---

[29] "The Over-the-Thrill Crowd," *Time*, May 28, 1979, p. 39.

also indicated a warming of public attitudes toward working mothers. More than half of those interviewed said that working mothers were better than, or as good as, their non-working counterparts. Only 40 percent said that working women would be worse mothers, compared to 48 percent who agreed in a similar poll conducted in 1970.[30]

"Men are beginning to recognize that they no longer need work all their lives at jobs they don't like to support wives and children. Women are beginning to question the ways in which women have adopted their careers to childbearing and some are questioning whether to have children at all."

Caroline Bird, *The Two-Paycheck Marriage* (1979)

Experts differ over the implications of these findings. Some see the growing acceptance of working wives and mothers as a positive step in the movement toward a more equitable society, while others see it as a threat to the stability of the family. Women who enter the marketplace develop "more self confidence . . . and gain a greater sense of economic worth," wrote Caroline Bird.[31] But they often have less time to spend on child care, homemaking and other functions that wives traditionally have performed. Psychologist Kenneth Keniston and other family experts have wondered if this change could have an unhealthy effect on "the content and nature of family life."[32]

Although most husbands welcome the additional income from their wives' jobs, many have a hard time adjusting to the new demands that go along with it. Being married to a woman with a busy schedule, an income of her own, and outside friendships and commitments may cause a husband to feel insecure and resentful. Numerous studies have shown that there is more divorce among families in which the wife works.[33] Once society has adjusted to women's new roles, the divorce rate might decline somewhat. But some observers believe that as the economic advances of women continue to alter their status in marriage, divorces are apt to increase.

---

[30] See *The New York Times,* Nov. 27, 1977.

[31] Bird, *op. cit.,* p. 11.

[32] Kenneth Keniston, *All Our Children: The Family Under Pressure* (1977), p. 5.

[33] See Heather L. Ross and Isabel V. Sawhill, *Time of Transition: The Growth of Families Headed by Women* (1975), pp. 35-66.

Closely related to this issue is the question of how the employment of women affects the division of labor within the home. In general, husbands of working wives engage in slightly more child care and housework than do husbands of non-working women. A 10-year study on housework by Professor John P. Robinson of Cleveland State University indicated that from 1965 to 1975 the amount of time working women devoted to doing household chores declined from 26 to 21 hours a week. The time men spent on housework during the same period increased from nine to 10 hours weekly. Robinson found that full-time homemakers in 1975 spent about 44 hours a week on housework, a drop from 50 hours in 1965.[34]

"The baby boomers . . . are a part of the instant-gratification, self-indulgent Me generation, which has a taste for high-priced gadgets and little interest in self-denial."

Time magazine, May 28, 1979

In many homes where both partners have jobs, the problem of dividing housework is often solved by hiring outside help. This has caused a shortage of domestic employees in some cities. It also has created a whole new service industry designed to meet the needs of working couples who do not have time to take care of routine domestic tasks, such as paying bills, handling deliveries and shopping. The owner of a San Francisco "errand" service called "Rent-a-Wife" described his business as an "idea whose time has come." "Someone has to be there for the phone company or the plumber," said a Los Angeles woman who runs a similar service. "People who work hard deserve to forget the little things," she said. "What's the sense of being successful if you can't enjoy it."[35]

Childless Couples; 'Commuter' Marriages

Many couples today are achievement-oriented.[36] They believe they are entitled to pursue their own interests — even if it

---

[34] See John P. Robinson, "Changes in Americans' Use of Time, 1965-1975," Cleveland State University, 1979.

[35] Both were quoted in the *Los Angeles Times*, Jan. 16, 1979.

[36] Two out of three parents interviewed in a 1976 survey conducted by Yankelovich, Skelly and White, a national market research and public opinion organization, said that parents should have their own lives and interests even if it means spending less time with their children. See "Raising Children in a Changing Society, The General Mills American Family Report, 1976-77."

means spending less time with their children, or not having children at all. The decision not to have children is often one that is not made consciously. Many times, it is the result of a tacit decision "not to decide," said Charles Westoff, head of the Princeton University Office of Population Research. Couples involved in their careers can gradually "back into childlessness," Westoff said.[37]

The U.S. birth rate in this decade is at its lowest point in history — the average family now has 1.8 children, about half the number of 20 years ago. Experts foresee a continued decline. A 1977 study on the falling birth rate by the Rand Corporation, a private research bureau, linked the drop to an increase in female employment. And as wages for women workers go up, the study predicted, the birth rate can be expected to decline even farther.[38]

"People are willing to take on any assignment, move to any location that promises a bigger paycheck — not for their family's well-being but for their own personal prestige."

William Raspberry, *The Washington Post,*
June 8, 1979

Among working couples who have children the trend is to rely on day-care centers and babysitters to supply the supervision they cannot. There also has been an increase in what sociologists call "latchkey children" — children unsupervised for portions of the day, usually between the end of the school day and the time when working parents return home.

Just as couples with careers tend to see less of their children, some, it seems, also see less of one another. Those with careers in separate cities sometimes practice what are being called "commuter" or "long distance" marriages, seeing each other on weekends or as time permits. The Census Bureau has no statistics to show how many couples actually maintain separate households. But, according to sociologist Betty F. Kirscher of Kent State University, such arrangements appear to be on the rise, especially in marriages where women hold "high-status" jobs that entail frequent transfers.

---

[37] Quoted in *The Washington Post,* April 9, 1979.
[38] See "The Emergence of Countercyclical U.S. Fertility," The Rand Corporation, 1977.

Company Couples

As an increasing number of women pursue professional careers, more and more companies find themselves in the position of having employees whose spouses work for clients, competitors or government regulators. As a result, many couples and companies face the delicate task of devising a new definition of conflict of interest. The situation has developed so rapidly, however, that few formal rules have been established.

"Conflict of interest between spouses is much more nebulous than something like owning stock in a supplier," said Lionel D. Norris of Atlantic Richfield. "We just have no specific policy." But the fact remains that many companies are afraid to hire people who might trade "business secrets" with their mates.

Despite the increase in working wives, many firms still have strict prohibitions against hiring married couples. A few companies have broken with that tradition, however. Citibank of New York, for example, lifted its ban against hiring husbands and wives in 1974. The federal Equal Employment Opportunity Commission has ruled that policies against hiring couples are legitimate if they are enforced without regard to sex. Nevertheless, couples that do work for the same company frequently are prohibited from working in the same department or having authority to promote each other. "The husband and wife may bend over backward to be professional," said Pamela Turner, director of placement for the Sloan School of Management at M.I.T., "but the situation makes other people feel awkward."

For both men and women, economic security has become a matter of paramount importance. Most people, wrote *Washington Post* columnist William Raspberry, "are willing to take on any assignment, move to any location that promises a bigger paycheck — not for their family's well-being but for their own personal prestige."[39] Too often, Raspberry concluded, the outcome is not more happiness, but less. In their quest "to stay ahead," many two-income couples have eliminated the problems caused by not having enough money. But in their haste, they could be setting the stage for future regrets — the kind that may surface when they begin to wonder if the pursuit of money was worth the price.

[39] Writing in *The Washington Post*, June 8, 1979.

Selected Bibliography

Books

Bird, Caroline, *Born Female: The High Cost of Keeping Women Down,* Pocket Books, 1971.

———— *Enterprising Women,* New American Library, 1976.

———— *The Two-Paycheck Family,* Rawson, Wade Publishers, 1979.

Chafe, William Henry, *The American Woman: Her Changing Social, Economic and Political Roles, 1920-1970,* Oxford University Press, 1972.

Jongeward, Dorothy and Dru Scott, *Affirmative Action for Women,* Addison-Wesley, 1975.

Kreps, Juanita, *Sex in the Marketplace: American Women at Work,* The Johns Hopkins Press, 1971.

Quinn, Jane Bryant, *Everyone's Money Book,* Delacorte, 1979.

Articles

"America's New Elite," *Time,* Aug. 21, 1978.

Bettleheim, Bruno, "Untying the Family," *The Center Magazine,* September-October 1976.

" 'Company Couples' Flourish," *Business Week,* Aug. 2, 1978.

Harris, Marlys, "Couples Wedded to the Same Careers," *Money,* Jan. 28, 1978.

Hayghe, Howard, "Families and the Rise of Working Wives — An Overview," *Monthly Labor Review,* May 1976.

Kron, Joan, "The Dual Career Dilemma," *New York,* Oct. 25, 1976.

Nulty, Leslie E., "How Inflation Hits the Majority," *Challenge,* January-February 1979.

Smith, Robert, ed., "The Equal Employment Opportunity Commission and How to Make it Work," *Ms.,* February 1977.

"The Over-the-Thrill Crowd," *Time,* Aug. 21, 1979.

Ware, Ciji, "Is a Baby Worth the Price?" *New West,* April 25, 1977.

Reports and Studies

Butz, William P. and Michael P. Ward, "The Emergence of Countercyclical U.S. Fertility," The Rand Corporation, 1977.

Editorial Research Reports, "Child Care," 1972 Vol. II, p. 439; "Single-Parent Families," 1976 Vol. II, p. 661; "Women in the Work Force," 1977 Vol. I, p. 121; "The Changing American Family," 1977 Vol. I, p. 412.

Espenshade, Thomas J., "The Value and Cost of Children," *Population Bulletin,* April 1977.

Nulty, Leslie E., "Understanding the New Inflation: The Importance of the Basic Necessities," Exploratory Project for Economic Alternatives, 1977.

The Conference Board, "The Two-Way Squeeze, 1979," April 1979.

U.S. Bureau of the Census, "The Social and Economic Status of the Black Population in the United States: An Historical View, 1790-1978," June 1979.

U.S. Department of Labor, "Why Women Work," 1976.

————, "1975 Handbook on Women Workers," 1975.

Women
IN THE
MILITARY

by

Marc Leepson

July 10
1 9 8 1

WOMEN IN THE MILITARY

WOMEN have come a long way in the U.S. military in the last decade. In 1973, the year the draft ended and the all-volunteer force came into being, women made up only 1.6 percent of total military personnel. Today there are more than 170,000 women on active duty in the Army, Navy, Marines and Air Force — 8.4 percent of the total.

The Pentagon began actively recruiting women soon after the draft ended when the armed forces came up short in the number of male recruits. To encourage female enlistments, the services opened up new opportunities for women. All but a handful of the hundreds of military job specialties — those directly involving combat — are now open to women. The service academies have been admitting women since 1976. And the separate-but-not-quite-equal women's auxiliary branches of the armed forces have been eliminated. Today, most aspects of military life, from basic training to K.P., are the same for men and women.

Many of the gains made by women in the armed forces came during the Carter administration. Harold Brown, Carter's secretary of defense, set a goal of increasing the percentage of women in the services to 12 percent by 1986. For advocates of equal rights for female military personnel, the future seemed bright. But under the Reagan administration the picture is changing. The 12 percent goal has been shelved, and signals from the Pentagon in the last six months strongly indicate a shift in policy. Feminists also are concerned about the implications of the June 25 Supreme Court ruling that Congress may exclude women from draft registration and, presumably, from the draft itself *(see p. 98)*.[1]

The first indication of a possible policy shift within the Reagan administration came on Feb. 26, 1981, when Defense Department officials told a Senate subcommittee[2] that the Army — which depends far more on women than any other branch of the service — was re-evaluating the Carter administration's plan to increase significantly the number of women in

---

[1] There has been no actual draft since 1973, and registration was suspended in 1975. President Carter reinstituted registration in 1980 in response to the Soviet invasion of Afghanistan. Congress would have to pass a new law to revive the draft.
[2] The Senate Armed Services Subcommittee on Manpower and Personnel.

the military. Lt. Gen. Robert G. Yerks, deputy chief of staff for Army personnel, said that the Army had begun a study to measure the impact of women on combat readiness. "We have seen indications in readiness reports and so forth that there may be some real adverse impact on readiness ... by just simply the large number [of women]," he testified. Maj. Gen. Robert Lewis Wetzel, who is in charge of the study, said it is focusing on such issues as pregnancy, single parenthood, attrition, physical strength and female health problems. Wetzel will make recommendations on the future role of women in the Army when the study is completed at the end of the year.

Gen. Edward C. Meyer, the Army chief of staff, announced June 4 that the Army will keep the percentage of women where it is today, at 8.9 percent. "I have called a pause to further increases in the number of Army women," he said in an address to the Associated Press Broadcasters Convention in Washington, D.C. "We will continue to recruit women at a rate sufficient to sustain the current level of 65,000 enlisted women — that is, we will recruit about 16,500 women in the coming year. During this pause an in-depth policy review of all the attendant issues will be conducted." Gen. Meyer said he, too, was concerned about the impact of women on combat readiness. "I'm simply not certain ... that the policies we have gradually arrived at [are] appropriate for a war-fighting Army," he said.

Lawrence J. Korb, assistant secretary of defense for manpower, reserve affairs and logistics, maintains that this "pause" does not constitute a fundamental break with the 8-year trend of expanding roles for women in the military. "We still want women," Korb said in a June 1 interview. "We want to increase the number of women in the military. There's been no slowdown in the number of women we'll take. ... But we will be guided not only by numbers but where we put the women based on the experience that we have."

Korb said the Pentagon generally is satisfied with the job performance of female military personnel. "Women, by and large, in the jobs they are in ... do as well and many times better than men," Korb said. "Women have made a positive contribution to the all-volunteer force, and we're committed to making the AVF work. The last thing we would do would be to take an action that would undermine it. ... Given the fact that you have a volunteer military, and women want to come in, I think they ought to be taken if they can meet the standards."

Reassessment of Women's Military Role

The Reagan administration's reassessment of the role of women in the military raises two related questions: (1) is mili-

Women on Active Duty in the Armed Forces*

Branch	Number of Women	Percentage of Total
Army	68,959	8.9%
Navy	34,683	6.6%
Marines	6,706	3.6%
Air Force	59,890	10.8%
Total	**170,238**	**8.4%**

U.S. Army photo

*As of Sept. 30, 1980

Source: Department of Defense

tary combat suited only to males, and (2) has the increasing number of women in the armed forces helped or hindered the nation's combat readiness? Columnist George F. Will is among those who oppose widening the role of women in the military. Will believes that a sexually integrated military runs counter to the "ancient practice" of excluding women from military service. "The military mission is not to replicate the civilian society's evolving notions of equity," Will wrote last year. "The mission is to be good at sustained, controlled violence.... The question is not just, or even primarily, whether women are physically 'tough' enough. The question, at bottom, is whether this society wants participation in war's brutality broadened to include women."[3]

The response to that argument comes from feminists and others who believe that women and men can make equal contributions in all segments of society, including the military. "Obviously there are some things ... that men undoubtedly do better than women," said Sara Lister, the former general counsel to the secretary of the Army. "But ... there are also obviously some women who can do things some men can't.... I don't see why the situation should be any different in a military unit than it is, for example, in a law firm where you may be fighting a serious litigation battle and you have women and men lawyers working on it, and it either works or it doesn't."[4]

[3] Writing in *Newsweek*, Feb. 18, 1980, p. 120.
[4] Interview, May 29, 1981. Lister is now an attorney with the Washington, D.C., law firm of Patterson, Belknap, Webb and Tyler.

James Webb, a former Marine officer who is now minority counsel to the House Veterans' Affairs Committee, is an outspoken critic of women in the armed forces. In a May 28 interview Webb characterized the Carter administration's effort to expand the role of women in the services as "a demonstrable disaster." "It is true that the recruitment of women has helped the armed forces meet their recruitment goals," Webb said. "But I think the military has by and large lost more than it has gained by bringing women in. Under the voluntary army syndrome, we seem to be more concerned with numbers . . . than with the efficiency of units and overall quality."

Webb believes that the large number of women holding combat-support jobs has significantly reduced the efficiency of combat units. "The most important thing in an operating unit is equality of treatment, the equality of conditions, the equality of sacrifice," he said. "But you end up having a double standard with men and women because of sexual differences — privacy needs, differences in physical abilities." He added: "Any time you have isolated operating units, working alone seven days a week, 24 hours a day, where unit morale and unit chemistry are the overriding military factors, women don't belong there."

Among those who disagree with Webb is Army Maj. Peter F. Herrly, like Webb a combat veteran. Herrly taught infantry tactics to male and female West Point cadets two years ago. "I . . . led first an all-male class and then two successive classes of men and women in weeks of dirty, dangerous, and uncomfortable conditions, at times as close to combat stress as professional officers and sergeants could make it," he said. "Observation and leadership scores indicate that women perform comparably to men. Their somewhat lesser physical abilities indicate fewer are ready for sustained infantry combat (not too many men are . . .) but virtually all were fit to handle the incidental combat required in a pinch of our support troops. . . . I am not close-minded enough to ignore the vastly increasing competence of today's women, or the ability of today's men to accept that competence at its worth."[5]

Lawrence Korb, giving the official Department of Defense position on the issue, termed allegations that combat readiness has suffered because of women "ridiculous." "Without women it would be lower than it is," Korb said.

Restricted Access to Combat Positions

Women are barred by law from serving aboard Navy combat vessels or Air Force combat aircraft. Internal Army policy directives prohibit women from holding combat jobs in that

---

[5] From a letter published in *The Washingtonian* magazine, January 1980, in response to Webb's November 1979 article "Women Can't Fight."

Women in the Military, 1970-1980

Year	Number of Women	Total Force	Percentage of Women in Total Force
1970	41,479	3,066,294	1.4%
1971	42,775	2,714,727	1.6
1972	45,033	2,323,079	1.9
1973	55,402	2,252,810	2.5
1974	74,715	2,162,005	3.5
1975	96,868	2,128,120	4.6
1976	109,133	2,083,581	5.2
1977	118,966	2,074,543	5.7
1978	134,312	2,062,404	6.5
1979	151,082	2,027,494	7.3
1980	170,238	2,050,627	8.4

Source: Department of Defense

branch of the service *(see p. 90)*. During the Carter administration, some Pentagon officials publicly advocated removing those restrictions, even though no other country's armed forces have women in combat positions.[6]

There have been no such suggestions from Reagan administration officials, but the issue remains alive primarily because women now are engaged in military tasks that put them close to combat. Army Chief of Staff Meyer, in his June 4 speech, questioned the practice of having women in combat-support roles. "I'm not comfortable with a policy that on one hand says no women in combat . . . and assignment policies on the other hand that are inconsistent with assuring that goal," he said. "We may have solved the problem of manning a peacetime volunteer Army while not fully evaluating the impact of current policies on the Army in wartime. . . . We cannot count on women as individual replacements on the battlefield — whatever their relative individual skill under other circumstances."

Those who believe that women should be allowed to fight say that combat positions are crucially important for the success of a military career, especially for officers. Commanding a combat unit is one of the "tickets" that an aspiring career officer must have "punched" in order to make his or her way up the ranks. "Command of a combat ship like a destroyer is the crowning

[6] In some battles during the early stages of Israel's 1948 war for independence, Israeli women joined men on the battlefield. Since then, Israeli women, contrary to popular opinion, have not served in combat jobs. As the German Army marched on Moscow in the winter of 1941-42, some Russian women were drafted and helped defend their homeland. But like the Israelis, the Russians have not allowed women to hold combat jobs since then. The Russian Army today has about 4 million men, but only about 10,000 women, all of whom hold traditional jobs such as nurses and clerks.

achievement for most of us in the Navy," said retired Rear Adm. Robert W. McNitt, head of admissions at the Naval Academy. "It could be a problem for women."[7]

Antonia Handler Chayes, Air Force assistant secretary for manpower, reserve affairs and installations during the Carter administration, is an outspoken advocate of allowing women to serve in combat. She told a House Armed Services subcommittee in the fall of 1979: "There must be changes to assure women that they can satisfy personal career goals and ambitions by moving up the ladder to senior management. . . . Combat roles are important to upward mobility in all the services and exclusion has a very clear impact on attainment of most high-level management positions."[8]

There is a feeling among officers and enlisted women that they are in the armed forces to defend their country, and they will do combat duty if called upon. "If we get attacked, I know that I could fight well," said Army Lt. Valerie Keim, a signal unit leader at Ft. Bragg, N.C. "My men respect me. They know I understand what's going on."[9] Sgt. Sharon Calabrisi of Ft. Benning, Ga., put it this way: "I wouldn't volunteer for combat, but I'd go if America was threatened. I think a lot of women can go to war and survive. Besides, I'd rather be hiding in the bush with an M-16 beside me."[10] Assistant Defense Secretary Korb said the main question raised by the issue of women in combat is whether the country is "ready to have women die in defense of the country in significant numbers."[11] He believes society, not the military, must decide the answer.

Changing Roles and Duties

WOMEN WERE NOT permitted to join the U.S. armed forces until 1901. But tens of thousands of women managed to serve in civilian status in the Revolutionary War, the War of 1812 and the Civil War. The Second Continental Congress in 1775 authorized the Continental Army to hire one woman for every 100 sick or wounded male soldiers. Over the course of the Revolutionary War an estimated 20,000 women volunteered to work as nurses, laundresses, cooks or clerks. A

---

[7] Quoted in *U.S. News & World Report*, May 26, 1980, p. 32.
[8] Testifying before the House Armed Services Subcommittee on Military Personnel, Nov. 18, 1979.
[9] Quoted in *U.S. News & World Report*, March 3, 1980, p. 31.
[10] Quoted in *The Washington Post*, Feb. 13, 1980.
[11] Interview, June 1, 1981.

Photo by Breton Littlehales

shipmen, U.S. Naval Academy, Annapolis, Md.

ademy officials — on the record at least — strongly
educational training. Lieut. Gen. Andrew J.
who is retiring after four years as superintendent of
, has recommended increasing the percentage of
he academy from the current 9 percent "to 12 to 15
that we can have women in every class in every cadet
It's part of the experience every cadet should
Goodpaster's counterpart at Annapolis, Rear Adm.
. Lawrence, thinks sexual integration of the Naval
has been a success. "The women have been immensely
here," Lawrence said last year. "As individuals, they
etent to do anything in the Navy. They are tough as

rmy began a study of women's experiences and prob-
West Point shortly after the first females were admitted
Maj. Jerome Adams, an Army psychologist, is in charge
study (called Project Athena), which focuses on five
military development, physical development, intellectual
pment, moral/ethical development and social develop-
The first phase of the study, completed in 1980, found
omen had few significant problems in most areas.[20] For
le, in the important category of military development,
nown as leadership ability, "women proved that they can
t lead," Adams said in a June 4 interview.

oted in *The New York Times*, May 27, 1981.
uoted in *U.S. News & World Report*, May 26, 1980, p. 32.
he second phase of the study will be completed in 1986.

few, including Mary Ludwig Hays McCauley, better known as
Molly Pitcher, even took part in combat. Molly Pitcher's claim
to fame came on June 28, 1778, when she took her wounded
husband's place at the Battle of Monmouth, and fought with
distinction. She was later made a non-commissioned officer by
Gen. George Washington.

Some women surreptitiously joined the Continental Army by
masquerading as men. But others, like Margaret Corbin, joined
under their own names. Corbin was wounded while fighting with
an artillery unit defending Fort Washington on Manhattan
Island in 1776. Three years later Congress voted her a pension.
Corbin is the only Revolutionary War veteran buried at the U.S.
Military Academy in West Point, N.Y.

"The women of the [Continental] Army were paid — at least
as frequently as the soldiers were — were provided with rations
for themselves and their children and were subject to military
discipline. . . ," historian Linda Grant DePauw has written.
"[T]hese women soldiers were not a bunch of eccentrics. They
were the sort of good, patriotic Americans from whom the
members of the DAR are proud to claim descent."[12]

During the War of 1812 at least one woman, Lucy Brewer,
disguised herself as a man and joined the Marines. She served
on the *U.S.S. Constitution.* Women served on both sides during
the Civil War, mostly as nurses, although some reportedly took
part in combat. Dorothea L. Dix and Clara Barton were
commissioned by President Lincoln during the war to organize a
regiment of women nurses.[13]

Following the Spanish-American War in 1901, Congress
established the Army Nurse Corps, the first official women's
component of the U.S. armed forces. The Navy Nurse Corps
was set up in 1908. The members of these two groups, although
recognized as military women, were not allowed to hold rank.
During World War I women took over some military jobs to free
men for combat duty. Some 13,000 women served in clerical and
administrative jobs with the U.S. Navy and Marine Corps.
These women were the first females given full rank and status in
the U.S. military. But after the war they were transferred to
inactive status, and eventually were discharged.

World War II, Korea and the Vietnam War

Women were not permitted to serve again until World War II
when five female auxiliary units were created — the Women's
Army Auxiliary Corps (WACs), the Navy Women's Reserve

[12] Writing in *The Washington Post*, April 6, 1980. DePauw is a history professor at
George Washington University in Washington, D.C.
[13] Barton founded the American Red Cross in 1881.

(also known as Women Accepted for Volunteer Emergency Service or WAVEs), the Coast Guard Women's Reserve, the Marine Corps Women's Reserve and the Women Airforce Service Pilots (WASPs). Overall, some 265,000 women enlisted in the auxiliary services during the war. They held jobs ranging from nurses and clerks to gunnery instructors, airplane mechanics and pilots of non-combat aircraft. The idea, as the recruiting slogan said, was "to free a man to fight."

Women nurses and other female military personnel were stationed in all the far-flung theaters of military operations in World War II. Eighty-three military nurses were taken prisoner by the Japanese on Guam and in the Philippines. Some of the 1,100 female pilots who flew non-combat missions during the war were killed or wounded in crashes. U.S. Navy nurse Lt. Ann A. Bernatitus won the Legion of Merit in 1942 — the first woman to be so honored. Thousands of women were decorated for bravery or meritorious service during the war.

In 1948 women were allowed for the first time to enlist in the regular armed forces. This came about when Congress passed the Women's Armed Forces Integration Act, giving women regular and reserve status in the Army, Navy, Marines and Air Force. The law also established a 2 percent ceiling on the number of enlisted women in the services, and limited the grade of female officers to lieutenant colonel, except for certain temporary appointments. The law also prohibited Air Force and Navy women from engaging in combat.[14]

Some women reservists were called to serve on active duty during the Korean War. About 10,800 women served in the Air Force alone. But after the war the number of women in the armed forces plummeted. In 1964, only 1.1 percent of uniformed personnel were women. From the mid-1950s to the late 1960s, sociologist Charles C. Moskos wrote, "the utilization of women as military personnel was essentially token."[15] Then, in 1967, Congress removed the 2 percent cap on the number of women allowed to serve in the military and the limitation on women's officer rank. One reason for the change was the large personnel needs generated by the Vietnam War. Some 193,000 women served in the armed forces during the Vietnam era (1964-75); an estimated 7,500 servicewomen — mostly nurses — served in Vietnam *(see box, p. 97).*

Two factors contributed to a fundamental change in the armed forces' recruitment and use of women in the early 1970s.

The first [...] forces, on[...] American [...] But many [...] war, and th[...] nities in the [...] observers cre[...] Pentagon to i[...] to begin remov[...]

President Ni[...] volunteers in t[...] military's recruit[...] forced the service[...] men. Because of a [...] 1960s, the supply [...] tary planners [hav[...] women as one mean[...] diminishing numbers[...] Gen. Meyers, the Ar[...]

Mid[...]

Women Admitted to [...]

It took an act of Co[...] Academy at West Point,[...] Md., the Air Force Acade[...] Coast Guard Academy at[...] women. There were 119 [...] class, compared to 1,539 [...] year. For the other acaden[...]

Wo[...]

Naval Academy
Air Force Academy
Coast Guard Academy

Military officials had fought [...] academies' status as all-male ins[...] that women would not be able to [...] psychological pressures of academ[...] the presence of women would destr[...] esprit de corps for which the milit[...] selves. But by the time the first co-ed[...] most cadets — male as well as fe[...] adjusted well.

Service ac[...] support co[...] Goodpaster[...] West Poin[...] women at t[...] percent, so[...] company.[...] have...."[...] William I[...] Academy[...] successfu[...] are comp[...] hell."[19]

The [...] lems at [...] in 1976[...] of the [...] areas: [...] develo[...] ment. [...] that [...] exam[...] also [...] in fa[...]

[14] The reason the law did not specifically exclude Army women from engaging in combat was that Col. Mary A. Hallaren, then director of the Women's Army Corps, convinced members of Congress that such a provision was unnecessary.
[15] Writing in *The Public Interest*, fall 1980, p. 18.

[16] See "Baby Boom's New Echo," *E.R.R.*, 1981 Vol. [...]
[17] The provision was part of the 1976 defense authoriz[...]
September 1975.
[18] Q[...]
[19] Q[...]
[20] [...]

The study did turn up some problems in the area of physical development. Women cadets lagged behind their male counterparts in running, chin-ups, sit-ups and rope climbing. Women, although physiologically similar to men in most respects, do not have the upper-body strength men possess. To offset this biological disadvantage, West Point set up different physical training standards for men and women. What might be a failing grade for men in physical education can be a C for women. But the two standards caused resentment among male cadets, who, Adams said, "felt that women should compete on the same physical standard that they do." As a result, "there's a kind of polarization."

Maj. Adams said there was "no difference" in the intellectual and moral/ethical development of male and female cadets: "Women are as prepared intellectually as men, and perform equally well in the classroom. In terms of moral and ethical value systems, they have the same ascribed values and standards of professionalism as men. So there is no problem in those areas." As far as social development — growth from adolescence to adulthood and the problems that go with it — men and women cadets "seem much more similar than different," Adams said. "They are all competitive. They are all assertive. They are independent. . . . The kind of attributes that we would ascribe to a leader . . . we see demonstrated both in men and women in their successful experiences here."

Advances for Women During Carter Years

When he took office in 1977 President Carter appointed a number of men and women to important policy-making posts in the Pentagon. The appointees' ideas about women in the military contrasted greatly with their predecessors under Presidents Nixon and Ford. Army Secretary Clifford Alexander, the first black appointed to that position, was chairman of the Equal Employment Opportunity Commission during the Johnson administration, and was particularly sensitive to the problems of blacks and women in the Army. Alexander believed that "the problems of women in the military paralleled those of blacks — a matter of society's repressive attitudes and civil rights denied. 'It is our responsibility,' he [said], 'to see to it that there is full opportunity for women, that their full talents to move ahead in the uniformed side can be, day by day, increased and enhanced.' "[21] During Alexander's four-year tenure, the WACs were dissolved, and women were integrated into all phases of the Army, including basic training, which is now co-educational and the same for men and women.

Alexander's two general counsels, Jill Wine Volner and Sara

---

[21] Quoted by Seth Cropsey in *The Public Interest*, fall 1980, p. 63.

Lister, also worked to improve the position of women in the all-volunteer Army. Lister, who succeded Volner in the fall of 1979 after serving two years as an attorney in the Navy's Legal Affairs Department, told Editorial Research Reports: "I think it is probably good for our society to have women in the military. We have women in the police forces, in fire departments and they are doing just fine. I think you have to have a large enough percentage and treat women well enough — that is, give them a real career, so that you have the right kind of women staying in and being role models and learning how to be leaders."

Among the others who worked for women's rights in the military during the Carter years were Antonia Handler Chayes, the Air Force assistant secretary for manpower, and Kathleen Carpenter, assistant secretary of defense for equal opportunity. Chayes placed great emphasis on expanding women's career fields in the Air Force. She strongly supported the Air Force's decision to assign women to ICBM missile-silo crews and lobbied to allow women pilots to fly C-141 cargo planes. Carpenter is credited with shifting the focus of the Pentagon's equal opportunity office from fighting racial discrimination to working for women's rights.

Mary Richardson, deputy director of West Virginia's Department of Health, served during the Carter years on the Defense Advisory Committee on Women in the Service, a 30-person civilian panel that advises the secretary of defense on women's issues. Richardson, who chaired the committee in 1979 and 1980, believes the Nixon and Ford administrations allowed the recruiting of women to "limp along," setting only minimal goals. "The driving force for increasing the number of women at that time was just to meet recruiting goals in general," she said in a recent interview.[22] Carter appointees, on the other hand, constituted a "unified force" dedicated to achieving equal rights for women in the military, she said.

The Carter Pentagon set a goal of having 233,000 women — about 12 percent of the active duty force — in the four armed services by 1986. The plan was to have 87,500 women in the Army, 90,000 in the Air Force, 47,000 in the Navy and 9,100 in the Marines. Those recruitment goals have been put on hold by the Reagan administration, although Pentagon officials say that they are still actively seeking qualified women *(see p. 84)*. The difference now, Lawrence Korb told Editorial Research Reports, is that there are no longer any numerical or percentage goals. "That's not our approach," Korb said. "Our approach is to take the best qualified people . . . [and] not to exclude people on the basis of race, creed, color, sex or national origin."

---

[22] Interview, June 4, 1981.

Overcoming Unique Problems

THE ADVANCES made by women in the armed forces have not come without significant problems, among them sexual harassment, unwanted pregnancies and low retention rates. Many view sexual harassment[23] as the biggest problem. In January 1980 Army Secretary Alexander and Gen. Meyer, the army chief of staff, sent a message to all Army commanders reminding them that sexual harassment was not to be condoned, and that offenders were to be disciplined "swiftly and fairly." The Army leadership was responding to a letter from Sen. William Proxmire, D-Wis., charging that there was "growing evidence that sexual abuse of women has become pervasive" at some Army bases. Proxmire based his complaint on evidence uncovered in a series of articles that ran in *The Baltimore Sun* in December 1979 and reports to his office from Army women.

There is disagreement on the extent of sexual harassment in the military. Maj. Gen. Mary Clarke, the highest-ranking woman in the military, does not think it is a widespread problem, although she said "that one case unresolved, is a problem." "Commanders are much more sensitive now than they've ever been...," she said. "I would say ... that there is [more] sexual harassment ... in units where the majority of personnel are male, where the women are in non-traditional jobs, where the men have not yet understood that women have been in the Army for 38 years."[24]

Rep. Patricia Schroeder, D-Colo., considers sexual harassment a serious problem in the military. Sexual harassment is "an everyday part of the lives of many military women...," she wrote. "Women complain of unsolicited and unwelcome advances by male soldiers that often go unpunished, and of mess hall stares that force them to eat off base. Such harassment will probably continue until women are fully accepted as equal and able members of the armed forces."[25] Schroeder's comments were seconded by retired Air Force Gen. Jeanne M. Holm, who had a pessimistic prediction for the future. "Deep down there's this feeling that women who join the military are asking for it," Gen. Holm said. "There's still this feeling that this is a man's Army. I don't think that's going to go away for a long time."[26]

[23] The Army defines sexual harassment as obscene language, gestures, coercion, humiliation, embarrassment and physical contact that is sexually related.
[24] Appearing on ABC-TV's "Good Morning America," March 4, 1981. Gen. Clarke is director of human resources development for the Army's deputy chief of staff for personnel at the Pentagon.
[25] Writing in *The Americana Annual*, 1981, p. 579.
[26] Quoted in *The Washington Post*, Jan. 29, 1980.

Dating, Homosexuality and Pregnancies

The widening sexual integration of the armed forces also has led to problems involving the inevitable fraternization among men and women. All four services have banned dating between officers and enlisted personnel. At the U.S. Military Academy plebes (freshmen) are not allowed to date upper class members, but dating among plebes and among upper class members is permitted. When women first came to West Point in 1976, "there was some social pressure against dating within the corps of cadets," said West Point psychologist Jerome Adams. "Those pressures are not as strong now as they were years ago. It's much more common to see couples in their own free time going to events together.... The number of engaged couples is increasing ... and I think that's healthy."[27]

Problems involving social relationships and sexual relationships can become particularly acute in the confining atmosphere of Navy ships at sea.[28] Women are barred from Navy combat vessels, but have been serving on communication, transportation and other non-combat ships since Nov. 1, 1978. This has led to morale problems among the wives of sailors worried about the presence of women on long sea voyages. Navy regulations forbid both heterosexual and homosexual activity on ships. Sailors are not permitted to make public displays of affection while on duty. "Their conduct on the beach is their own business," said Capt. Harry A. Spencer Jr., commanding officer of the repair ship *Vulcan.* "But their conduct on this ship cannot be in any way non-military."[29] In spite of these strictures, there have been several incidents involving sexual misconduct aboard Navy ships in the last year.

When the *Vulcan* returned to Norfolk, Va., from its first sexually integrated cruise in March 1980, three sailors were pregnant and several males and females were disciplined for public displays of affection. On July 11, 1980, a Navy court-martial convicted a 22-year-old petty officer of having repeatedly sexually harassed four female sailors aboard the missile test ship *Norton Sound.* The petty officer was given a bad conduct discharge, and reduced to the lowest enlisted rank. In a separate and highly publicized incident involving the *Norton Sound* last year, six of the 61 women serving aboard the ship were charged with homosexual activity. Homosexuality is not totally unknown in any of the services. In fiscal year 1979, for example, the Navy discharged 778 men and 76 women for homosexuality.

---

[27] Interview, June 4, 1981.
[28] As of Jan. 31, 1981, the Navy had some 1,500 enlisted women serving on 16 ships and 158 female officers aboard 29 ships.
[29] Quoted in *Working Women,* February 1980, p. 50.

Psychological Problems of
Female Vietnam Veterans

Psychologists discovered several years ago that hundreds of thousands of Vietnam veterans still experience emotional problems directly related to their war experiences. While the overwhelming majority of the 2.7 million Vietnam vets have adjusted well, a significant minority — primarily combat veterans — are suffering from what has been called delayed stress syndrome. It appears that the same situation is true of female Vietnam veterans.

Lynda Van Devanter, who served as an Army surgical nurse in Vietnam and now heads the women's unit of the Vietnam Veterans of America, is given credit for publicizing the psychological and other problems of women who served in Vietnam. She has traveled across the country contacting other female Vietnam veterans and referring those in need of counseling and other help to the "storefront" centers run by the Veterans Administration. Van Devanter has helped train center counselors to deal with women vets' special needs. She is currently involved in a long-term project to assess the problems unique to female Vietnam veterans.

Of the 7,500 women who served in Vietnam, most were nurses who had to deal with the carnage of war on a daily basis. Former Army nurse Gayle Smith, who served a year's tour of duty at the 3rd Surgical Hospital in Binh Thuy in 1971, spoke recently about what her homecoming was like: "When I came home I cried when I saw my parents, but that was the last time I cried for a very long time.... I had no interest in sex, no interest in anybody. Then one day ... I fell and hurt my thumb. It hurt really bad and I started to cry. It wasn't because I was crying about my thumb.... I was beginning to realize that the problem was I didn't feel anything about anybody anymore. I had no feelings, no feelings of love or hate or anything. Just nothing. And I didn't know why. I guess it was because I was emotionally exhausted. I had been through the highs and the lows and the fears and the hatred and the caring for a year and I had nothing left to give anymore. There was nothing that could compare with what had happened to me."*

*Quoted by Al Santoli in *Everything We Had* (1981), p. 138.

At one time pregnancy was a ground for discharge from the service. Today pregnancy is classified by the military as a "temporary physical disability." Women are eligible for as many as six weeks paid leave after bearing their children, or they may be released from the service if they choose. In 1979, the last year for which complete statistics are available, 14 percent of all Army women became pregnant. It is estimated that between 8-10 percent of all enlisted women are pregnant at any one time. "Pregnancy is thus a question of lost time — actually a lot of lost time," wrote Seth Cropsey. "The average pregnancy carried to term causes 105 days absence. The statistic should be insignificant except for the movement of women into 'non-traditional skills.' In the Army, pregnant women are returned home from overseas posts after the 13th week. With man-power shortages what they are, this is a strain on units in the field."[30]

Others maintain that pregnancy in the military is not a significant problem. According to Kathleen Carpenter, former assistant secretary of defense for equal opportunity, pregnancy affects fewer than .01 percent of all those serving in the military. Lawrence Korb said that a larger percentage of servicemen are absent from their jobs than servicewomen. "If you take a look at people who are absent, and you compare women and men, men have a higher absentee rate than women," Korb told Editorial Research Reports. "But the reasons are different. With women, obviously it's pregnancy and medical. With men it's the more traditional AWOL, desertion and alcohol. But if you look at the overall statistics, the women are on the job more than men."

Retaining trained personnel is one of the all-volunteer force's biggest problems.[31] And the dropout rate for women exceeds that for men. According to Department of Defense statistics, of all those who joined the four branches of the military in fiscal year 1977, 37.4 percent of the women failed to complete their first enlistments, compared to 30.8 percent of the men. For the Army alone, the figures were 37.9 percent for males and 45.4 percent for females. Kathleen Carpenter said one reason for the disparity is that servicewomen working in non-traditional jobs are subject to more sexual harassment and psychological pres-sures, working in what she termed a "fishbowl environment in which they are very closely scrutinized."[32]

Impact of Supreme Court Ruling on Draft

The fate of women in the armed forces could be affected by the Supreme Court's June 25 decision that male-only draft registration is constitutional. The Court, in overturning a July 1980 ruling by a three-judge federal district court in Pennsylva-nia, said it is not a form of sex discrimination to require only young men to register. The issue of drafting women should be left to Congress, the court said, since Congress has "especially broad constitutional power" over military matters. "The fact that Congress and the executive have decided that women should not serve in combat fully justifies Congress in not au-thorizing their registration, since the purpose of registration is

---

[30] Cropsey, *op. cit.*, p. 68.
[31] See "Draft Registration," *E.R.R.*, 1980 Vol. I, p. 425.
[32] Quoted by the Associated Press in *The New York Times*, Aug. 19, 1980.

to develop a pool of potential combat troops," declared Justice William H. Rehnquist, writing for the court's 6-3 majority.

The court noted that Congress fully considered President Carter's request that women as well as men be required to register for the draft. The decision to exclude women was not an "accidental byproduct" of the traditional view of women but rather a considered judgment, Rehnquist said. Congress had every right, in shaping registration for the draft, "to focus on the question of military need rather than equity," he added.

Reaction to the court's decision was mixed. Conservatives were elated, calling the ruling a vindication of traditional values. Phyllis Schlafly, an outspoken opponent of the Equal Rights Amendment, said the decision was "a tremendous victory for everything we've been fighting for." Feminists viewed the ruling as a setback for the cause of equal rights. "What this court says to us is that when women are compared to men under the Constitution, there are always going to be overriding concerns," said Judith Lichtman of the Women's Legal Defense Fund. "Today it happens to be the military; tomorrow it will be something else."[33]

Eleanor Smeal, president of the National Organization for Women, called the ruling "blatant discrimination." She predicted that the decision would be used "to perpetuate the myth that women are incapable of doing certain things."[34] Smeal and other feminists are worried that the decision could spell further trouble for the beleaguered Equal Rights Amendment. With the June 30, 1982, ratification deadline just a year away, the ERA still needs the approval of three more state legislatures.[35]

For the short-term, at least, the impact of the Supreme Court's ruling is likely to be more symbolic than real. President Reagan has said on a number of occasions that he supports the concept of an all-volunteer army and opposes a resumption of the draft. There has been talk in Washington that Reagan might end draft registration for males by not funding the Selective Service System in fiscal year 1982, which begins Oct. 1. But most defense analysts believe this is unlikely.

As for the future of women in the military, the "pause" in recruiting will be in effect at least until the end of the year. By that time, Pentagon planners will have received the final report on the impact of women on the nation's military readiness *(see p. 84)*. The findings of this report will likely influence the administration's future policies on women military personnel.

---

[33] Quoted in *Newsweek*, July 6, 1981, p. 65.
[34] Smeal and Schlafly were quoted in *The New York Times*, June 26, 1981.
[35] See "Equal Rights Fight," *E.R.R.*, 1978 Vol. II, pp. 925-944.

Selected Bibliography

Books

Binkin, Martin and Shirley J. Bach, *Women in the Military,* Brookings Institution, 1977.

Bliven, Bruce Jr., *Volunteers One and All,* Reader's Digest Press, 1976.

Fallows, James, *National Defense,* Random House, 1981.

Hoeber, Francis P. et al., *Arms, Men and Military Budgets: Issues for Fiscal 1981,* Transaction Books, 1980.

Moore, John L., ed., *U.S. Defense Policy: Weapons, Strategy and Commitments,* 2nd edition, Congressional Quarterly, 1980.

Stiehm, Judith Hicks, *Bring Me Men and Women: Mandated Change at The Air Force Academy,* University of California Press, 1981.

Articles

Adams, Virginia, "Jane Crow in the Army: Obstacles to Sexual Integration," *Psychology Today,* October 1980.

Beck, Melinda et al., "Women in the Armed Forces," *Newsweek,* Feb. 18, 1980.

Chaze, William, "Academy Women: Ready to Take Command?" *U.S. News & World Report,* May 26, 1980.

Cropsey, Seth, "Women in Combat?" *The Public Interest,* fall 1980.

Gilder, George, "The Case Against Women in Combat," *The New York Times Magazine,* Jan. 28, 1979.

Marshall, Kathryn, "Who are the Women who Join the Marines?" *Ms.,* February 1981.

Moskos, Charles, "The All-Volunteer Force," *The Wilson Quarterly,* spring 1979.

Myers, Lisa, "A Giant Step Toward Equality?" *The New Republic,* March 1, 1980.

Perry, Susan, "Female Veterans: Their Fight is Not Over," *Graduate Woman,* May-June 1980.

Rose, Frank, "The Captain is a Lady," *Esquire,* January 1981.

Stern, Linda, "Launch a Career With Basic Training," *Working Woman,* February 1980.

Webb, James, "Women Can't Fight," *The Washingtonian,* November 1979.

Reports and Studies

Editorial Research Reports: "Draft Registration," 1980 Vol. I, p. 425; "Military Pay and Benefits," 1978 Vol. I, p. 421; "Volunteer Army," 1975 Vol. I, p. 443.

Laird, Melvin R., "The Problem of Military Readiness," American Enterprise Institute, 1980.

U.S. Department of Defense, Office of the Assistant Secretary of Defense for Manpower, Reserve Affairs and Logistics, "Use of Women in the Military," 1977.

WOMEN AND AGING

by

Jean Rosenblatt

Sept. 25
1 9 8 1

WOMEN AND AGING

ONE WOMAN, aged 65, said she felt an occasional pang about the loss of her sexual attractiveness. She also said that when she went back to work at age 50, the younger people in her office ignored her at first. She felt invisible. Now, she is happily retired and has friends, interests, health, some money and a husband. She relishes the assurance she has gained over the years, although she worries about the death of those she loves, particularly her husband, and fears infirmity.

Another woman, 81 years old, has been widowed for 16 years and lives on her husband's Social Security benefits, now $400 a month. She misses her husband. Soon the room she gets in exchange for sorting clothes at a church community center will no longer be available. She does not know where she will go, but she would prefer not to live in a nursing home.

The lives of these two women embody some of the problems women face as they grow older. The number of women over 65 is increasing faster than any other segment of the population; women comprise 60 percent of those over 65. Women who became 65 in 1977 could expect to live an average of 18 more years, compared to the 14 years for men the same age. The most rapidly growing segment of the. elderly are those over 75, of whom 65 percent are women.

These statistics underscore the fact that the problems of aging are to a great extent the problems of women. But according to a recent study, "[o]lder women in America have been largely invisible, the reality of their lives obscured by myth and benign neglect."[1] In many instances, the reality of older women's lives includes loneliness, failing health and poverty. Besides being the fastest growing segment of the population, women 65 and older are also the poorest. In 1980, 18 percent of elderly women were classified as poor by the U.S. Census Bureau. Their poverty was largely the result of a lifetime of dependence, low wages and the fact that they live longer than men.

In October 1980, a White House Mini-Conference on Older Women was held in Des Moines, Iowa, in preparation for the White House Conference on Aging scheduled for December

[1] "Older Women: The Economics of Aging," The Women's Studies Program and Policy Center at George Washington University, October 1980, p. 1.

1981. Held every 10 years, the White House Conference on Aging has had considerable impact. The conclusions of the two previous conferences, held in 1961 and 1971, helped to increase Social Security benefits and to generate Medicare, Medicaid and laws prohibiting discrimination based on age. The 1980 mini-conference produced an advocacy group for and of middle-aged and older women, the Older Women's League (OWL), which made a number of recommendations to the White House Conference on Aging concerning adequate income, health and quality of life. "The emergence of OWL is both timely and inevitable," said the group's president, Tish Sommers. "Under the guise of combating inflation, there is a concerted across-the-board push to reduce collectively won benefits and to assure that no new entitlements are created. . . . Older women are ripe for action, strongly motivated by self-interest."[2]

Older women are emerging as a potentially powerful political group. More older people vote than do younger people and among them, women make up the majority. Older women are also becoming more organized. Groups such as the National Association of Retired Persons and the National Council of Senior Citizens report expanding predominantly female memberships and increasing activism concerning retirement income issues. These groups are working to influence public policies that affect older women and to combat the myths that the elderly are sexless, useless and powerless. Their messages and the social changes they advocate concern everyone, for by the year 2020 about 40 million people will be over 65, compared to the current 25 million.

Widowhood Inevitable for Most Women

In *Alone: Surviving as a Widow* (1981), Elizabeth C. Mooney wrote: "A widow has the image of one of life's losers. Ask anyone for free association and he'll offer gray hair, loneliness, matinees, dependence on children and grandchildren, attachment to television commentators. Even in the printer's world the widow has a bad name. It's a leftover word, taking up a whole line, that must be pruned from the end of a paragraph."

Although widows are thought of and often treated as outcasts, they comprise a large portion of the U.S. population *(see box p. 108)*. Over half of all women over 65 and 10 percent of all middle-aged women are widows. In contrast, only 14 percent of men over age 65 are widowed. A number of factors account for these statistics. Men die sooner than women, women tend to marry older men and only a small portion of older women remarry, primarily because there are so few eligible males.

---

[2] Quoted in "Growing Numbers, Growing Force: A Report from the White House Mini-Conference on Older Women," October 1980, p. 54.

While it is acceptable for older men to marry younger women, social norms do not condone women marrying men much younger than themselves.

The fact that the average age of widowhood is 56 and that only one woman in 12 will die before her husband are among the reasons women should know how to take care of themselves. But preparation for the loss of a husband may not make the adjustment to widowhood any easier. One 1975 study found that "older widows who experienced an extended period of grief in anticipation of a spouse's death adjusted no better to the loss than those widows who experienced the sudden loss of a spouse."[3] Dr. Robert N. Butler, director of the National Institute on Aging (NIA) in Bethesda, Md., suggests that husbands and wives teach each other the skills they use in everyday life so that neither will be helpless upon the death of the other. Women should know the financial affairs of the family, for example, and what their survivor's benefits are likely to be.

Dr. Butler also advises women not to move out of their homes immediately after their husband's death. A woman "does not need to upset the social fabric of her life so suddenly," he said. "She should give herself time to allow all the anniversaries she shared with her husband to pass at least once before she moves to a new home."[4] According to most experts it takes about two years for a widow to navigate the painful transition from being part of a couple to being alone. At first the widow is numb and still thinks of herself as a wife. After the numbness comes awareness, and feelings of anger, bitterness, self-hate and abandonment. Often women in this stage, which usually lasts about a year, feel as if they are going crazy. Eventually, although the widow does not recover from her grief, she adjusts to her loss and begins building a new life.

Medical problems brought on by the stress of watching a spouse die (if illness precedes the death), financial need, interrupted plans and lack of daily interaction all may add to the stress of mourning. According to sociologist Helena Z. Lopata of Chicago's Loyola University, the needs of widows fall into five areas: expression of grief, companionship, solution of immediate problems, building of self-confidence and competence, and help in regaining connections with friends and activities. Some experts believe that the most important of these is the expression of grief. Widows need to be encouraged to talk about how badly they feel, to cry, to talk about their late husbands. But this "grief work" can be easily stymied because other people sometimes find it difficult to talk about death.

---

[3] Quoted by Marilyn R. Block and others in "Uncharted Territory: Issues and Concerns of Women Over 40," University of Maryland Center on Aging, 1978.
[4] Quoted in *The Washington Post*, April 20, 1981.

Widowhood can be particularly difficult if money is tight, which is the case for many widows. A third of all widows live below the poverty level ($4,190 in 1980 for a single person). Less than 10 percent receive pension survivor benefits. About 60 percent of all single and widowed women over age 65 have as their sole source of income Social Security benefits averaging under $300 a month *(see p. 116)*. Although widows have to overcome enormous problems, there are compensations. "We are women who have learned to depend on ourselves, stronger women who are more than a leftover," Elizabeth Mooney wrote. "It is a gift that comes after the fire."

Living Arrangements, Social Networks

In her famous essay "A Room of One's Own," novelist and critic Virginia Woolf said that women ultimately have "no arm to cling to [and] ... go alone." Increasing numbers of older women are, willingly or not, going it alone. According to a recent study by the Women's Studies Program and Policy Center at George Washington University, women aged 55 and over are more likely to live alone than people in any other age group. Partly because of the high percentage of widows in this group, older women are more likely to live alone than older men, and the proportion doing so increases with age. "Almost half of the women 75 and older lived alone in 1978, compared to 21 percent of the men in this age group," the study noted.[5] In this vulnerable age group, only 21 percent lived with husbands while 20 percent lived with another family member.

The trend toward more older women living alone is in part related to the fact that 30 percent of all women now in their 70s have no children. According to Dr. Butler of the National Institute on Aging,[6] this is the result of the low fertility rates of women born between 1905 and 1910 — the lowest for any group of women in the United States. When these women would have been having children in the 1930s, the Great Depression struck. About 22 percent had no children, 23 percent had only one child and another 22 percent had two.

There are other factors accounting for the high number of older women living alone. Couples are having smaller families and live in smaller dwellings that cannot always accommodate another generation. With more women working, there may be no one at home to care for an aging parent. In addition, older women may not want to live with their children because of incompatible values or lifestyles. Despite these trends, the fam-

---

[5] "Older Women: The Economics of Aging," *op. cit.*, p. 5.
[6] Speaking at a conference on the health issues of older women held April 1, 1981, at the State University of New York at Stony Brook. Copies of the talks are available from School of Allied Health Professions, Health Sciences Center, SUNY at Stony Brook, N.Y. 11794.

ily remains the primary caretaker of older persons in the United States. Only 5 percent of men and women over 65 live in nursing homes. But of this number, 75 percent are women.

Retirement communities are one solution to isolation for predominantly middle-class and upper-middle-class people. These communities have been criticized as "hedonistic in spirit and devoted only to pleasure, recreation and leisure activities."[7] For people who can afford them, however, retirement communities shield residents from loss of status and give them an opportunity to remain active and involved with other people.

Single women often spontaneously form their own social networks. One researcher described an informal community that emerged in a small apartment building in San Francisco, where 37 of the 43 residents were women, mostly widowed, in their 60s, 70s and 80s. The women planned and participated in activities together and visited nearby nursing homes. Friendships were confined mainly to each floor. "This neighboring is a way of relaying information and also a way to detect sickness," said Marilyn Block, director of the National Policy Center on Women and Aging.[8]

Various forms of communal living may be the wave of the future for older women. Marilyn Pearlman, a psychiatric social worker in Washington, D.C., said that women now in their 30s more than women currently in their 50s and 60s may be the ones to eventually adopt such living arrangements as a way to retain their autonomy and stay out of nursing homes. Older women now "are not as open to having non-competitive relationships with other women," Pearlman told Editorial Research Reports. "But younger and middle-aged women are thinking of ways to design their retirement years rather than be helpless in them." Group and shared housing, in which women may live with others their own age or different ages, reduces living expenses, wards off loneliness and fosters mutual assistance as an alternative to doing without or relying on government programs.

Health Issues Affecting Older Women

Because of their longevity, women are at greater risk of disease than men; 85 percent of all women over age 65 have at least one chronic health problem. According to Nancy King, co-director of the National Action Forum for Older Women in Washington, D.C., "most of these problems do not seriously threaten a woman's ability to be mobile and independent but do

---

[7] G. F. Streib, "Social Stratification and Aging," in *Handbook of Aging and the Social Sciences* (1976), p. 172.

[8] "Uncharted Territory," *op. cit.*, p. 105. The National Policy Center is a research group funded by the Administration on Aging that analyzes federal policy affecting middle-aged and older women.

Marital Status of Men and Women Over 65

	Men	Women
Never married	5.4%	6.1%
Married	77.1	38.5
Living with spouse	74.6	36.9
Widowed	14.1	52.2
Divorced	3.3	3.3

Source: U.S. Department of Commerce, Bureau of Census

involve major expenses and a fear of living alone, perhaps without the necessary financial resources to afford quality health care."[9]

Arthritis, hypertension, diabetes, visual and hearing impairments, and strokes are all more common among women than men. Osteoporosis, or brittle bones, afflicts mainly post-menopausal women and because of it, women are three to five times more likely than men to have impairments of the hip, back and spine. Breast cancer is the most prevalent kind of malignancy in women and strikes one out of 15 in the United States between the ages of 35 and 55. The incidence increases among older women, although the number of new cancers drops because fewer women are still alive. Mastectomies — removal of the cancerous breast — are among the most frequently performed surgeries in the United States and may cause psychological problems for post-menopausal women, who are often dealing with other issues related to their femininity and sexuality at this time of their lives.

As women grow older, it may be increasingly difficult for them to obtain adequate health care. For example, an unemployed woman covered by her husband's health insurance plan may suddenly find herself without coverage if she gets divorced or her husband dies. The White House Mini-Conference on Older Women estimated that 4 million women between ages 45 and 65 do not have health insurance.

"Older women can not count on the medical profession," Dr. Butler wrote in *Aging and Mental Health* (1977). "Few doctors are interested in them. Their physical and emotional discomforts are often characterized as post-menopausal syndrome, until they have lived too long for this to be an even faintly reasonable diagnosis. After that they are assigned the category of senility." Yet experts agree that health care is one of the most important features in helping to keep older women independent, functional and out of institutions. A health delivery sys-

[9] Nancy King, "Older in America: A Background Paper," National Action Forum for Older Women, 1980, p. 4.

tem that provides for preventive self-care and home health care — cheaper than nursing home or hospital care in five out of six cases[10] — is important not only for the well-being of the elderly but also as a way to limit escalating health care costs.

Elder Abuse: Violence in the Family

Although battered children and wives have received much attention in recent years,[11] violence against older family members is not as well known. Like the other problems of the elderly, physical and mental abuse are largely women's issues. Older women are four times more likely than older men to be abused and make up 80 percent of all elder abuse victims, according to Marilyn Block of the National Policy Center on Women and Aging.[12]

Battered elders are most often battered parents and in many ways resemble battered children. Both are vulnerable because they are usually dependent on their caretakers for basic survival needs. In addition, both children and elderly parents "are *assumed* to be protected by virtue of the love and caring most people expect between parents and children," said Suzanne Steinmetz, associate professor of individual and family studies in the University of Delaware's College of Human Resources. Caretakers of both dependent children and parents often perceive their wards as a source of physical, emotional and financial stress. But "[w]hile the costs of caring for one's children are at least a recognized burden," Steinmetz wrote, "the emotional and economic responsibility for caring for one's elderly parent over a prolonged period of time has not been fully acknowledged."[13]

Violence against the elderly takes many forms, including physical assault, neglect, verbal and psychological abuse, and financial abuse — diverting assets, for example. Abused elders may have their medication withheld, be oversedated or not given the proper food. Definitions of abuse and neglect vary, and reported cases of abuse may comprise only a small number of incidents. Older women, like battered wives, may also be unwilling or unable to report abuse. Older women may fear reprisals or more abuse if they report it, they may be ashamed to admit they are being abused, or they may prefer abuse to living alone, in a nursing home or some other unfamiliar arrangement. According to one of the most recent studies on

---

[10] See Claude Pepper, "Congress and the Aging," *Journal of Home Economics*, fall 1978, pp. 21-22.
[11] See "Violence in the Family," *E.R.R.*, 1979 Vol. I, pp. 305-324.
[12] Experts estimate that about 4 percent of the total elderly population is at risk of being abused.
[13] Suzanne Steinmetz, "Investigating Family Violence," *Journal of Home Economics*, summer 1980, p. 34.

elder abuse,[14] someone other than the victim reported the abuse in 70 percent of the cases.

Studies indicate that older women are most likely to be abused by their adult children, particularly daughters and daughters-in-law. "It makes sense that women would be abusers," Marilyn Block told Editorial Research Reports, "given that women usually assume the caretaking role, regardless of whose parent comes to the house. A number of women . . . are expected to assume the caretaking responsibilities no matter what else they are doing. That increases the frustration level, the anger, and makes her a prime candidate to be an abuser." Limited financial resources, the continual demands of caring for a dependent elderly person and insufficient help with daily chores all contribute to an abusive situation.

Concerns Of Middle Age

MIDDLESCENCE is a word coined to describe a period in people's lives when they must adjust to emotional, physical and situational changes as inexorable and potentially disturbing as those of adolescence. Middle age usually is a time of self-examination that may reveal painful shortcomings or unaccomplished goals. Because of what author and critic Susan Sontag has called "the double standard of aging"[15] — by which men are judged by their achievements, personality and earning power, and women by their physical appearance — middle age is sometimes a more difficult period for women than for men.

Loss of physical attractiveness is not the only problem confronting women in their middle years. They also worry about the loss of a longtime spouse — and wage earner — through death or divorce, the end of the ability to bear children, the departure of children from the home — the so-called empty nest syndrome — and entry or re-entry into the job market. The growing number of very elderly people also has implications for middle-aged women, since they are the primary caretakers of aging parents.

Most women adjust to the biological and social changes associated with middle age. But for some, age-related stress leads to psychological problems that manifest in depression, suicide, drug abuse or alcoholism. In the population as a whole, the

---

[14] Legal Research and Services for the Elderly, "Elder Abuse in Massachusetts: A Survey of Professionals and Paraprofessionals," 1979. See also Marilyn Block and Jan Sinnott, eds., *The Battered Elder Syndrome* (1979).
[15] Susan Sontag, "The Double Standard of Aging," *Saturday Review*, Sept. 23, 1972.

The "Old-Old"		
	Women	Men
75-79	2,945,482	1,847,115
80-84	1,915,370	1,018,859
85+	1,558,293	681,428

Source: U.S. Department of Commerce, Bureau of Census, 1980 figures

suicide rate is highest for those in their 70s. But for women the suicide rate peaks between the ages of 45 and 54. Middle-aged and older women are the major consumers of prescription drugs. Over half the adult women in the country have used prescription tranquilizers, stimulants or sleeping pills.

Middle-aged women are frequent targets of pharmaceutical companies, who advertise their drugs as treatments for everything from the empty-nest syndrome to menopause, which some in the medical profession view as a disorder or a disease rather than a natural biological change. "Doctors will advise a male patient to 'work out' his problems in the gym or on the golf course, while a female patient with the *identical* symptoms is likely to get a prescription for Valium," noted the final report from the White House Mini-Conference on Older Women.[16]

Women account for about 20 percent of the nation's 10 million problem drinkers and alcoholics. According to Marian Sandmaier, author of *The Invisible Alcoholics* (1980), alcohol abuse is more widespread among women than is generally believed because women are more apt to indulge in secret or to minimize an alcohol-related problem. "The invisibility of women drinkers is reinforced at the public level as well," Sandmaier wrote. "Despite recent pressure from activist groups, some centers for alcoholism still refuse to admit women; many others limit their number. Organized efforts to identify and account for problem-drinking women in the community are often lackadaisical or non-existent, while outreach programs for men are energetically pursued. Thus, by the time many women finally do get help, their condition has resulted in extensive physical or emotional damage."[17]

Sandmaier contends that working women are more than twice as likely to have drinking problems as housewives and that married professionals are especially susceptible. Single, divorced and separated career-women also have a high rate of excessive drinking, she said. "While sex-role differences are breaking down, women are still largely encouraged to base their self-worth on relationships with men rather than on achieve-

[16] "Growing Numbers, Growing Force," *op. cit.*, p. 35.
[17] Marian Sandmaier, "The 'Closest Alcoholics,' " *Harper's Bazaar,* September 1981, p. 312.

ments and activities of their own," she wrote. "This can make them particularly vulnerable to the ups and downs of a marriage or affair, propelling them toward destructive drinking or drugs when 'something goes wrong.' "

Empty Nest Syndrome: Myth or Reality

The changes associated with middle age are not necessarily negative ones. For many women, the period after their children are grown is a high point in the life cycle — a time to refocus their energies on their own talents, interests and needs. On the other hand, "a woman who [has] put achievement first up to this point in life might now put more effort into friendships, community activities, relationships with men and other women, and the spiritual side of life."[18]

The departure of children from the home can be traumatic, especially for women who have gained their sense of worth primarily from the motherhood role. But many women also enjoy the freedom from the constant demands and responsibilities of child-rearing. In her book *Women of a Certain Age: The Midlife Search for Self* (1979), sociologist Lillian B. Rubin concluded that the empty-nest syndrome has been over-dramatized because of the widely held view that motherhood "is a woman's ineluctable destiny, her sacred calling, her singular area of fulfillment."

"Since mothers usually don't miss any part of the process, the end of active mothering doesn't come with any sudden wrench," Rubin wrote. "Indeed, for women who can look at their children and think: 'There's a job well done,' the sense of accomplishment transcends any feelings of loss; the relief is unequivocal. For those who suffer disappointment, the relief is mixed with painful feelings of failure. And yet, not one of those women yearned for another chance. For good or ill, they were glad the job was done, ready to move on to the next stage of life."

Menopause; Sexuality Beyond Mid-Life

In a culture that worships youth, menopause is frequently seen as the end of a woman's sexuality. Menopausal women are often pictured as unattractive, irritable, irrational and hysterical. Such stereotypes make a woman's adjustment to middle age more difficult than it needs to be. Menopausal women may also receive biased treatment from male physicians, who sometimes prescribe medication such as tranquilizers, anti-depressants or estrogen to suppress symptoms that may be unrelated to menopause or that require other treatment.

Women usually go through menopause between the ages of 45 and 50. It is a period — lasting from three months to three years

---

[18] Block, *et al.*, "Uncharted Territory: Issues and Concerns of Women Over 40," p. 76.

Crime Against the Elderly

Although older women are less likely to be victims of homicide, crimes such as rape, robbery, assault and fraud are common. Statistics are difficult to obtain since over half the crimes against women over 60 go unreported — particularly those involving abuse and fraud.

Fraud is the most prevalent crime against the elderly and in at least two-thirds of all cases the victim is an older woman. Schemes to bilk them out of their bank savings, phony medical plans, quick "cures" for chronic health problems, mail-order fraud, and fraudulent home and car repairs all take advantage of the fact that many older women are easily intimidated. These women are less likely than others to understand what they need and less likely to recognize what they are getting.

Frequently the elderly do not report fraud because they are embarrassed that they were "taken" while trying to get something for nothing. They may also fear that they will lose their independence, since their adult children may take the crime as proof that they should not be living alone. Even when the elderly do report fraudulent crimes, it is difficult to convict the con artists. If the case goes to trial, a defense attorney can use the hearing or vision impairment of elderly witnesses to invalidate their testimony.

A problem just as significant as crime against older people is their fear of being victimized. This fear as well as the crimes themselves "engender the loss of physical mobility, economic security, self-confidence and trust in others, thus contributing to the unhappy ending of the lives of many older women."*

*"Growing Numbers, Growing Force," 1980, p. 48.

or longer — of hormonal changes marked by the cessation of menstruation and ovulation. Although much is made of this "change of life," 65 percent of all women experience no significant physical or emotional symptoms. According to the Women's Medical Center of Washington, D.C., 20 percent of all women have no symptoms at all, and only 15 percent have severe symptoms requiring treatment.

Hot flashes and vaginal atrophy are thought to be the only symptoms directly related to the decreased estrogen levels that accompany menopause. Hot flashes are sudden, brief waves of heat that sweep over a woman's body. In vaginal atrophy, the walls of the vagina become drier, thinner and less elastic. This can lead to painful intercourse for some women, particularly those who have had intercourse infrequently. Decreased estrogen levels also cause loss of skin tone and elasticity, resulting in sagging breasts and wrinkles. Other symptoms associated with menopause — depression, anxiety, insomnia and weight gain, for example — are thought to result from psychological problems with aging and role changes rather than any physiological state.

Replacing the estrogen that a woman's body no longer produces after menopause has been a highly controversial practice in recent years. A panel of experts convened by the National Institute on Aging in 1979 concluded that although estrogen does relieve hot flashes and vaginal atrophy and might help prevent osteoporosis, it also increases the incidence of endometrial cancer. The panel recommended that physicians inform candidates for estrogen replacement about risks and benefits before deciding with the patient on a course of action.

Women who have gone through menopause are often considered too old to be interested in sex. In fact, menopause is often sexually liberating because a woman no longer has to fear unwanted pregnancies. Women who enjoy sex as young adults can continue to enjoy it at least into their 80s. Any decline in women's sexual activity has more to do with the aging of their partners or lack of available partners, researchers say. A study conducted at Duke University with couples over 60 found that of the men who were interested in sex, 87 percent were sexually active while 60 percent of the interested women were active. But 10 years later, the same proportion of women were active while only 30 percent of the men were; 75 percent of the couples agreed that the husbands were responsible for the cessation of intercourse.

A recent study by Bernard Starr and Marcella Bakur Weiner, two New York City psychologists, found that men and women over 60 "*are* interested in sex. They need it. They get it whenever they can."[19] Of the 800 60- to 91-year-olds Starr and Weiner surveyed, 75 percent said that sex was the same or better than when they were younger. Two predictors of continuing sexuality, Starr and Weiner found, were an active sex life and a positive attitude toward aging and life in general.

The myth that the middle and older years are devoid of sex is sometimes said to be perpetrated by adult children "bound by a primitive childhood need to deny their parents a sex life and to lock them into purely parental roles."[20] In any case, many couples report that their sex lives improve after their children grow up and move away. "After youngsters leave, couples can enjoy greater intimacy and start relating to each other again as husband and wife instead of Mom and Dad," said Dr. Ruth Westheimer, adjunct associate professor in the department of psychiatry at The New York Hospital-Cornell Medical Center. "This is the time when Saturday mornings in bed, for years just a remembered luxury, become possible once more."[21]

---

[19] Quoted in *The Washington Post*, July 23, 1981.
[20] Robert N. Butler and Myrna I. Lewis, *Love and Sex After Sixty* (1976), p. 7.
[21] Quoted by Abby Avin Belson in "Prime Time for Sex," *Harper's Bazaar*, September 1981, p. 58.

The Economics of Aging

EITHER by economic necessity or choice, increasing numbers of women are entering the work force. For the first time, more adult women are workers than are full-time homemakers. Nearly half of the nation's 44 million women workers are widowed, divorced or single. One out of every three women who work is 45 or older, a proportion that has increased significantly in the last 30 years. It has been estimated that another 3.5 million women between the ages 45 and 54 will be looking for work by the end of this century.[22] The most steady increases among older women workers have been in the 50-59 age group, a time when many women must become self-supporting for the first time because of the death of their spouse.

Although older women's labor force participation rates have increased, their earnings have not. "Mature women earn even less than younger women relative to the earnings of males in their own age groups," the Women's Study Program at George Washington University reported. "While white men's earning potential increases with age, women's earning potential stagnates and even declines in later years. The wage gap between men and women broadens with age until age 55, after which women recover minimally."[23]

In 1978, the average income for women 45 years and older who worked full-time, year-round was $8,941 — only slightly higher than for women 25-44 years of age whose income averaged $8,902. Like younger women workers, mature women are concentrated in dead-end, low-paying jobs. Nearly a third of older women workers hold clerical positions.[24]

Unemployment rates for women over 40 are about one-third higher than for men that age. Unemployed older women also stay out of work longer than younger women even though studies indicate that they try harder to find jobs. Half a million women over age 45 work part-time because they cannot get full-time jobs. Among the women who have the most difficulty finding jobs are displaced homemakers — persons who after being out of the work force for an extended period suddenly find themselves in need of work because of divorce or the death of the supporting spouse.

After three years of lobbying by women's rights groups, dis-

[22] See "Vanished Dreams: Age Discrimination and the Older Woman Worker," Working Women, National Association of Office Workers, 1980, p. 3.
[23] "Older Women: The Economics of Aging," op. cit., p. 14.
[24] See "Equal Pay Fight," E.R.R., 1981 Vol. I, pp. 209-228.

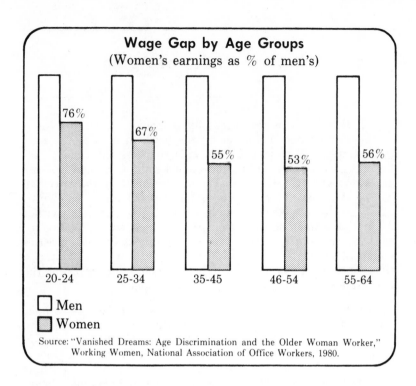

Wage Gap by Age Groups
(Women's earnings as % of men's)

76%
67%
55%
53%
56%

20-24   25-34   35-45   46-54   55-64

☐ Men
◼ Women

Source: "Vanished Dreams: Age Discrimination and the Older Woman Worker,"
Working Women, National Association of Office Workers, 1980.

placed homemakers became eligible for federal assistance under a 1978 law extending the Comprehensive Employment and Training Act (CETA). Title III of the act authorized job training and placement services specifically for displaced homemakers. Although this year's budget cuts hurt or killed several CETA-funded programs, the cuts were less than feared, according to Sandra Burton, director of the Displaced Homemakers Network in Washington, D.C. But, she added, the Reagan administration's preference for consolidating aid into block grants to the states will undoubtedly affect many programs established to help displaced homemakers.

Inequities in Social Security System

Although Social Security was never intended as the only means of support for older Americans, some 60 percent of all unmarried women over age 65 depend on Social Security as their sole source of income. To examine the treatment of women under the current system, Rep. Claude Pepper, D-Fla., chairman of the House Select Committee on Aging, in 1979 created the Task Force on Social Security and Women. Headed by Rep. Mary Rose Oakar, D-Ohio, the task force — which is still in existence — found many inequities in the system relating to widows, homemakers and working women.

Under the current system, which has not changed much in 40

years, married women generally receive Social Security protection as dependents of their husbands. If women do work, they can be covered as dependents of their husbands or on their own, but not both. Should the marriage end in divorce, the woman would lose Social Security protection if the marriage lasted less than 10 years. Widowed homemakers under age 60 cannot receive benefits unless they are at least age 50 and disabled or caring for children under age 18. Widows who remarry after age 60 retain their widows benefits, but divorced women forfeit their dependent's benefits upon remarriage at any age.

Because married women cannot receive both spouse and worker benefits, the protection they receive as workers often duplicates rather than supplements the protection they receive as spouses. In addition, benefits are often higher for couples where one spouse earned most or all of the income than for couples where both spouses had roughly equal earnings, even though the total family earnings in both cases are the same.

A study completed by the Department of Health, Education and Welfare (now the Department of Health and Human Services) in 1979 recommended several changes in the Social Security system to make it more equitable for women. Among other things, it said Congress could require that 50 percent of the total annual earnings of a couple be credited to each spouse's individual earnings record. The benefits of each spouse then would be based on one-half of the couple's earnings during years of marriage and on individual earnings while unmarried. "The idea underlying earnings sharing," the report said, "is that each spouse is an equal partner in marriage and each — whether a worker in paid employment or an unpaid homemaker — should have equal credit for total family earnings."

Older women would be the group most seriously affected by the Reagan administration's proposal, approved by Congress July 31, to eliminate the minimum Social Security benefit of $122.[25] This goes to workers who would otherwise receive a lesser amount based on their earnings record. The administration maintains that the chief beneficiaries of the program are people who have worked only a short time in employment covered by Social Security — many of them federal retirees with generous federal pensions. But according to the Women's Equity Action League, "double dippers" comprise only about 15 percent of the minimum beneficiaries. The minimum benefit cut caused such an uproar that the House of Representatives voted to restore it. The Senate referred the measure to its Finance Committee, which will consider it in the fall as part of an overall revision of the Social Security system.

---

[25] The cut in minimum benfits was included in the budget reconciliation package (HR 3982) that President Reagan signed into law Aug. 13.

Pension Issues Affecting Older Women

Pensions are the primary supplement to Social Security for most older Americans. But according to statistics compiled for the White House Mini-Conference on Older Women, only 20 percent of retirement-age women receive either public or private pensions based on their own or their husband's employment record. "For one reason, women are often employed in those industries and jobs where there is no pension coverage. Second, even those who work in covered employment receive pensions less often because they have alternated work force participation with homemaker/child-rearing roles."[26] In most cases, an employee must work for the same company for at least 10 years in order to qualify for a pension when he or she retires.

Many women are also adversely affected by provisions pertaining to their husband's pension benefits. Since few pension plans automatically provide survivor annuities, a woman will not receive pension income if her employed spouse dies before he reaches early retirement age or if he chooses not to provide survivor benefits in favor of a higher annuity while he lives.

For divorced women, the problems can be even greater. Many divorce courts do not treat retirement income or survivor's benefits as joint property, depriving divorced women of benefits accrued while they were contributing to the economy of the marriage. Even in community property states, where retirement income is considered divisible property in case of divorce, many women have trouble collecting it.

Proposed Legislation to Ease Poverty

To remedy some of the problems found in the Social Security system's treatment of older women, Reps. Oaker and Pepper introduced six bills, now pending before the Subcommittee on Social Security of the House Ways and Means Committee. One bill proposes that the combined earnings of a husband and wife be divided equally between them to determine eligibility for and amount of old age and disability benefits. Another would allow couples to split their earnings for Social Security purposes, which would equalize their Social Security payments.

A third bill concerns widows and surviving divorced spouses. Under the proposed legislation, the survivor or surviving divorced spouse would inherit the deceased's earnings credits that were earned during the marriage. The couple would have to have been married for at least five years before the spouse's death or the date the divorce became final. In another bill, a transition benefit would be provided to a widow of an insured

---

[26] "Growing Numbers, Growing Force," *op. cit.*, p. 12.

individual if the survivor was at least 50 years old and not otherwise eligible for benefits. The benefit, set at 71.5 percent of the wage earner's benefit, would cover only the first four months after the spouse's death.

Oakar and Pepper also proposed that, when a disabled spouse is entitled to benefits before age 50, the amount be not less than 71.5 percent of the benefits the deceased spouse would be entitled to at age 60. Another Oakar-Pepper bill would, if passed, allow a divorced spouse to qualify for benefits on the basis of a marriage that lasted five or more years. Currently, to receive benefits a woman must have been married to the wage earner for at least 10 years. The provision would apply only when the marriage existed for at least five years after the younger spouse reached 50.

Objections to these proposals have been raised by the House Subcommittee on Social Security. According to subcommittee spokesman Joseph Hall, "these bills, if passed, will add billions to the cost [of Social Security]. All the experts agree that women have an advantage under Social Security as dependents; they don't feel that women are badly treated, except in isolated incidents."[27]

Last April, three Republican senators — David Durenberg, Minn., and Mark O. Hatfield and Bob Packwood, Ore. — introduced the Economic Equity Act, a package of legislation intended to eliminate some of the economic inequities borne by women. Among other things, the act would:

Amend ERISA (Employment Retirement Income Security Act) to provide mandatory survivor's benefits for spouses of participants who die before retirement age; provide automatic joint and survivor's options; and eliminate the two-year waiting period between electing and receiving survivor's benefits.

Allow homemakers and women with low incomes to establish individual retirement accounts in their own names.

Assume that pensions of federal workers are part of marital property to enable ex-wives and widows of workers with federal pensions to collect a pro-rata share of retirement coverage.

Give tax credits to employers who hire displaced homemakers.

Reduce estate taxes for women who inherit farms and businesses.

Although legislation may alleviate some of the difficulties older women face, experts regard this as merely a first step to solving the larger problem of society's negative stereotyping of older women. By seeing older women as individuals and responding to their needs, we will, in the words of Dr. Robert Butler, be taking care of "our futures and our future selves."

---

[27] Quoted in *The Christian Science Monitor*, April 15, 1981.

Selected Bibliography

Books

Block, Marilyn R. et al., *Women Over 40,* Springer, 1981.
Butler, Robert N. and Myrna I. Lewis, *Love and Sex After Sixty,* Harper & Row, 1976.
Bequaert, Lucia H., *Single Women, Alone and Together,* Beacon Press, 1976.
Fuller, Marie Marschall and Cora Ann Martin, *The Older Woman,* Charles C. Thomas, 1980.
Mooney, Elizabeth C., *Alone: Surviving as a Widow,* Putnam, 1981.
Rubin, Lillian B., *Women of a Certain Age: The Midlife Search for Self,* Harper & Row, 1979.
Shields, Laurie, *Displaced Homemakers: Organizing for a New Life,* McGraw-Hill Paperbacks, 1981.

Articles

Gastel, Barabara et al., "Estrogen Use and Postmenopausal Women: A Basis for Informed Decisions," *Journey of Family Practice,* Vol. 11, no. 6, 1980.
Journal of Home Economics, selected issues.
Sontag, Susan, "The Double Standard of Aging," *Saturday Review,* September 23, 1972.

Reports and Studies

Block, Marilyn R. et al., "Uncharted Territory: Issues and Concerns of Women Over 40," Center on Aging, University of Maryland, August 1978.
Editorial Research Reports: "Retirement Income in Jeopardy," 1981 Vol. I, p. 169; "Social Security Reassessment," 1979 Vol. I, p. 461.
"Growing Numbers, Growing Force: A Report from the White House Mini-Conference on Older Women," October 1980.
Hooyman, Nancy R., "Older Women as Victims of Family Violence," University of Washington, 1980.
Moore, Emily C., "Women and Health: United States, 1980," Public Health Service, October 1980.
Oakar, Mary Rose, "Women and Social Security: The Challenge of the Eighties," National Action Forum for Older Women, 1980.
Older Women's League Educational Fund, "Older Women and Health Care: Strategy for Survival," January 1980; "The Disillusionment of Divorce for Older Women," August 1980.
"Older Women: The Economics of Aging," Women's Studies Program and Policy Center, George Washington University, October 1980.
"The Older Woman: Continuities and Discontinuities," National Institute on Aging and National Institute of Mental Health, October 1979.
"Vanished Dreams: Age Discrimination and the Older Woman Worker," Working Women, National Association of Office Workers, August 1980.

Cover art by Staff Artist Robert Redding

BABY BOOM'S NEW ECHO

by

Julia McCue

June 26
1 9 8 1

BABY BOOM'S NEW ECHO

BABIES ARE STAGING a comeback on the American scene these days. They have always been around, of course, but in the past two decades they have suffered from a certain obscurity. The postwar baby boom faded into the youth culture of the 1960s, followed by the singles society of the 1970s. But infant visibility again is rising, suggesting that another baby boom may be in the making. Though the statistical evidence is scant and tentative, the subject of childbearing is gaining attention. "Suddenly, having babies is back in fashion," Naomi Munson noted recently in *Commentary* magazine.[1] The news media aside, many people, using the evidence under their eyes, believe a second baby boom is under way. "Everyone I know is having a baby," a 31-year-old Washington lawyer commented recently. "This is a baby year."

Demographic conditions in the United States are uniquely primed to set off the largest baby boom in the country's history. This year, approximately 29 million women span the traditional childbearing years of ages 20 to 35. Never before has this group been so large. Ten million others in their upper teens will enter prime childbearing years during this decade. So far, however, this "mother bomb," as it is known, has been somewhat of a dud. Comparatively few of these women have chosen to bear children, and those that have usually opted for small families. But, enhancing the growing perception that a second baby boom may be under way, a slightly higher percentage of them have decided to have babies in the past three years.

By the end of 1980, the country's fertility rate *(see Definitions, p. 125)* had risen 4 points above the all-time low of 65.8 in 1976. This rise in fertility is not attributed to a massive, across-the-board embracing of motherhood, but rather to women having postponed childbearing and, upon reaching their late twenties and early thirties, deciding to begin a family. In 1978, the last year for which fertility rates have been compiled by specific ages, the rate for women 30-34 rose 2.8 percent. Although figures for 1979 and 1980 are not yet available, demographers believe that this trend is continuing.

---

[1] Naomi Munson, "Having Babies Again," *Commentary,* April 1981.

Even if this is an unusual and temporary situation, the possibility of another baby boom will not disappear until young women now 15 to 19 pass into their late twenties. However, many demographers believe that a baby boom could occur only if the childless women in their early thirties — the "postponers" — were joined in the childbearing urge by women in their twenties. If these two groups of women were to have an average of 1.8 children, the number predicted for them by the 1981 *total fertility rate*, the U.S. population would swell enormously for a time but would eventually settle down to zero population growth.[2]

The most extreme scenario that can be envisioned, given this country's demographic makeup, is that women of all ages will, like their mothers, have families of more than three children. During the postwar baby boom, the total fertility rate stayed above 3.0 for 18 years. In 1972, the presidential Commission on Population Growth and the American Future predicted that, given the prevailing rate of immigration, the population of the United States would reach 322 million in the year 2072 if women limited themselves to an average of two children. If three children were the norm, the population would approach one billion.

Demographers have long predicted that the birth rate would rise when the postwar baby boom generation began to have children. This is known as the "echo effect" and occurs simply because a large number of fertile women will have more children than a small number, almost regardless of the fertility rate. Richard A. Easterlin, a University of Pennsylvania economist, claims to detect more than an echo effect. He theorizes that population and the economy go through 15- to 25-year cycles and that, in the next decade, the time will be ripe for another explosion in birth rates.

Parents of the postwar babies were likely to have come of age in the Depression when times were hard and family size tended to be small. But they, in turn, had many children — the "baby boomers." These children grew up in relative affluence and had high expectations. Many of their expectations, Easterlin reasons, will remain unfulfilled because the sheer size of this generation has increased the competition for jobs. So as the baby boomers grow up and marry, they decide to have few children. But these children — sons and daughters of the baby boomers — will have lower expectations and will be happily surprised by what they are able to achieve, according to Easterlin. They will

[2] Without taking immigration into account, an average of 2.1 children per woman is needed to maintain a population with low mortality rates at a constant size — zero population growth. The United States has been below replacement-level fertility since 1972.

Demographic Definitions

Birth rate. The annual number of births per 1,000 people.

Cohort. The entire group of people born during a specified time. Those born in 1941, for instance, or in 1940-45.

Fertility rate. The annual number of births per 1,000 women of ages 15 through 44, considered their childbearing years.

Total fertility rate. A measure expressing births in a year in terms of the implied average number of children per women during her lifetime. This calculation takes into account the fertility rates for each age of women in childbearing years. The 1981 total fertility rate for the United States is 1.8.

face less competition for entry-level jobs and will have greater opportunity for advancement. They will be so optimistic about the future they, in turn, will produce an abundance of offspring.

Factors Underlying the Fertility Decline

Among demographers, Easterlin's is the minority view. Most of them regard the postwar baby boom as a bizarre anomaly that will not soon be repeated. The so-called "baby bust" or "birth dearth" that occurred immediately after the baby boom[3] can, Princeton sociologist Charles F. Westoff noted, "be regarded as a resumption of a long-term historical downward trend of fertility."[4] With the exception of the baby boom years, the fertility rate in the United States has been in a fairly steady decline since the 19th century.

Because the United States, like most developed countries, has made great strides toward reducing its mortality rate, decreasing fertility is a kind of Malthusian substitute for pestilence, famine and war — the traditional population controls throughout history. In 1972, the Commission on Population and the American Future characterized the population of the United States as being in transition "from a stabilized population maintained by high birthrates, high and erratic death rates, and short lifetimes, toward a stabilized population characterized by low birth rates, low death rates, and long lifetimes."[5]

America traces its fertility decline back to the last century. The underlying cause usually is regarded as the great urban

---

[3] The years most often given for the baby boom are 1946-61. In 1962, the U.S. fertility rate made its first sharp decline. However, the actual number of births remained high until 1965.

[4] Writing in *Demographic Dynamics in America* (1977), p. 54. The book is a collection of essays by Westoff and Wilbur J. Cohen, a former secretary of health, education and welfare.

[5] Commission on Population Growth and the American Future, "Population and the American Future," March 1972, p. 16. The commission was established jointly by President Nixon and Congress in 1969. John D. Rockefeller 3rd was chairman and Charles F. Westoff was executive director.

migration. Unlike on the farm, children in cities are not needed as laborers, and they are expensive to house and feed. There are also other reasons to account for the return of low fertility after the baby boom had run its course in the early 1960s. First, more effective contraception became available, and, second, women were making fundamental and far-reaching changes in their priorities regarding families and careers.

On May 9, 1960, the Food and Drug Administration approved the sale of a pill for use as a contraceptive. Around the same time, the medical establishment gave its sanction to interuterine devices. A decade later, in 1973, abortion laws were liberalized.[6] Public acceptance of new and effective birth control was not immediate but grew quickly. According to Selma Taffel of the National Center for Health Statistics, the number of unwanted births dropped by 36 percent between 1961 and 1970. "It was estimated," she wrote, "that about half of the drop in fertility between 1965 and 1970 was due to greater control of unwanted births."[7]

The dominant view of demographers is that improved methods of contraception alone did not cause the baby bust; women will attempt to achieve or prevent conception depending on the number of children they want. But effective contraceptives did take much of the guesswork out of family planning. The critical question is why, in any given time span, women are more inclined to have — or not to have — children. Two economists for the Rand Corp., William P. Butz and Michael P. Ward, advance the idea that the entrance of a large number of women into the labor force during the 1960s and 1970s caused the drop in fertility rates. In 1960, 37.7 percent of all adult women worked outside the home. By 1970, this figure had risen to 43.3 and by 1980 to 51.6. Butz and Ward believe that after 1960 it was the affluence of women workers that determined and continues to determine fertility rates.

When a working woman gives birth to a child, inevitably she must take time off from her job, forfeiting salary and perhaps experience that would lead to her advancement. Butz and Ward note: "In a society where mothers usually take principal responsibility for raising children, the income they do without as a result is a significant part of the cost of the child."[8] These "opportunity costs" may raise the expense of having several children to a prohibitive level. The Department of Agriculture

---

[6] See "Contraceptives and Society," *E.R.R.*, 1972 Vol. II, pp. 415-438, and "Abortion Politics," *E.R.R.*, 1976 Vol. II, pp. 765-784.
[7] Selma Taffel, "Trends in Fertility in the United States," Department of Health, Education and Welfare Publication No. (HRA) 78-1906, September 1977, pp. 17-18.
[8] William P. Butz and Michael P. Ward, "Baby Boom and Baby Bust: A New View," *American Demographics*, September 1979, p. 13.

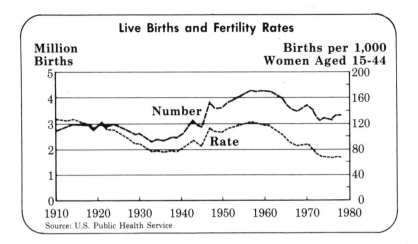

Live Births and Fertility Rates

Million Births

Births per 1,000 Women Aged 15-44

Number

Rate

1910 1920 1930 1940 1950 1960 1970 1980

Source: U.S. Public Health Service

estimated that the average cost of raising a child from birth to age 18 was approximately $77,000 at 1980 price levels. This figure does not, of course, include the cost of college or "opportunity costs" of the mother.

Further, a working mother essentially holds down two jobs, those of housewife and wage earner. A study conducted by the Survey Research Center of the University of Michigan indicated that in 1975 married men spent an average of 25 minutes a day doing housework, whereas married women spent two hours and 23 minutes. The average amount of time married men spent in caring for their children decreased from 17 minutes a day in 1965 to 15 minutes in 1975, according to the same findings. The married woman's time spent in child care increased from 29 to 31 minutes a day.[9]

Other studies have indicated that men do not increase the amount of time they spend working in the home in proportion to the number of children they have. For all these reasons, Ward and Butz maintain, working women are more likely to postpone having children and to have fewer children than women who do not work. And they add that as long as large numbers of women work, the fertility rate will be depressed.

Postponed Pregnancy and Its Hazards

Mothers of infants are traditionally pictured as being young. The term "young mother" is understood to denote not only the youth of the woman but also the tender age of the child. This picture of mothers of very young children is changing. Nowadays, "young mothers" may be anywhere from 30 to 40 years old. Women who postpone having children generally do so because of career aspirations or simply because they no longer feel

[9] Figures cited by Frank P. Stafford, "Women's Use of Time Converging with Men's," *Monthly Labor Review,* December 1980.

expected to marry and promptly start bearing children upon leaving school. Deborah Baldwin, a writer and editor, is a typical "postponer." In 1978 she wrote about "Motherhood and the Liberated Woman," describing her reasons for delay:

> I am 28 years old and working in a white-collar professional job. I am childless, as are practically all the other women I know of my generation and class. We are today's women — perseveringly independent, mobile, our own best friends. Many of us have taken great pains to free ourselves from the sticky bindings of family, but the bindings of a career are ones we have eagerly assumed.
>
> There's a new wave of books and movies that show heroic women casting off the bonds of housewifedom and striking out on their own. Women like me, who have built our lives around avoiding that trap in the first place, have gone largely unrecorded, but still we can identify with the tales of our slightly older sisters, the ones who made the 'mistakes' we've steered clear of.[10]

Now in 1981, Deborah Baldwin is 31 years old and is expecting her first child. She describes her decision to have a child as a complicated one: "I think that it was deciding 'Well, now or never.' Also realizing that if you want kids, that you want to be young enough to enjoy them. Even though doctors say that you can wait until you're 40, you sort of have this image of growing old before they are grown up and you feel 'why wait that long?' "[11] Baldwin also said that waiting much longer might make it risky to have children.

There are increased health risks to a pregnant woman in her thirties and to her unborn child. First, the chances of conceiving a child decrease as a woman gets older. Pregnant women over the age of 35 are twice as likely as women in their twenties to develop toxemia, a disorder characterized by high blood pressure that can lead to convulsions and coma. A woman of 35 is also three times as likely to miscarry as a woman of 25. Dangers to the child of an older mother are even greater. There is only one chance in 2,500 that children born of American mothers in their twenties will have an extra chromosome, causing Down's Syndrome or mongolism. Children born of mothers in their late thirties have one chance in 280 of developing this chromosomal defect.

Certain chromosomal and nervous disorders, including Down's Syndrome, can be detected by amniocentesis, a test routinely given to pregnant women over 35. Amniotic fluid is withdrawn from the womb and is checked for Down's Syndrome and certain hereditary diseases. However, amniocentesis does

---

[10] Deborah Baldwin, "Motherhood and the Liberated Woman," *The Washington Monthly*, July-August, 1978.
[11] Interview, May 21, 1981.

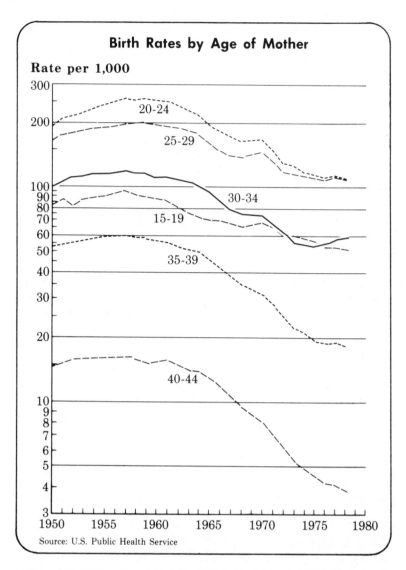

Birth Rates by Age of Mother

Rate per 1,000

20-24

25-29

30-34

15-19

35-39

40-44

300
200
100
90
80
70
60
50
40
30
20
10
9
8
7
6
5
4
3

1950   1955   1960   1965   1970   1975   1980

Source: U.S. Public Health Service

not reveal all development problems to which a fetus is prey. A study made by the Center for Disease Control in Atlanta in 1979 found that if all pregnant women between the ages of 35 to 45 underwent amniocentesis and if those found to be carrying abnormal babies took the only remedy available, abortion, the risk of these women actually bearing a child with a serious defect would be reduced to that of a younger woman.

The chances that a woman over 45 would bear a severely retarded child increase greatly, however. Even if all pregnant women over 45 had amniocentesis and decided to abort fetuses found to have severe abnormalities, the study found, their chances of bearing abnormal children would still be twice as likely as for a much younger woman. Cynthia Green of the Population Crisis Committee in Washington, D.C., predicts that medical science may react to the lengthening of the childbearing years by developing prenatal tests for a wider range of fetal disorders. "I think in the future we are going to see many more women 35 to 40 and on up to 45 who are having their first or second child," she said.[12] This trend may be reinforced by the failure of many first marriages and the desire of women to begin a family during a second marriage.

The Postwar Baby Boom

THE UPSURGE in the birth rate touched off after World War II is the single most unusual and intriguing event in the demographic history of the United States. Preceded and followed by small cohorts *(see Definitions)*, the baby boom generation appears on demographic charts as a mammoth lump, often described as looking like a python that swallowed a pig. From 1946 through 1961, 64 million babies were born in this country, whereas only 41.5 million were born in the 16 years immediately before the end of the war. The fertility rate jumped from 85.9 in 1945 to 101.9 in 1946, and on up to 122.7 at the height of the baby boom in 1957.

This leap in the fertility rate immediately after the end of the war led to the label "postwar baby boom." Dr. Leon F. Bouvier of the Population Reference Bureau Inc., a nonprofit research organization in Washington, D.C., believes the term is misleading — that it falsely suggests that the "prime cause was the ending of hostilities" and the return of the troops, "some to wives and others to fianceés." He points out that after 1947, both the rate and the number of births fell off for the next three years. "It was not until 1951 that the real baby boom got under way. Postwar family reunification and/or formation does not explain the high fertility that lasted for well over the next decade.[13]

High birth rates are, however, a traditional byproduct of a war's aftermath. In the years immediately following World War II, Western Europe, Australia, Canada and New Zealand also experienced a rise in fertility. For European countries, this "boomlet" was of short duration and they soon returned to their

---

[12] Interview, May 28, 1981. The Population Crisis Committee is a non-profit interest and educational group based in Washington, D.C.
[13] Leon F. Bouvier, "America's Baby Boom Generation: The Fateful Bulge," *Population Bulletin*, Vol. 35, No. 1, Population Reference Bureau Inc., 1980.

U.S. Births Since World War II

Year	Births	Year	Births
1980	3,473,000	1962	4,167,362
1979	3,598,000	1961	4,268,326
1978	3,333,279	1960	4,257,850
1977	3,326,632	1959	4,244,796
1976	3,167,788	1958	4,246,000
1975	3,144,198	1957	4,300,000
1974	3,159,958	1956	4,210,000
1973	3,136,965	1955	4,097,000
1972	3,258,411	1954	4,071,000
1971	3,555,970	1953	3,959,000
1970	3,731,386	1952	3,909,000
1969	3,600,206	1951	3,820,000
1968	3,501,564	1950	3,632,000
1967	3,520,959	1949	3,649,000
1966	3,606,274	1948	3,637,000
1965	3,760,358	1947	3,817,000
1964	4,027,490	1946	3,411,000
1963	4,098,020	1945	2,858,000

Source: Bureau of the Census

historic pattern of diminishing birth rates. Of the countries that took part in the war, only Canada, Australia, New Zealand and the United States exhibited an extended rise in fertility. "These were countries of hope, new worlds where lives could begin again," writes journalist Landon Y. Jones in his book *Great Expectations*. He believes more was at work than a wartime legacy of "pentup birth demand."[14]

Any explanation of a given fluctuation in the birth rate of a developed country must take into account many factors affecting the decision of millions of women to bear children. Changing social, economic and political conditions are reflected in the ascending and descending lines on demographic charts. Americans were generally optimistic about their future in the late 1940s and during the 1950s, according to most social indexes of the time. The United States emerged from World War II victorious, its territory unscathed, its international reputation enhanced and, after years of prewar depression, its industries healthy. The country was, in the words of President Truman's 1949 State of the Union address, "better able than ever before to meet the needs of the American people and to give them their fair chance in the pursuit of happiness."

For many Americans, the pursuit of happiness seemed to entail starting a family; marriage and fertility patterns underwent an abrupt change. Women suddenly began marrying

---

[14] Phrase used by Landon Y. Jones in *Great Expectations*, (1980), p. 20.

U.S. Birth Rates

Record	Rate	Period
Lowest	14.8 births per 1,000 population	1975, 1976
Previous low	14.9 births per 1,000 population	1973, 1974
Depression low	18.4 births per 1,000 population	1936
Postwar high	25.3 births per 1,000 population	1957

younger and having children sooner than their mothers did. The median age at first marriage for women in 1930 was 21.3 and by 1956 it was 20.1. Almost half of the women embarking on first marriages in that year were, therefore, teen-agers. In 1960, near the end of the baby boom, 71 percent of all women aged 20-24 had been married once. Half of the births in 1955-1964 took place during the first 15 months of marriage, compared to the 25- to 26-month average for first births in 1930. In the 1950s, second children were also born sooner, and the average age of mothers giving birth to second children dropped to 24.7.

Younger women bore most of the children in the baby boom. However, there is evidence that older women who delayed having children during the Depression and war years also began to have them. Birth rates were very high for older women as well as for younger women during this period. Not only was childbearing extended into middle age, but fewer women than in the preceding generation remained childless. Childlessness declined to a new low. Before the baby boom, 20.8 percent of all women who had ever been married never had children; in the baby boom the percentage dropped to 10.6.[15]

What prompted women, from teen-agers to those in middle age, suddenly to begin having children in greater numbers than their mothers did? Those women who had spent the war years in traditionally male civilian jobs withdrew from the labor force after the war and returned to the home and childbearing. Whether because of patriotism ("let the vet have the job"), traditional values or prejudice against women in the work force, women left the business world to men. When labor shortages developed, Richard A. Easterlin theorizes, the population tried to compensate with an enormous onslaught of future workers, the baby boom. Whatever the reasons — whether it was a population's response to economic bounty, or simply a pervad-

---

[15] Figures cited in published congressional hearings, "Domestic Consequences of United States Population Change," Select Committee on Population, U.S. House of Representatives, Government Printing Office, 1978.

ing optimism — millions of babies (as many as 4.3 million in 1957) arrived yearly on the American scene.[16]

Population Bulge; Its Far-Reaching Effects

Once America was well on its way to producing these 64 million infants, it faced the task of providing for them. As they passed through each phase of life, their effect on the institutions that served them was "like a baseball being shoved through a straw."[17] For a few years this army of infants was kept relatively quiescent in cribs and playpens. The crunch came when they reached school age. Between 1950 and 1970, elementary school enrollment zoomed by 63 percent. Between 1946 and 1956, the number of students in kindergarten through the eighth grade rose from 17.6 million to 24.3 million. This wave of youngsters caused shortages of elementary schools in the mid-1950s and secondary schools in the 1960s. The nation's high school population doubled between 1950 and 1975.

The growth of the college-age population naturally lagged behind, increasing only from 16 million in 1950 to 16.1 million in 1960. By 1970, this age group had expanded to 24.7 million. There were not only more people of college age but a higher percentage of them were actually in college. This was due, in part, to increased affluence and expectations but also because of the war in Vietnam and student deferments.

After struggling along somewhat uneasily in the overcrowded classrooms of the 1950s, the first wave of the baby boomers and their younger brothers and sisters found a certain measure of unity as they set the tone of the decade of youth, the 1960s. Joined together by the commonality of the college experience, objections to the war and a knowledge that their numbers gave them strength, the baby boom generation laid its stamp on that decade so that now "the sixties" conjures up the vision of rebellious youth.

As the baby boom generation came of age in the 1970s, its effect on society was more subtle but perhaps also more profound. During the 1970s, the labor force grew by 22 million, compared with 12 million in the 1960s and 7.5 million in the 1950s. This influx of young, inexperienced workers is sometimes blamed for a slowdown in the growth of productivity. Capital

---

[16] Easterlin wrote: "[S]everely restrictive immigration legislation of the 1920s meant a sharp curtailment in the labor reserve that had traditionally supplied the demands of major economic booms. Thus, in the 1940s and 1950s when labor force growth from native sources was at an all-time low, a massive influx of immigrants to satisfy the labor demand of a major economic boom did not occur as in the past. In effect, the role that immigration had served to buffer the impact of economic booms on the native population was eliminated by the restrictive legislation." — "What Will 1984 Be Like? Socioeconomic Implications of Recent Twists in Age Structure," *Demography*, Vol. 15, No. 4, November 1978.

[17] Dr. Martin O'Connell, chief of fertility statistics, U.S. Bureau of the Census, quoted in *The New York Times Magazine*, May 31, 1981.

investment could not keep up with the expanding labor market and industry investment in equipment per worker grew more slowly, causing productivity growth to be slugglish. The labor surplus depressed real income for younger workers.

According to Data Resources, a Massachusetts-based economic consulting firm, 25- to 29-year-olds now earn $300 less (after salaries are adjusted for inflation) than that age group earned in 1970. Male college graduates now in their late forties and early fifties are relatively scarce, and they earn 63 percent more than workers in their twenties and thirties. In 1968, the advantage of older college graduates over younger workers was only 38 percent. Almost one-fifth of the number of Americans holding college degrees are products of the baby boom and have received those degrees since 1975. It has been estimated that among those graduates who find jobs, almost one-quarter of them will be overeducated for their jobs — a situation that is expected to last through 1990.[18] Many do not find jobs. The unemployment rate averaged 6.2 percent during the 1970s, compared to 4.6 percent between 1947 and 1969.

If members of the baby boom have lowered productivity, they have also contributed to inflation. Now at a time in their lives to make major purchases, such as houses and cars, they are buying on credit and heating up the economy. Because young people do not save as much as those in middle age, the rate of savings has dropped. The baby boom cohort has had other effects on the country. Younger people move more than older ones and the baby boomers' travels have made geographic shifts more pronounced. Their numbers have made an all-volunteer armed forces possible. They have even been blamed for the drop in voter participation, from 62.8 percent of the voting age population in 1960 to 51.8 percent in 1980. Younger voters stay away from the polls in greater numbers than older ones.

The effects of the baby boom are, and were, staggering. Because the arrival of children in such large numbers took the country unawares, the dislocations they caused were perhaps greater than they had to be. Services, especially government services geared to certain age groups, such as education and Social Security, are extremely sensitive to demographic age shifts. The federal government recently recognized the importance of demographic analysis by including studies on the long-range effects of population changes in the federal budget.[19] Although such predictions are admittedly speculative, they may alert government planners to future population trends and their effect on society.

---

[18] See "The Baby Boomers Come of Age," *Newsweek*, March 30, 1981.
[19] The federal budget for fiscal year 1981 included an analysis of those effects.

Cyclic View of Successive Generations

In studying population trends and their ramifications, it is difficult to ignore the idea that there may be a certain amount of demographic determinism affecting our lives. It may simply be, as Easterlin suggests, that the size of one generation affects the next. It may extend further and affect the whole generation's outlook on life. It has been suggested that there are "good" years and decades in which to be born. The fewer the number of births, the better life will be, the theory goes. Children born in the 1930s formed a small cohort, the first in 150 years to be smaller than that which preceded it, and it is often called the "good times cohort." Americans born during that decade benefited, when they grew up, from the labor shortages their numbers had caused.

Members of large cohorts are generally supposed to suffer from anxiety based on the feeling that if they falter once at school or at work, there are many others equally willing and capable of taking their places. Whether a large generation will go down in history as being more productive than a small one because of this competition is hard to foretell and perhaps not fair to judge. Some people do, however, look upon the size of the generation they were born into as a kind of demographic zodiac sign promising good fortune and happiness or struggle and unfulfilled expectations.

The baby boom generation would seem to bear out the theory that a large generation does not necessarily confer happiness on its members. Although they enjoyed a certain exhilerating feeling of unity during the youth revolution of the 1960s, members of the baby boom did not sail smoothly through the 1970s. Landon Y. Jones describes the baby boomers' changing perceptions as they matured and discovered that the idealism of youth did not last long in a world crowded with competitors:

> [T]hey originally saw themselves as the beneficiaries of progress. To prepare for it, they had been educated like no other generation. With their education came high mobility and high aspirations. These baby boomers will be satisfied not simply with an affluent society but only with one that will fulfill the expectations that their self-confidence and sophistication have fostered. Women want both careers and families. Men want to equal the incredible achievements of their parents. They would be strong of body and fulfilled of mind.

> Now, as it washes up in the 1980s, the baby-boom generation is experiencing a shift in the way it thinks about itself and its future. Optimism is yielding to pessimism. Altruism is yielding to

narcissism. The generation that grew up convinced of its special place in society is not finding it. The maternity wards were too crowded: there were too few pediatricians; the schools were crowded; they were sent to Vietnam; they couldn't find jobs; they couldn't get promoted. Instead, they found themselves causing booms in crime, in suicide, in divorce, in childlessness, in venereal disease, in housing prices and in property taxes.[20]

In 1959, when the "good times cohort" was in its twenties, Americans believed that the future would be an improvement on the present and the past. In 1979, with the baby boom generation in its twenties and early thirties, the Bureau of the Census found that "the past of five years ago is now given a higher rating than the present, and the five-year future was given a lower rating than the present or the past."[21] The future, in short, is not as bright as it used to be.

Demographics of the Future

H OWEVER GLOOMILY the coming years look to the baby boomers, a brighter future for the country as a whole is expected when they enter middle age. Dr. Bouvier writes: "The baby boom generation is on the verge of entering the most productive phase of life. It has all but completed the earliest troublesome phases and U.S. society has survived!"[22] Planners expect that it will begin to contribute to society in the same massive way in which it has, in the past, disrupted society.

The economy is expected to benefit most from the aging of the work force. Older, more experienced workers tend to raise productivity. Moreover, fewer young workers will then be entering the labor market, and less money will be needed to train and equip them. According to this line of reasoning, industries will therefore have more money for capital investment, and for research and development. Equally important, unemployment should drop as fewer young people enter the labor force, and labor shortages usually translate into higher wages.

The future for the labor force is not all rosy. Competition for coveted positions will increase in the next decade, and in the long term retirement will cause a severe problem. According to

---

[20] Landon Y. Jones, *op. cit.*, p, 330.
[21] Conrad Taeuber, preface, "America Enters the Eighties, Some Social Indicators," *The Annals of the American Academy of Political and Social Science*, January 1981, p. vii. Taeuber is a former assistant director of the Bureau of the Census and currently is director of the Center for Population Research at Georgetown University. See also "America's Next Century," *E.R.R.*, 1976 Vol. I, pp. 1-20.
[22] Leon F. Bouvier, "America's Baby Boom Generation: The Fateful Bulge," *Population Bulletin*, 1980, p. 32.

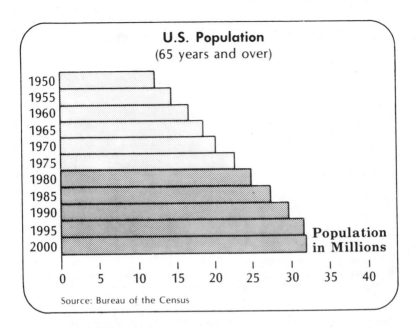

U.S. Population
(65 years and over)

1950	
1955	
1960	
1965	
1970	
1975	
1980	
1985	
1990	
1995	Population
2000	in Millions

0　5　10　15　20　25　30　35　40

Source: Bureau of the Census

the 1981 federal budget's long-range projections, the elderly population — those over 65 — will grow from approximately 25 million this year to over 52 million by 2030. And the work force, which will support the retirees, is destined to shrink. The ratio of workers to retirees is currently 5 to 1, but by 2005 it is expected to be only 2 to 1. The Office of Management and Budget estimates that even now almost 38 percent of the federal budget goes to retirement and health care benefits for those Americans over the age of 65. Because of demographic trends and rising life expectancy,[23] there is the prospect of far higher outlays in the next century.

As the number of old people rises, so will the demand for long-term health care and economic security. Unless measures are taken to shore up the Social Security system, the baby boom generation will perhaps face deprivation in old age. Because they will have few children, baby boomers will not be able to rely on their offspring for support if the government cannot help them. However, because of their numbers, they can look forward to exerting tremendous political power in middle and old age to ensure adequate retirement benefits.[24]

Perils of Forecasting Population Trends

While it is the job of demographers to predict population trends, forecasting is fraught with the probability of error. Fabian Linden, director of consumer research for the Conference

---

[23] Life expectancy has risen steadily in the United States. In 1968, average life expectancy was 70.2 years. In 1978, the last year for which data is available, it was 73.8. This trend is expected to continue.
[24] See "Retirement Income in Jeopardy," *E.R.R.*, 1981 Vol. I, pp. 171-187.

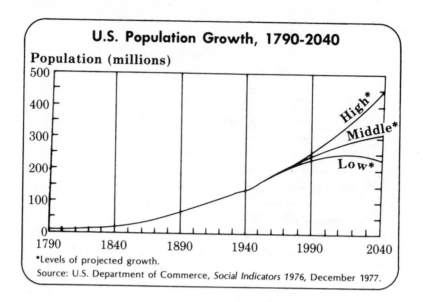

U.S. Population Growth, 1790-2040

Population (millions)

High*
Middle*
Low*

1790   1840   1890   1940   1990   2040

*Levels of projected growth.
Source: U.S. Department of Commerce, *Social Indicators 1976*, December 1977.

Board, a New York-based business research organization, observes that demography "is a very nervous way to make a living." Demographers "have a forecasting accuracy which just rates marginally better than the meteorologists; it is very difficult to forecast the disposition of women to have . . . babies."[25]

Demographers try to devine the future by making mathematical projections that are based on a given set of circumstances and assumptions. Predictions are made by selecting what seems to be the most likely projection. Dr. Bouvier recalls that in 1938, "one of our great demographers, Jacob Siegel," projected that the U.S. population would level off in 1990 at about 160 million. "He predicted the right total fertility rate but he missed the baby boom."[26]

Population projections are calculated for the government by the Bureau of the Census, which issues three sets of projections every few years. Each set is based on assumptions of low, moderate and high fertility. The most recent projections were made in 1977, and re-analyzed in 1979. When the bureau estimated the size of the U.S. population on July 1, 1979, the number corresponded closely to the one predicted in the 1977 moderate projection.

However, once the 1980 census was taken, the Census Bureau discovered that it had woefully underestimated the number of people living in the United States. On the day of the census, April 1, 1981, the bureau estimated that the population stood at 222 million. The number actually counted was significantly

---
[25] Quoted in *The Wall Street Journal*, July 19, 1978.
[26] Interview, May 29, 1981.

larger, 226.5 million. Even the highest growth projections made in 1977 were several million below the census figure.

Prospects for Zero and Negative Growth

Zero population growth is a term that gained currency in the late 1960s when the dangers of the worldwide population explosion impinged on the consciousness of the United States.[27] Zero growth means not just limiting births but also restricting immigration so that a country's population gain is balanced by emigration and deaths. If 2.1 children were the average per family, the so-called replacement rate ("zero population growth") would be achieved — assuming that the number of people leaving the country equaled the number of people coming in.[28]

Low fertility has given rise to talk of "demographic suicide" in Western Europe, but it does not look to immigration to replenish its stock. Sagging economic conditions have prompted some of the countries to restrict the inflow of immigrants ("guest workers") from southern Europe. Because of low fertility, France and West Germany have a median age that is 15 percent higher than America's. Both have instituted larger allowances for families with more than two or three children.

While the concept of zero population growth has drawn many adherents,[29] negative growth has not. It is viewed as ultimately detrimental to the economy of a country and on its standard of living. But in the short term, as the "good times cohort" of the 1930s illustrates, a declining population seems good. According to Gerard Calot of the National Institute of Demographic Studies in Paris, "for perhaps 20 years, everyone finds it to his advantage. A falling population is good for the short term."[30] If a population keeps declining, however, markets can be expected to shrink so severely that the economy will falter.

It is extremely doubtful that the scenario of a doomed civilization is a realistic one for the United States, with its continuing high immigration and the possibility of another baby boom, or at least an "echo" of the first. While it may seem likely that the U.S. population is fairly stable, the current "boomlet" is being watched closely for its portents. Since the postwar baby boom surprised the demographers, they are hesitant to say outright that another one is not in the making.

---

[27] See "Zero Population Growth," *E.R.R.*, 1971 Vol. II, pp. 903-924.

[28] See Leon F. Bouvier,"The Impact of Immigration on U.S. Population Sizes," Population Reference Bureau Inc.

[29] They include the Commission on Population Growth and the American Future, which stated in its 1972 report: "We have looked for, and not found, any convincing economic argument for continued national population growth. The health of our economy does not depend on it. The vitality of business does not depend on it. The welfare of the average person certainly does not depend on it."

[30] Quoted in *The Wall Street Journal*, Aug. 23, 1979.

Selected Bibliography

Books

Cohen, Wilbur J. and Charles F. Westoff, *Demographic Dynamics in America*, The Free Press, 1977.

Jones, Landon Y., *Great Expectations*, Coward, McCann & Geoghegan, 1980.

Sternlieb, George and James W. Hughes, *Current Population Trends in the United States*, Center for Urban Policy Research, 1978.

Articles

Adams, Arvil V., "The American Work Force in the Eighties: New Problems and Policy Interests Require Improved Labor Force Data," *The Annals of the American Academy of Political and Social Science,* January 1981.

Beck, Melinda et al., "The Baby Boomers Come of Age," *Newsweek,* March 30, 1981.

Butz, William P. and Michael P. Ward, "Baby Boom and Baby Bust: A New View," *American Demographics,* September 1979.

Easterlin, Richard A., "What Will 1948 Be Like?: Socioeconomic Implications of Recent Twists in Age Structure," *Demography,* November 1978.

Munson, Naomi, "Having Babies Again," *Commentary,* April 1981.

Otten, Alan L., "Western European States See Economic Troubles As Birth Rates Decline," *The Wall Street Journal,* Aug. 29, 1979.

Wolfe, Linda, "The Coming Baby Boom," *New York,* Jan. 10, 1977.

Reports and Studies

Bouvier, Leon F., "America's Baby Boom Generation: The Fateful Bulge," *Population Bulletin,* Population Reference Bureau Inc., April 1980.

"Domestic Consequnces of United States Population Change," Report of the Select Committee on Population, U.S. House of Representatives, 95th Congress, December 1978.

Editorial Research Reports: "The Changing American Family," 1977 Vol. I, p. 415; "Retirement Income in Jeopardy," Vol. I, p. 171; "Zero Population Growth," 1971 Vol. II, p. 903.

Harter, Carl L., "The 'Good Times' Cohort of the 1930s," Population Reference Bureau Inc., April 1977.

Population and the American Future, Report of the Commission on Population Growth and the American Future, 1972.

"Projections of the Population of the United States: 1977-2050," *Current Population Reports,* Bureau of the Census, Series P-25, No. 704, July 1977.

"The State of the World Population, 1981," United Nations Fund for Population Activities, 1981.

Taffel, Selma, "Trends in Fertility in the United States," Bureau of the Census, Series 21, No. 28, September 1977.

Waite, Linda J., "U.S. Women at Work," *Population Bulletin,* Population Reference Bureau Inc., May 1981.

VIOLENCE IN THE FAMILY

by

Sandra Stencel

Apr. 27
1 9 7 9

Editor's Note: Legislation that would have authorized a new federal program aimed at combating domestic violence died in November 1980, at the end of the 96th Congress. Opposition from conservative groups, including the Moral Majority, helped kill the bill, which passed the House easily in December 1979 but ran into trouble in the Senate. The Senate passed the measure by only a five-vote margin, and when conservative senators threatened to filibuster the conference report, it was withdrawn from the floor and never brought up for a final vote. The bill would have authorized $65 million over three years to aid victims of physical abuse by family members. Most of the money would have gone to local centers that provided emergency shelter to women who left home because their husbands beat them.

In January 1981 the Office on Domestic Violence merged with the National Center on Child Abuse and Neglect in the Department of Health and Human Services' Administration on Children, Youth and Families.

The Fifth National Conference on Child Abuse and Neglect was held in April 1981 in Milwaukee, Wis. It was cosponsored by the National Center on Child Abuse and Neglect and the Milwaukee-based Region 5 Child Abuse and Neglect Resource Center. The first national conference on violence in military families was held March 10-13, 1981, in Savannah, Ga. The conference was cosponsored by the Washington-based Center for Women Policy Studies and the Coastal Area Community Mental Health Center's Family Violence Project.

VIOLENCE IN THE FAMILY

THE IMAGE of the family as a refuge from the strains and stresses of the outside world is one most Americans hold dear. Our unwillingness to abandon this idealized picture of family life, despite rising divorce rates and other signs of family discord,[1] is perhaps an indication that the American family is here to stay. This optimistic assessment of the future of the family draws general agreement. But there also seems to be a growing recognition that this idyllic concept of family life has contributed to the conspiracy of silence that, until very recently, surrounded the problem of violence in the family.

Evidence of violent confrontations among family members, especially extreme cases of child abuse and neglect, were never completely ignored by law enforcement personnel, social workers, psychologists or the news media. But the tendency was to view these cases as abnormalities, as exceptions to the usual state of affairs. Family violence also was seen as primarily a working-class phenomenon. In recent years, however, it has become increasingly apparent that violence in the family is a much more serious problem than many realized — or were willing to admit. Consider these statistics:

> In 1977, according to the FBI Uniform Crime Reports, nearly 20 percent of all murder victims in the United States were related to the assailants. About half of these intra-family murders were husband-wife killings.[2]

> In any one year, according to one study,[3] approximately 1.8 million wives are beaten by their husbands. Over one-fourth of all American couples engage in at least one violent episode during their relationship.

> Over one million children are abused each year, physically, sexually or through neglect, the Department of Health, Education and Welfare (HEW) reports. About 240,000 children are victims of physical abuse and at least 2,000 of them die of their injuries.[4]

---

[1] See "The Changing American Family," *E.R.R.*, 1977 Vol. I, pp. 413-432.

[2] U.S. Department of Justice, "FBI Uniform Crime Reports: Crime in the United States, 1977," Oct. 18, 1978, p. 9.

[3] See Murray A. Straus, "Wife Beating: How Common and Why?" *Victimology: An International Journal*, November 1977, p. 445.

[4] U.S. Department of Health, Education and Welfare, "New Light on an Old Problem: 9 Questions and Answers on Child Abuse and Neglect," 1978, p. 5.

"The family is both the most loving and supportive of human groups and also by far the most physically violent group or institution except for the police or the military during a war," Professor Murray A. Straus of the University of New Hampshire said at a meeting of the American Psychological Association in Toronto, Aug. 29, 1978. "Violence in the home is a far more serious problem than violence in the streets, in the classrooms, or anywhere else."

Violence within the family does not necessarily have to involve physical abuse. While Professor Straus notes that "the most common of all forms of intra-family violence" is the physical punishment of children *(see p. 153),* psychologists and sociologists also are beginning to recognize the toll so-called "emotional violence" takes on family members. The most common tactics in emotional warfare are the withholding of sex, love or money. An increasingly popular strategy is the "honesty or openness maneuver, where being brutally frank is often times an excuse for being brutal."[5]

Increased Attention From the Government

In recent years the problem of domestic violence has been receiving more attention. Child abuse and wife battering have been the subject of numerous newspaper and magazine articles, radio and television talk shows and even a few made-for-television movies. Social service agencies, church groups, schools, colleges and other organizations are offering courses, seminars and lectures on various aspects of the problem.

The women's movement has encouraged battered women to speak more openly about their predicament and to demand protection from the police and the courts. Some police departments are beginning to train officers in family crisis intervention. Social workers are being trained better to detect domestic violence when rendering other services. And prosecutors show a new willingness to bring domestic violence cases to trial.

Hearings have been held at the state and local level to measure the prevalence of domestic violence and to consider such remedies as legislation and coordination of social services. In the past decade most states have strengthened their laws to encourage prompt reporting of suspected cases of child battering. In many states, telephone "hot lines" have been set up to assist the public in reporting suspected cases of child abuse and to offer advice to victims of domestic violence *(see p. 157).* Emergency shelters for battered wives and their dependents are being opened in a growing number of communities.

---

[5] Remarks of Barbara O'Connor, a New York social worker, at a seminar on emotional violence within the family held Nov. 18, 1978, at the New School for Social Research in New York.

Murders in the Family

Year	All reported murders	Spouse killing spouse	Parent killing child	Other relative killings
		(in percentages)		
1969	14,680	13.1	3.7	8.4
1970	15,910	12.1	3.1	8.1
1971	17,680	12.8	3.5	8.4
1972	18,570	12.5	2.9	8.9
1973	19,530	12.3	3.2	7.7
1974	20,600	12.1	2.7	8.0
1975	20,510	11.5	3.0	7.9
1976	18,780	*	*	*
1977	19,120	10.6	3.1	5.3

*In 1976 available figures show that a total of 27.2 percent of all reported murders were by relatives.

Source: FBI Uniform Crime Reports

Growing awareness of the problem also prompted action at the federal level. The Child Abuse Prevention and Treatment Act, passed by Congress on Jan. 31, 1974, authorized $85 million over a three-year period for federal aid to programs for the prevention, identification and treatment of child abuse. At least half of the funds were assigned to demonstration programs and to training programs for professionals involved in child abuse work. The National Center on Child Abuse and Neglect was created by the Child Abuse Prevention and Treatment Act to administer these funds. The National Center, within HEW, also is responsible for studying the incidence of child abuse nationwide and for maintaining a central clearinghouse of information on child abuse and neglect.

In 1977 Congress extended the Child Abuse Prevention and Treatment Act for two years, through fiscal 1979. The reauthorization bill broadened the definition of child abuse under the bill to include "sexual abuse and exploitation." Some $2 million was authorized in fiscal 1978 and again in 1979 for programs and projects designed to prevent, identify and treat sexual abuse of children. In a report issued in August 1978, the National Center on Child Abuse and Neglect estimated that the current annual incidence of sexual abuse of children is between 60,000 and 100,000 cases a year.[6]

Last year the Senate passed but the House voted down separate bills to establish a new federal program for financing spouse-abuse shelters and other community activities intended to prevent family violence and treat its victims. The bills pro-

---

[6] National Center on Child Abuse and Neglect, "Child Sexual Abuse: Incest, Assault, and Sexual Exploitation," August 1978, p. 3.

posed to establish a National Center on Domestic Violence within HEW.[7] Women's groups, pushing for reintroduction of the bills this year, cite the continuing need for additional federal funding for spouse abuse shelters.[8] As late as 1976, only 30 such houses were known to exist. By 1978, over 170 shelters were operating in the United States, according to a survey conducted by the Center for Women Policy Studies in Washington, D.C.[9]

Police Response to Wife-Battering Cases

It is generally agreed that available statistics greatly under-estimate the extent of violence within the family. Many cases of child abuse and spouse battering still go unreported, even though every state now requires physicians to report suspected cases of child abuse. In most states the reporting requirements also apply to other medical personnel, including nurses, dentists, interns, coroners and medical examiners. Since 1973, according to the National Center on Child Abuse and Neglect, many states have broadened their reporting requirements to cover non-medical professionals, including teachers and law-enforcement and child-care personnel.[10]

States and localities have been slower to respond to the problem of spouse abuse. Police authorities often are reluctant to get involved in such cases since wife beating traditionally has been thought of not as a crime, but as a private marital squabble. Police indifference is thought to have contributed to the reluctance of many battered wives to even call the police. The FBI has said that wife battering may be the most underreported crime in the nation.

Police intervention in domestic violence can be dangerous. About 20 percent of the deaths and 40 percent of injuries suffered by the police occur when officers seek to intervene in such cases. But the primary reason police are reluctant to get involved in domestic fights, according to James Bannon, executive deputy chief of the Detroit Police Department, "is because we

---

[7] The Senate bill was introduced by Alan Cranston, D-Calif.; the House version was sponsored by Reps. George Miller, D-Calif., Lindy Boggs, D-La., Newton Steers, R-Md., and Barbara Mikulski, D-Md. See *CQ Weekly Report* of May 27, 1978, p. 1335, and Sept. 16, 1978, p. 2485.

[8] Some federal funding for shelters is provided under Title XX of the Social Security Act. Title XX, which took effect Oct. 1, 1975, authorized federal payments to the states for provision of social services directed at the goals of (1) economic self-support, (2) personal self-sufficiency, (3) prevention or correction of neglect of children or adults and preservation of families, (4) prevention of inappropriate institutional care through community-based care programs and (5) provision of institutional care where appropriate.

[9] Center for Women Policy Studies, "Programs Providing Services to Battered Women," April 1978. The Center for Women Policy Studies received two grants from the Law Enforcement Assistance Administration (LEAA) to develop a clearinghouse and a newsletter to gather and share information on domestic violence, child sexual abuse and rape. The center recently received another LEAA grant to provide assistance to LEAA-funded Family Violence Programs in 17 communities across the nation.

[10] National Center on Child Abuse and Neglect, "Child Abuse and Neglect: State Reporting Laws," May 1978, pp. 7-8. See also "Child Abuse," *E.R.R.*, 1976 Vol. I, pp. 65-84.

Battered Husbands

"The most unreported crime is not wife beating — it's husband beating," according to University of Delaware sociologist Suzanne Steinmetz. "Unless a man is battered to the degree where he requires medical attention, he is not going to report it." Extrapolating from her studies of domestic quarreling in New Castle County, Del., Steinmetz has estimated that each year at least 250,000 American husbands are severely thrashed by their wives.

"Most battered men are too ashamed to admit they've been beaten by their wives," Roger Langley and Richard C. Levy noted in their book *Wife Beating: The Silent Crisis* (1977). "The humiliation a battered woman suffers is multiplied enormously for a man who must stand before a police sergeant and file a complaint. Not many men have the courage to face the snickers, innuendos, and open sarcasm inherent in this situation."

Langley and Levy also observed that there are few places a battered man can go for help. "When he does reach out," they wrote, "or if circumstances propel the family problem into the public arena, a man can find his life bewildering and frustrating. He can conclude as easily as does the battered wife that the police, the courts, the clergy, and the social-service agencies are all stacked against him."

do not know how to cope with them."[11] To overcome this problem, a growing number of police departments are forming specially trained units. In Atlanta, for example, police are taught through role-playing to defuse family fights by projecting a calm, mediating manner rather than the aggressive posture of an arresting officer.

A training guide on wife beating published by the International Association of Chiefs of Police in 1976 reflected changing police attitudes toward domestic violence. It urged police to distinguish between situations where there is a threat of violence, and where mediation might be effective, and situations where violence already has occurred. "Where an attack has already taken place," it stated, "the police officer must be prepared to conduct an assault investigation. . . . 'Family disturbances' and 'wife beatings' should not be viewed synonymously; nor should wife abuse be considered a victimless crime or solely a manifestation of a poor marraige. A wife beating is foremost an assault — a crime that must be investigated."

Several states have modified their laws to make it easier to arrest wife batterers. An Oregon law that took effect in October 1977 states that a police officer called to a domestic disturbance must take the assailant into custody when the officer has reasonable cause to believe an assault has occurred or a person

---

[11] Quoted by Joan Potter in "Police and the Battered Wife: The Search for Understanding," *Police Magazine*, September 1978, p. 41.

has been placed in fear of injury. A similar law went into effect in Minnesota in April 1978. Until that time Minnesota police could make an arrest for a misdemeanor assault only if the assault was committed in their presence. Under the new law an officer can make an arrest for a domestic assault he did not witness if he has probable cause to believe it happened within the preceding four hours or if there is visible injury to the victim.

Many changes in police attitudes and in domestic violence laws are attributed to a class-action suit filed in December 1976 against the New York City Police Department. The suit was filed on behalf of 71 wives who accused the police of denying them assistance after they reported being assaulted by their husbands. In June 1978 the police department agreed in an out-of-court settlement to arrest wife beaters when there was reasonable cause to believe the men had committed the crime. New York City Counsel Allan G. Schwartz said the new stipulation did not change existing law but "recognizes that, in practice in the past, married women in assault cases have been treated differently from unmarried women."[12]

The out-of-court settlement stipulated that the police department would send one or more officers in response to every call from a woman who said that her husband had assaulted her or was threatening her with assault. The police also agreed to inform a battered wife of her rights; to protect the wife or aid her in getting medical help if she needs it; and to try to locate the assailant if he had left the scene.

One reason police have been reluctant to respond to wife battering cases is that many women are reluctant to prosecute their husbands. Only about 2 percent of the accused males are ever prosecuted. Many feminists argue that this is because prosecutors make it very difficult to press charges. "Prosecutors impose extraordinary conditions on a woman complaining of assaults or harassment by her husband or former husband," wrote Marjory D. Fields, a lawyer with the Brooklyn Legal Services Corporation. "After she passes these tests of her intent to prosecute, pleas to minor infractions are accepted and suspended sentences . . . recommended to the court. Judges impose light or suspended sentences even without the prosecutor's suggestion. Thus, the injured wife who persists does not receive the protection of having her assaultive husband jailed."[13]

According to Fields, "prompt and certain punishment" is the only answer to wife abuse. Others believe that traditional prosecution is not always appropriate. Charles Benjamin Schudson, an assistant district attorney in Milwaukee, Wis., said: "Crimi-

[12] Quoted in *The New York Times*, June 27, 1978.
[13] Marjory D. Fields, "Representing Battered Wives, or What To Do Until the Police Arrive," *The Family Law Reporter*, April 5, 1977.

nal prosecution is an act of desperation. It's something done when all else has failed. Sometimes it is necessary, sometimes it must be done. But what I'm saying is that . . . criminal prosecution does not solve the problem."[14]

Self-Defense Pleas in Wife-Husband Killings

Frustrated by the criminal justice system, some battered wives have taken the law into their own hands — and many of them have gotten away with it, as a number of press reports indicate:

> Marlene Roan Eagle, a pregnant American Indian in South Dakota, stabbed her husband through the heart after he came at her with a broken broomstick. It was established that he had beaten her on several occasions and, in July 1977, she was acquitted of murder on the ground that she acted in self-defense.
>
> Sharon McNearney was found innocent of murdering her husband in November 1977. The Marquette, Mich., housewife fired a shotgun at him as he walked through the front door. Police described her as a battered wife who had long been abused. Marquette County Circuit Court Judge John E. McDonald said the prosecution failed to prove she had not acted in self-defense.
>
> The same month Evelyn Ware was found not guilty of murdering her husband after pleading self-defense in Superior Court in Orange County, Calif. She shot her husband five times. Evidence of past beatings was used as part of her defense.
>
> In the spring of 1977 a jury in Bellingham, Wash., acquitted Janice Hornbuckle of first-degree murder. One night, after her husband beat her and threatened her at knife-point, she grabbed a shotgun from her teenage son and shot her husband. She had sought police protection on several occasions.
>
> In Chicago, Juan Malonado was shot and killed by his wife, Gloria, after he beat his eight-year-old son with a shoe. The State's Attorney's office ruled there was "insufficient evidence" to warrant her prosecution.
>
> In a well-publicized case in Lansing, Mich., Francine Hughes claimed that years of physical abuse drove her to pour gasoline around her sleeping husband and light it. A jury acquitted her of murder on the ground of temporary insanity.

These and other similar cases have attracted national attention and generated considerable controversy. Indeed, it has been suggested that the acquittals could result in an "open season on men."[15] Despite the controversy, lawyers increasingly are using

---

[14] Interview on "The MacNeil/Lehrer Report," Public Broadcasting System, Oct. 19, 1978.

[15] See "Thirteen Ways to Leave Your Lover," *New Times*, Feb. 6, 1978, p. 6. See also "A Killing Excuse," *Time*, Nov. 28, 1977, p. 108; "The Right to Kill," *Newsweek*, Sept. 1, 1975, p. 69; "Wives Who Batter Back," *Newsweek*, Jan. 30, 1978, p. 54; and "Wives Accused of Slayings Turning to Self-Defense Pleas," *The Washington Post*, Dec. 4, 1977.

Marital Rape

One aspect of spouse abuse that until recently received very little attention is marital rape. That was before the celebrated Rideout case in Oregon. Last October, Greta Rideout, then 23, charged her husband John with rape. Filing such a charge would have been unthinkable and, in fact, impossible until the Oregon legislature changed the state's rape law in 1977 to remove marriage or cohabitation as a defense.

John Rideout was acquitted of the rape charge in January. But that did not end the debate on marital rape. Besides Oregon, at least three other states — New Jersey, Delaware and Iowa — have revised their rape laws to allow women to charge their husbands with sexual assault. Several other states, including California, are considering similar legal changes.

The Rideouts, when last heard from, were granted a divorce after a brief reconciliation.

the self-defense plea in wife-husband murders. Two lawyers associated with the Center for Constitutional Rights in New York last year published a report intended to help attorneys representing women who commit homicide after they or their children have been physically or sexually assaulted.[16] "Ten years ago women didn't talk about being raped," said one of the lawyers, Elizabeth M. Schneider. "Ten years ago women didn't talk about being battered. If they fought back, society and they themselves thought they were wrong to do it; they pleaded guilty and they went to jail. The climate of the times now is that more battered women are ready to say, 'It's either him or me at this moment and I choose me.' You can't really assert self-defense until you feel you have a self to defend; that's what women finally are developing."[17]

In many states, to prove self-defense the defendant has to show a reasonable apprehension of imminent danger of great bodily harm. Lawyers have effectively used evidence of past beatings and threats to show reasonable apprehension, even in cases where the husband's actions at the moment of the killing are inconclusive or negligible. Lawyers also have successfully argued that it is not an unreasonable response for a physically outmatched wife to resort to a lethal weapon such as a gun or a knife if a husband comes at her with his fists.

Acceptance of self-defense pleas is not universal. In Birmingham, Ala., Hazel Kontos was convicted and sentenced to life in prison in December 1977 for shooting her husband despite her contention that he had slapped her around and once held

---

[16] Elizabeth M. Schneider and Susan B. Jordan, "Representation of Women Who Defend Themselves In Response to Physical or Sexual Assault," Center for Constitutional Rights, 1978.
[17] Quoted in *The New York Times*, March 10, 1978.

her at gunpoint. In Waupaca, Wis., Jennifer Patri, a Sunday school teacher and PTA president, was convicted and sentenced to 10 years in prison for the shooting death of her auto-repairman husband. Patri had pleaded self-defense. Her lawyer argued that her husband beat and sexually abused her and that he also molested their 12-year-old daughter. Like many battered women, Patri said she had never called the police for help because of feelings of shame.

Generational Theory of Violence

WHAT MAKES someone physically abuse their children or their spouse? No one knows for sure, but recent studies seem to confirm the long-held belief that children who witness violent acts between their parents or who are victims of parental violence themselves often grow up to become the wife abusers and child abusers of their generation. "Family violence is usually a learned pattern of behavior," according to psychologist B.L. Daley. "Often the behavior is modeled on the father or other adult male figures. The mother also contributes by accepting this behavior."[18]

A 1975 British study of 100 abusive husbands indicated that over half of them had witnessed their fathers battering their mothers.[19] A 1975 study by John D. Flynn of Western Michigan University on spouse abuse in the area around Kalamazoo, Mich., indicated that two-fifths of the wife beaters studied had been abused as children.[20] A study by D.G. Gil, author of *Violence Against Children: Physical Child Abuse in the United States* (1970), found that 14 percent of the abusive mothers studied and 7 percent of the abusive fathers had been abused as children.

"The chances of a battered child becoming a battering adult are very, very strong," said sociologist Suzanne K. Steinmetz. "I found that there were patterns that extended over three generations. So that if you had a grandmother and a grandfather who perhaps screamed and yelled at each other and maybe occasionally slapped each other, they tended to use those methods on their children, and their children tended to use those methods

---

[18] Quoted by Roger Langley and Richard C. Levy in *Wife Beating: The Silent Crisis* (1977), p. 50.

[19] J.J. Gayford, "Wife Battering: A Preliminary Survey of 100 Cases," *British Medical Journal*, Jan. 25, 1977, pp. 194-197.

[20] John D. Flynn, "Spouse Assault: Its Dimension and Characteristics in Kalamazoo County, Michigan," Unpublished field studies in research and practice. School of Social Work, Western Michigan University, 1975.

on their brothers and sisters. And then when these children married, they tended to use the same methods on their husbands and wives and similarly on their children, and of course their children repeated it. So for three generations I found very consistent patterns on the way they resolved conflict . . . the monkey see, monkey do idea."[21]

According to psychologist Lenore E. Walker, author of *The Battered Woman* (1979), children who live in homes where spouse abuse is a problem "experience the most insidious form of child abuse."

> Whether or not they are physically abused by either parent [she wrote] is less important than the psychological scars they bear from watching their fathers beat their mothers. They learn to become part of a dishonest conspiracy of silence. . . . Like many children who suffer from overt physical abuse, these children learn to be accommodating and cooperative. They blend into the background. They do not express anger. They do not acknowledge tension. They do expend a lot of energy avoiding problems. They live in a world of make-believe. When the screaming and yelling begin they stare transfixed but inconspicuous, watching in terror.[22]

Tolerance for Violence in Family Setting

According to Murray Straus, the norms within the family are far more accepting of physical violence than are the rules governing behavior outside the family. Straus observed that most parents are much more tolerant of physical fights among their children than they would be if their children got into a fight with someone else's child. A recent study by Straus and others found that the same children are far more violent to their own siblings than they are to other children. For example, 62 percent of the high school seniors they interviewed had hit a brother or sister during the preceding year, but "only" 35 percent had hit someone outside the family during the same year.[23]

Violence generally is tolerated in the family setting when it is labeled as discipline or punishment. "In general," Straus told the American Psychological Association last year, "the rule in the family is that if someone is doing wrong and 'won't listen to reason,' it is OK to hit. In the case of children, it is more than just OK. Most American parents see it as an obligation." A poll taken for the National Commission on the Causes and Prevention of Violence in 1969 found that the overwhelming majority of Americans (93 percent) approved of a parental spanking. About

---

[21] Quoted by Langley and Levy, *op. cit.*, p. 51.

[22] Lenore E. Walker, *The Battered Woman* (1979), pp. 149-150.

[23] Results to be included in a forthcoming book, *Violence in the American Family* by Murray Straus, Suzanne Steinmetz and Richard Gelles.

Disciplinary Measures Used by Parents

Yelled at or scolded the children	52%
Spanked them	50
Made them stay in their rooms	38
Didn't allow them to go out to play	32
Didn't let them watch television	25
Made them go to bed	23
Threatened them	15
Gave them extra chores	12
Took away their allowances	9

Source: "The General Mills American Family Report 1976-77"

20 percent of those interviewed approved of a husband slapping his wife's face in certain circumstances.[24]

After yelling and scolding, spanking still is the principal form of punishment in most families with children under 13 years of age, according to a survey conducted by Yankelovich, Skelly and White, the national market research and public opinion organization.[25] Half of the parents interviewed said they recently had spanked their children. The study found that younger parents (60 percent) were more likely to spank their children than were parents over age 35 (37 percent). Spanking also was slightly more common in families with incomes under $12,000 a year (56 percent).

Society's Mixed Views of Punishing Kids

Most parents are quick to defend their right to raise their children as they see fit. The idea of parental rights has been culturally ingrained in society from the beginning and it includes the widely accepted notion that children are taught acceptable behavior through punishment — including physical punishment. But many psychologists and sociologists have warned that parents who use physical punishment run the risk of teaching their children that the only way to cope with stress is through the use of violence. "Violence begets violence, however peaceful and altruistic the motivation," said a 1974 study.[26]

Another study found that adults who were hit frequently as children were more likely to be violent with their mates than people who were never hit as children. "Not only does the family expose individuals to violence and techniques of violence," it said, "the family teaches approval for the use of violence."[27]

---

[24] See "Violence and the Media: A Staff Report to the National Commission on the Causes and Prevention of Violence," November 1969, p. 343. The National Commission on the Causes and Prevention of Violence was set up by President Johnson in 1968 after the assassinations of Sen. Robert F. Kennedy, D-N.Y., and Dr. Martin Luther King Jr.

[25] "Raising Children in a Changing Society, The General Mills American Family Report 1976-1977," p. 104.

[26] Suzanne K. Steinmetz and Murray A. Straus, eds., *Violence in the Family* (1974), p. 3.

[27] Richard Gelles, *The Violent Home* (1972), p. 171.

Seven years later, Lenore E. Walker wrote: "When we correct our children by hitting them, we teach them that it is possible to love someone and physically hurt the person at the same time, all in the name of discipline. We need to find ways of disciplining our children that do not include transmitting this message to them."[28]

The results of one of the most recent studies on the effects of physical punishment on children were published in the February 1979 issue of *Human Behavior* magazine. Sociologist Brian G. Gilmartin reported that "children who are frequently spanked tend to become highly resentful and distrustful of authority. Indeed, sometimes their often blind feelings of extreme hostility for, and distrust of, any and all authority figures reach the point of being dangerous to both themselves and others." He went on to say that "children who are often spanked tend to be conspicuously quieter, less articulate and more sullen than those who grow up under milder, more democratic forms of discipline. In addition, harshly disciplined offspring tend to display a large amount of negativity in their approach to people and to life."[29]

Evidence of a link between physical punishment and later tendencies toward violence so impressed Swedish legislators that they recently voted to outlaw spanking.[30] The new law is meant to be primarily "educational." The statute carries no penalties for spanking, but it is hoped that it will encourage children and concerned neighbors to file complaints with police or social workers. A similar ban is not likely to be enacted soon in the United States. In April 1977, for example, the U.S. Supreme Court voted 5 to 4 in favor of continuing to permit the use of corporal punishment in public schools *(Ingraham v. Wright).*

The majority held that the Eighth Amendment ban on cruel and unusual punishment "was designed to protect those convicted of crimes ... [and] does not apply to the paddling of children as a means of maintaining discipline in public schools." Commenting on the Supreme Court's decision, Gilmartin wrote: "Banning the use of physical punishment in the schools is not going to end its use in the home. But public schools can and should be expected to set a positive example for parents to follow."

---

[28] Walker, *op. cit.*, p. 252.

[29] Brian G. Gilmartin, "The Case Against Spanking," *Human Behavior*, February 1979, p. 18.

[30] See *Newsweek*, April 16, 1979, p. 63.

New Efforts to Help Abusers

BREAKING the chain of violence from one generation to the next will have to involve efforts to help abusers as well as the victims of family violence. At the National Center for the Prevention of Child Abuse and Neglect in Denver, Colo., professionals directed by Dr. C. Henry Kempe[31] teach lay therapists to work in the home with abusive parents. The therapists try to help the parents become aware of their tendency to react to crises with violence. The center also operates a therapeutic day-care center for abused children, a residential treatment program for parents and children who are undergoing therapy, and a "crisis nursery" open 24 hours a day where parents can leave their children when things get tense at home.

Dr. Kempe and his colleagues have developed a screening method that may help predict which parents will abuse their children. The profile of abuse-prone parents emerged during a four-year study of 150 couples at Colorado General Hospital in Denver. Each mother was observed during labor, delivery and the post-partum period for clues that might determine how she would treat her baby. Among the things researchers were looking for was whether the mother was depressed, not affectionate with the infant, bothered by its cries, disappointed with its sex, quick to make disparaging remarks about its physical characteristics. The researchers also observed each husband, looking to see whether he was supportive and how he reacted during the delivery process.

After interviews and further observation, the mothers were divided into high- and low-risk groups. Half of the high-risk mothers were provided with intensive post-natal help and therapy; the rest received routine care. When the children were a little over two years old, 25 families in each of the three groups were randomly chosen for evaluation. The researchers found that five children in the high-risk/ordinary-care group had required hospitalization for serious injuries that were thought to have involved parental mistreatment. No such injuries were found among the children of the high-risk group that received special help or among the children of the low-risk parents.

Kempe and his colleagues insist that their study has not produced any "magic formula" for detecting parents who might be likely to harm or neglect their children. But they believe the clues they have gathered will make it easier for observant hospital personnel to spot warning signals early and try to help the

---

[31] In a paper presented to the American Academy of Pediatricians in 1961, Dr. Kempe coined the phrase "the battered child syndrome" and described the symptoms of the abnormality.

new parents adjust to their new responsibility. "Families identified early as being in need of extra parent-preparedness services must have access to intensive, continuous intervention," said one of the researchers, Dr. Jane Gray. "It makes little sense to provide excellent prenatal, obstetric and neonatal care only to abandon the most needy young families at the hospital door and leave the child rearing to chance."[32]

The National Center on Child Abuse and Neglect has observed that "even if it is possible to identify successfully a high-risk group of parents, the next step, intervention, is by no means easy. Ethical and legal problems involving the rights of parents to privacy versus the rights of children, and the states' right to intervene if parents object, are not easily solved. There is an additional concern about labeling these parents 'potential abusers' and the possibility that this can become a self-fulfilling prophecy."[33]

Preventing Abuse and Treating Abusers

Many people think the best cure for child abuse is a dose of prevention in the form of training for parents. "It's ironic that the most important job many of us will ever do is one for which most of us receive absolutely no training," Kitty Ward of the Massachusetts Society for the Prevention of Cruelty to Children said in 1977.[34] Studies have found that abusive parents often lack specific knowledge of what children do at various stages of their development and therefore have unrealistic expectations for their children. When the children fail to meet these expectations, the parents often erupt in violence.

Many experts think child care should become a required part of the curriculum in high schools. Education for Parenthood, a program sponsored by the Department of Health, Education and Welfare, attempts to teach students the "joys and responsibilities" of being a parent. The course currently is being given to approximately 121,000 high school students across the country.

One of the most successful treatment methods for abusive parents was started in 1970 by a California mother who prefers to be known as Jolly K. She is a former abusive parent who in one instance threw a kitchen knife at her six-year-old daughter and in another tried to strangle her. When Jolly could find no agency providing the kind of help she wanted, she founded her own and called it Mothers Anonymous. Known today as Parents

---

[32] Quoted in *Human Behavior*, May 1978, p. 67. See also Jane Gray et al., "Perinatal Assessment of Mother-Baby Interaction," in *Child Abuse and Neglect: The Family and the Community* (1976) edited by R.E. Helfer and C. Henry Kempe.

[33] National Center on Child Abuse and Neglect: "1977 Analysis of Child Abuse and Neglect Research," January 1978, p. 22.

[34] Quoted in *Newsweek*, Oct. 10, 1977, p. 115.

Anonymous, the organization claims to have over 500 chapters in the United States and Canada. Patterned after Alcoholics Anonymous, the group gives parents an opportunity to meet each other and share their problems. "Child abusers are going through hell," Jolly K. said in an interview in 1975. "We have a vision of how powerful our anger can be, a concept of where this anger will take us if we are pushed too far, and the constant dread that we will be pushed that far."[35]

Besides giving psychological support to each other at meetings, members of Parents Anonymous also contact one another by telephone when a crisis develops at home. Emergency "hot lines" are sponsored by many groups interested in helping abusive parents. A survey conducted by the National Center on Child Abuse and Neglect in 1978 found child abuse hot lines in at least 52 communities across the country.[36] According to the center, hot lines "provide isolated parents with a sympathetic, concerned individual who will listen as the caller airs frustrations, vents anger (which might otherwise have been directed at the children), or simply expresses feelings which cannot be confided to friends or relatives."

Besides the emergency hot lines serving the needs of anxiety-ridden parents, there also are a growing number of telephone lines set up to encourage neighbors, relatives, social workers and others to report suspected cases of child abuse. The National Center on Child Abuse and Neglect reports that at least 10 states — Arkansas, Colorado, Iowa, Mississippi, Missouri, New Jersey, New York, Pennsylvania, Virginia and West Virginia — have established these child abuse reporting lines through legislation. Hot line services also are being made available to spouse abusers, according to a recent survey by the Center for Women Policy Studies.[37]

Special Aid Programs for Wife Batterers

A 24-hour-a-day hot line is run by the Victims Information Bureau of Suffolk Inc. (VIBS) in Hauppauge, N.Y. "The majority of women coming to VIBS want to remain in their marriages, but without the violence," said Executive Director James Walsh. "We believe that battering will not stop unless both partners are involved in counseling. The emphasis . . . is on restructuring relationships. . . ."

In its survey, the Center for Women Policy Studies found

---

[35] Quoted by Judith Reed in "Working with Abusive Parents; A Parent's View," *Children Today,* May-June 1975, p. 6.

[36] National Center on Child Abuse and Neglect, "Child Abuse and Neglect Helplines," August 1978.

[37] See the October 1978 issue of *Response,* a newsletter published by the Center for Women Policy Studies.

several programs that work exclusively with abusive men. One is EMERGE in Somerville, Mass. It grew out of the concern of women working in local shelters who saw the need for such a service. The program emphasizes that "it is important for men to begin to talk about battering — why it starts, what leads to it, how it affects individuals and relationships, and what can be done to stop it." To encourage this, EMERGE provides "a safe environment for men to explore the roots of their violence and to learn ways to change their behavior."

Another program concerned directly with the abuser is Therapy for Abusive Behavior (TAB) in Baltimore, Md. The program is run by three women volunteers with the assistance and cooperation of the Southern Baltimore Police District commander and one of his community relations officers. It was started to give abusers the "opportunity for self-help in the areas of personal growth and development by actively participating in a program designed to identify and change violent behavior patterns." TAB teaches men more effective techniques for handling situations and relationships, while it provides a supportive network for the men during and after the program.

According to the Center for Women Policy Studies, the TAB program "is unique in that it intervenes to help the abuser at the initial stages of his contact with the courts. . . . Instead of allowing the litigation to continue, a judge may place the abuser in the TAB program, under the condition that he attend the program regularly or else re-enter the judicial system."

Minneapolis, Minn., has several programs to help spouse abusers. These include the Citizens' Dispute Settlement Project, the Walk-in Counseling Center, the Twin Cities Men's Center and men's groups within the state's Family and Children's Services department. Other efforts to help spouse abusers have been established in Seattle, Wash., Portland, Ore., and Pittsburgh, Pa. The relatively small number of programs operating to help abusive husbands is perhaps an indication of the reluctance of many men to seek help. "It must be understood that the husband is caught by the same societal values as his wife," explained James Walsh of the VIBS program. "He has been taught that men are not supposed to express feelings and that he must handle his own problems and not ask for help."

Therapy Techniques for Troubled Couples

If the husband is willing to undergo treatment or counseling, successful changes in his behavior can be accomplished in up to 80 percent of the cases, according to Sanford Sherman, executive director of Jewish Family Services in New York.[38] Sherman

---

[38] Quoted in Langley and Levy, *op. cit.*, p. 201.

recommends having the husband and wife visit the therapist together. "It's important for both partners to understand that [the husband is] afraid. He fears loss of status, loss of life, and paradoxically, loss of his wife. The fear is intolerable to him. He must choose either fight or flight. With a vulnerable woman present, the tendency is to fight." Sherman said the man must be taught non-violent ways of behaving when he is enraged, to get him to translate his anger into words or to take it out on objects rather than people.

The assumption that most men will stop their abusive behavior if they participate in therapy is not universally accepted. Among those who disagree is Lenore E. Walker. "Very few traditional techniques of couples therapy apply to battering couples," she wrote. "Many of these methods include teaching couples how to fight fairer and better.... Battering couples do not need to learn new fighting behavior. Rather, they need to learn to control their anger."[39]

Another problem with traditional couples therapy, Walker said, is that its primary goal is to make the relationship better. "With battering couples, the survival of the relationship [should be] secondary. The goal is to strengthen each individual to be able to build a new, healthier relationship. Success is achieved if the individuals are strengthened, even if the relationship itself is not able to survive." Walker and her late husband, Dr. Morton Flax, a psychologist, developed a technique which, she said, "has been successful in limiting the severity of battering incidents, although it has not yet eliminated battering incidents completely." Most couples in a battering relationship have extremely poor communications skills. "Their verbal and non-verbal communication is fraught with distortion and misinterpretation...," Walker said. "We begin by teaching the couple a signal to use with each other when either one begins to feel tension rising.... Often it takes a lot of work to teach the couples to recognize their own cues. Once they learn to feel their tension at minimum levels, we can begin to prevent the tension build-up that causes an acute battering incident."

Dr. Walker admitted that this type of therapy is "time-consuming, expensive and exhausting for both the couple and the therapists." And while it may help the two parties involved, therapy does little to address the broader problem of violence in the family. Both spouse abuse and child abuse are symptomatic of deep, underlying stress within the family. Until the dynamics of the problem are better understood, more support systems must be provided the growing number of victims of domestic violence.

[39] Walker, *op. cit.*, p. 245.

Selected Bibliography

Books

Gelles, Richard J., *The Violent Home: A Study of Physical Aggression Between Husbands and Wives*, Sage Publications, 1972.

Langley, Roger and Richard C. Levy, *Wife Beating: The Silent Crisis*, E.P. Dutton, 1977.

Martin, Del, *Battered Wives*, Glide Publications, 1976.

Pizzey, Erin, *Scream Quietly or the Neighbors Will Hear*, Anchor Press, 1974.

Steinmetz, Suzanne K. and Murray A. Straus, eds., *Violence in the Family*, Harper & Row, 1974.

Walker, Lenore E., *The Battered Woman*, Harper & Row, 1979.

Walters, David R., *Physical and Sexual Abuse of Children: Causes and Treatment*, Indiana University Press, 1975.

Articles

"Authorities Face Up to the Child Abuse Problem," *U.S. News & World Report*, May 3, 1976.

Eisenberg, Susan and Patricia Micklow, "The Assaulted Wife: 'Catch 22' Revisited," *Women's Rights Law Reporter*, spring-summer 1977.

Fields, Marjory D., "Wife Beating: the Hidden Offense," *New York Law Journal*, April 29, 1976.

Franke, Linda Bird, "Battered Women," *Newsweek*, Feb. 2, 1976.

Gelles, Richard J., "Abused Wives: Why Do They Stay," *Journal of Marriage and the Family*, November 1976.

Gingold, Judith, "One of these days — Pow — right in the kisser," *Ms.*, August 1976.

Jacobson, Beverly, "Battered Women," *Civil Rights Digest*, summer 1977.

Potter, Joan, "Police and the Battered Wife: The Search for Understanding," *Police Magazine*, September 1978.

Shiels, Merrill, "The Battered Children," *Newsweek*, Oct. 10, 1977.

Straus, Murray A., "Wife Beating: How Common and Why?" *Victimology*, November 1977.

"The Battered Husbands," *Time*, March 20, 1978.

Reports and Studies

"Battered Women: Issues of Public Policy," A Consultation Sponsored by the U.S. Commission on Civil Rights, Washington, D.C., Jan. 30-31, 1978.

Editorial Research Reports: "Child Abuse," 1976 Vol. I, pp. 65-84; "The Changing American Family," 1977 Vol. I, pp. 413-432.

National Center on Child Abuse and Neglect, "1977 Analysis of Child Abuse and Neglect Research," January 1978.

Schneider, Elizabeth M. and Susan B. Jordan, "Representation of Women Who Defend Themselves In Response to Physical or Sexual Assault," Center for Constitutional Rights, 1978.

Straus, Murray A., Suzanne K. Steinmetz and Richard J. Gelles, "Violence in the Family: An Assessment of Knowledge and Needs," paper presented to the American Association for the Advancement of Science, Feb. 23, 1976.

Changing Male Image

by

William V. Thomas

**Aug. 29
1 9 8 0**

CHANGING MALE IMAGE

I F the 1960s was the decade of youth, and the 1970s was the decade of women, then the 1980s could be the decade of men — at least in the opinion of some social trend watchers. "American men are on the edge of a tidal wave of change — a change in their very identity as men," feminist Betty Friedan said recently.[1] It is a change not yet clearly visible or completely understood, but its effects could be as important and far-reaching as those wrought by the women's movement, she added. "Men's liberation," as the new phenomenon sometimes is called, is seen by many as the "second stage" in the sexual revolution. "Now it is the male consciousness that is being raised," said Dallas psychologist Michael E. McGill. "The whole way men look at themselves — their work, their social responsibilities and their emotional lives — is undergoing a tremendous readjustment."[2]

A generation ago, the accepted male role emphasized such traits as competitiveness and aggressiveness, while the accepted female role stressed such qualities as gentleness and passivity. In the past, "those polarities were relied on as evidence of psychological health," said Evan Leepson, a behavioral psychologist who practices in New York City. "Today, however, established sex-role definitions are being replaced with more meaningful descriptions of human behavior."[3]

This is reflected in alterations in family life and sexual attitudes that have begun to blur traditional male and female roles. The rapid increase in the number of working women has forced men to redefine their responsibilities both at work and at home. As wives have assumed a greater part of the economic burden of supporting their families, husbands have had to share in more of the domestic tasks of homemaking. At the same time, psychologists say, men have been freed from many of the "functions of dominance" — pressures to

---

[1] Betty Friedan, "Their Turn: How Men Are Changing," *Redbook*, May 1980, p. 23. Friedan is the author of *The Feminine Mystique* (1963), often referred to as the bible of the feminist movement.

[2] Interview, July 21, 1980. McGill teaches psychology at Southern Methodist University in Dallas.

[3] Interview, Aug. 7, 1980.

conform to society's demands that they act as aggressive bread-winners, always keeping their feelings under wraps.

In the popular terminology, the male image is "softening." The process has been going on for over a decade. The Vietnam War and the counterculture of the late 1960s, as well as the women's movement, are credited with debunking the "he-man mystique" and causing men to turn "inward." The Vietnam era was a "watershed," Friedan wrote, a time when many men decided to stop "defining themselves by going to war or getting power from jobs women can't have" and to start putting "a new value on personal qualities once considered the exclusive domain of women." Once a man admits to those feelings and emotions that men as well as women have, Friedan said, "he can't be the same kind of man anymore."

The transformation is not always easy. "It would seem that men would be eager to shed the burdens of [their] programming," sociologist Bob Brannon told a National Conference on Men and Masculinity held in December 1978 at the University of California at Los Angeles. "But one of the ironies of our preoccupation with masculine men and feminine women is that people have become proud of the very traits that are impeding their own happiness."

Factors Perpetuating Old Value Systems

"Who finally will wash the dishes?" That is the question of our age, Norman Mailer wrote in the *Prisoner of Sex* (1971). Mailer's answer pleased few women: "A man might love a woman and she might even sprain her back before a hundred sinks of dishes in a month. Even so, I would not be happy to help her if my work should suffer." According to Michael E. McGill, there are "millions of men today who feel exactly the same way."

In an age when even *Playboy* editor and publisher Hugh Hefner supports the Equal Rights Amendment, the days when men can openly embrace a philosophy of sexual and social dominance over women may be numbered. But some trace of what writer Bob Green called the "dinosaur" part of the male personality still lurks in many men. "The nation's social fabric has been embellished in recent years by the arrival of something called the New American Man," Green wrote. "He's a staunch supporter of feminist theology [and] is constantly searching for the feminine side of his own personality. . . . But in isolated pockets of male America, there are men who, if the feminine side of [their] personality were ever to reveal itself, would probably stomp on it."[4]

---

[4] Bob Green, writing in *Esquire*, September 1980.

Men Who Cry

Edmund Muskie cried, Lou Gehrig cried and so did Richard Nixon. But many men just cannot bring themselves to do the same thing. "As boys, they're given the message it's not okay, or it's feminine or weak to cry," said Washington psychologist Barton Kraff. By the time they're adults, he added, some men have so completely suppressed the urge to cry that they have difficulty expressing any feelings at all.

"An infant's cry is a signal of some state of displeasure," said Kraff. "The infant is anxious or angry and wants to get rid of the discomfort. When we cry as adults, we are acting like our natural selves. . . ."

Is it possible that more men will take up weeping as male expressions of emotion become more acceptable? "What I see happening," Kraff said, "is women moving into business situations where they want to cry but feel they can't. As male and female roles are drawing closer, we seem to be moving in both directions — some men may be finding it easier to show emotion and cry, but some women may be finding it harder."

Psychologist Warren Farrell, author of *The Liberated Man* (1977), concedes that many men exist as they always have, locked in "a straightjacket" of masculinity. The sensitive, caring, sharing male is largely an inhabitant of white, middle-class America, Farrell said. Although he may be making inroads elsewhere, he is still the exception rather than the rule in most areas of society. In business and labor, "reality is defined by a masculine value system that has changed very little," Farrell wrote. "Feminine values may be considered 'nice' but not 'realistic.' "[5] Much the same is true in the blue-collar world, where the traditional masculine attributes of toughness and aggression have both practical and cultural functions.

Some men have changed their ideas about the proper male role and become more demonstrative of their feelings. Many of them admit that they made these changes largely in response to the women's movement. Ironically, "the great unvoiced paranoia" among men, according to film critic Peter Rainer, is that they "will liberate themselves only to discover that women really don't want liberated men after all."[6] A similar fear was voiced by psychologist Herb Goldberg, author of *The Hazards of Being Male: Surviving the Myth of Masculine Privilege* (1977). "Women want men who are successful, powerful, who take charge but who are also soft, warm, loving — qualities almost impossible to have in the same person," he said. "The kinds of internal mechanisms that make a man extremely powerful and highly successful are frequently in total contradiction to being a good companion."

---

[5] Warren Farrell, *The Liberated Man* (1977), p. 18.
[6] Peter Rainer, "Is There Life After Sex Roles?" *Mademoiselle*, May 1979, p. 254.

Men's Altered Family Roles

A DECADE AGO, when the women's movement was first gathering momentum, the family was regarded by many feminists as the linchpin in the "male power structure." In her radical "classic" *The Dialectic of Sex* (1971), Shulamith Firestone depicted the family as a debased and hopeless institution that men for centuries had used to imprison their mates. Since then, attitudes toward the family, and the male role in it, have been modified.

By and large, the family no longer is seen as a tool of oppression, but rather as an indispensable social structure that often provides men and women with the best opportunity to function on equal terms. This interpretation of the family, wrote political scientist Jean Bethke Elshtain, "involves a commitment to a particular ideal of . . . existence that does not repeat earlier terms of female exploitation. It begins with the affirmation that family ties and childrearing are essential to . . . human social existence."[7]

At a time when the family is facing many challenges,[8] the current generation of young husbands and fathers seems to be rediscovering the values of family life. "Men are rethinking what it means to be a man, especially what it means to be a family man," said Gary Simpson, director of the Men's Center, a counseling service of Planned Parenthood in Washington, D.C. "Fathers are looking at the world and realizing how important families really are. Many also are finding there are rewards in raising children that you don't get from work."

Pollster Daniel Yankelovich says that men today "have come to feel that success is not enough to satisfy their yearnings for self-fulfillment. They are reaching out for something different."[9] Managers say their male employees are more apt today than in the past to reject transfers, decline promotions, switch jobs or refuse to work overtime for personal reasons. Workers also are demanding more time off from the job, flexible hours and other changes in work schedules to help them cope with family responsibilities.

Gail Sheehy, the author of *Passages: Predictable Crises of Adult Life* (1976), also detected a change in men's attitudes

---

[7] Jean Bethke Elshtain, "Family Reconstruction," *Commonweal*, Aug. 1, 1980, p. 430. Elshtain is a professor of political science at the University of Massachusetts.
[8] See "The Changing American Family," *E.R.R.*, 1977 Vol. I, pp. 412-432.
[9] Quoted by Bernard Lefkowitz in *Breaktime: Living Without Work in a Nine to Five World* (1979), p. 14.

toward work. "Following their father's route to happiness is seen by many younger men as a fate marginally better than early suicide," she wrote last year in *Esquire* magazine. "They dread waking up at the age of 55 from the money-power-fame-success grind they watched their fathers pursue to find they have only a few years left to enjoy life between the first and the final heart attacks."[10]

New Division of Labor Within the Home

As women are pushing for an equal share of power in the world outside the home, men are assuming more of the household responsibilities and, according to Gary Simpson, gaining more of the "inner benefits" attached to home life. The new frontier for men, many psychologists now believe, is the "domestic side" of their personalities. The division of household chores and child care responsibilities exposes men to feelings that ground them in the task of actually caring for others as opposed to simply providing financial support.

Feminists contend that the so-called "liberated" marriage, in which there is a rough parity of "hard work and glory," is a long way from being a reality. "There is still no set of beliefs that allows men to value themselves without regard to the marketplace," stated Robin Gordon of the National Organization for Women (NOW). "Many men want to be closer to their children, but the old assumption that mother means

[10] Gail Sheehy, "Introducing the Postponing Generation: The Truth About Today's Young Men," *Esquire*, October 1979, p. 25.

'mommy' and father means 'breadwinner' refuses to be ignored."[11]

In general, husbands of working wives engage in slightly more child care and housework than do husbands of non-working women. A 10-year study on housework by Professor John P. Robinson of Cleveland State University indicated that from 1965 to 1975 the amount of time working women devoted to doing household chores declined from 26 to 21 hours a week. The time men spent on housework during the same period increased from nine to 10 hours weekly. Robinson found that full-time homemakers in 1975 spent about 44 hours a week on housework, a drop from 50 hours in 1965.[12]

The Emotional Impact of Divorce on Men

The way parents relate to their children and to one another has become a growing concern in light of the nation's high divorce rate. Today, over 40 percent of all new marriages are expected to end in divorce. Such separations affect every member of the family. But over the years, it was the impact of divorce on children and their mothers that received most attention. Until recently, the problems of divorced husbands and fathers went largely unnoticed.

Divorce can be a traumatic event for anyone. For men, however, the readjustment to living alone can be particularly trying. The practical problems of day-to-day living prove especially difficult for newly divorced men. Men whose wives had not worked tend to have the hardest time maintaining a household routine. For the first year or two after divorce, a man's lifestyle is frequently erratic. A 1977 survey conducted for *Psychology Today* magazine said that divorced men usually get less sleep, have a harder time organizing their finances, and generally feel less competent handling basic day-to-day tasks.

During the first year following divorce, the survey found, many men also faced serious emotional problems. They "complained of not knowing who they were, of being rootless, of having no structure . . . in their lives. Their separation induced profound feelings of loss, previously unrecognized dependency needs, guilt, anxiety and depression."[13] To fill the void created by divorce, men often take up diversionary pursuits, such as adult education courses and athletics.

While divorced mothers frequently say they feel "trapped," divorced fathers commonly admit to feeling "shut out." Many

---

[11] Robin Gordon, "The Ties that Bind: The Price of Pursuing the Male Mystique," *PEER Report* (a publication of the National Organization for Women), 1980.
[12] John P. Robinson, "Changes in Americans' Use of Time, 1965-1975," Cleveland State University, 1979. See also "Two-Income Families," *E.R.R.*, 1979 Vol. II, pp. 501-520.
[13] E. Mavis Hetherington, Martha Cox and Roger Cox, "Divorced Fathers," *Psychology Today*, April 1977, p. 42.

U.S. Marriages and Divorces

Year	Marriages	Divorces	Divorce Rate (per 1,000 marriages)
1920	1,274,000	170,000	1.6
1930	1,127,000	195,000	1.6
1940	1,596,000	264,000	2.0
1950	1,667,000	385,000	2.6
1960	1,523,000	393,000	2.2
1970	2,159,000	708,000	3.5
1975	2,153,000	1,036,000	4.9
1979	2,317,000	1,170,000	5.3

Source: U.S. Bureau of the Census

divorced fathers see their children less and less as time goes by. Fathers who leave marriages in which there was a high degree of conflict, sometimes find relations with their children improved after divorce. But many say that "a great sense of loss" accompanies separation from their children.

Fathers' Attempts to Gain Custody of Kids

For years, divorced fathers deferred to the conventional wisdom that women were better nurturers than men. But now, increasingly, they are demanding exclusive custody of their children — and sometimes getting it. "That whole 'male mystique' about men not caring as much or not wanting to be with their children is balderdash," said *Newsweek* senior writer Douglas M. Davis, who won exclusive custody of his two daughters after an eight-year legal battle with his former wife. "Yes, it was terrifying to think of raising them alone, because as men we're not raised to think we can do it. But I found delight and joy in being a single parent."[14]

The U.S. Census Bureau reports that there were about 570,000 bachelor fathers in the United States in 1979, up from 500,000 in 1975. Although adoption by single males has contributed to the increase, the main reason is the liberalized attitude of the courts about awarding custody of the children to the father in divorce cases. In the past, fathers had almost no chance of being awarded custody unless they could prove their wives were unfit mothers. Women still wind up with the children in 90 percent of the divorce cases, but this percentage is slowly decreasing. New York, California and Illinois are among those states which have abandoned the "tender years" doctrine — which holds that children generally are better off with their mothers — and amended their laws to specify that either parent can be awarded custody.

Liberalized custody laws are just one sign of the courts' growing recognition of fathers' rights. Earlier this month a jury

[14] Quoted by Daniel D. Molinoff in *The New York Times Magazine*, May 22, 1977.

in Fairfax County, Va., awarded $25,000 to a divorced father who claimed he suffered severe emotional problems because his ex-wife prevented him from seeing his children. An official of the American Bar Association's family law section called the verdict "precedent-setting" and said it would serve as "a warning" to divorced parents who attempt to evade court orders granting visitation rights to their former spouses. "I think this is very important," agreed Paul M. Robinson, acting president of the Washington-area chapter of Fathers United for Equal Rights, a national organization of divorced fathers. "It has always been hard to get the courts to enforce visitation rights."

What happens when a father does win custody? Does he find himself drowning in a sea of peanut butter and jelly, utterly unable to cope? Not necessarily, according to psychologist Frederick Phillips of Washington, D.C. "When men become single fathers they experience anxiety and say to themselves, 'I cannot be what the mother is.' But they can. They can learn how to do the traditional tasks like cooking. Anybody can learn to cook by reading a book." Phillips, speaking at a June 13 conference in Washington on "The Changing Roles of Fathering In Our Society," said that one of the biggest hurdles for new single fathers is learning how to reorder priorities. Instead of earning money, the children become primary, he said, even if that means skipping a business meeting to go to a school play.

Insights Into Male Sexuality

EVERY AGE has had its say about love. But it is doubtful that any era has devoted as much attention to the problems of mating as our own. Never before have there been so many experts — as distinct from sages — to tell people how to conduct themselves in bed. This emphasis on sexual gratification is an outgrowth of the revolt against 19th century Victorianism, which held that sexual relations were a necessary albeit an unsavory part of life. Freud and other prophets of the "new freedom" taught the post-World War I generation that uninhibited sex was a sinless joy.

Next came the sex manuals spelling out what to do, and how to do it. As the social climate became increasingly permissive, these books, and the advice given by a new class of professional sex counselors, became more and more explicit. Today's experts advise variations of sexual behavior once considered "unnatural," if not illegal. Some urge not only a variety of techniques but a variety of partners, before and after marriage.

The current ethos of sexual freedom, reinforced by the ubiquity of the sex motif in plays, movies, television programs and literature, may be less liberating than once assumed. In fact, many mental health specialists believe that the increased attention paid to sexual performance has produced a new generation of psychological problems for both sexes. For many men and women, expectations of erotic performance are simply too high. One therapist put it this way: "Nowadays, you're expected to be great in bed — even on the first date. There's the feeling that if you're not good enough, your partner won't ever want to see you again. . . . This kind of pressure to perform often turns a man or woman off to sex."[15]

Celibacy: Rewards of Doing Without Sex

Some "victims" of the sexual revolution apparently have decided to withdraw from the fray — at least temporarily. They have made a conscious decision to stop having sexual relations. "Just as fasting helps rejuvenate and cleanse the body after too much eating, celibacy affords the soul respite and refreshment when sexual energy needs to be understood," wrote one advocate of the celibate lifestyle.[16]

"The best way to tell if you might be ready to be celibate for a long time is if it feels natural," Gabrielle Brown wrote in *The New Celibacy* (1980). The results of being celibate may lead some men and women back to sex, she speculated. But others may choose to remain celibate because non-sexual experience often "turns out to be more fascinating to them."

The prevalence of the new celibacy is difficult to measure, but sex counselors and therapists report a growing number of patients expressing a lack of interest in sexual intercourse. "Older people have always reported low interest for cultural, psychological and sometimes physical reasons," said Shirley Zussman of the American Association of Sex Educators, Counselors and Therapists. "But now we're seeing more and more of this among young people, males and females in their late twenties and early thirties."

Dr. Bernard Zilbergeld, a clinical psychologist in the human sexuality program at the University of California in San Francisco, has found more men who are contemplating abstinence

---

[15] Quoted by Rose Hartman in "Asexuality: Is Everybody Not Doing It?" *Forum*, January 1979, p. 12.
[16] Carmen Kerr, *Sex For Women Who Want to Have Fun and Loving Relationships With Equals* (1977), p. 109.

than actually practicing it. "The idea is still strange for most guys," he said. "They are afraid they'll end up thinking more about sex than they already are. . . . With women, it's somehow more permissible, but for a man it is still considered 'weird.' "[17]

Men and women always have exhibited different attitudes toward abstinence, according to Paul Solomon. "Throughout the centuries, the sexes have practiced celibacy for very different reasons, with women remaining chaste largely because men *ordered* them to," he wrote last year in *Cosmopolitan* magazine. "Females were best kept celibate, it was thought, lest their rampaging libidinous appetites cause them to betray their husbands and eventually bring the whole of a monogamous society tumbling down. . . ."

"For men, though, chastity has rarely had these 'moral' implications," Solomon continued. "When practiced, it has generally been because the man believed, either expressly or subconsciously, that too-frequent indulgence would drain his power, that women rob men of their potency during the act of sex. Creative geniuses were particularly susceptible to this belief. . . . Modern men, however, have usually been chaste by default, because they couldn't find a woman willing to serve as a sex partner. And with the New Chastity, this problem, rampant in the randy-but-repressed fifties, is back with us again."

While most men do not voluntarily choose sexual abstinence, Solomon said a few are refraining from sex because they find it difficult to relate to today's "liberated" woman. "The woman's movement which accompanied the advent of our sexual freedoms also decreed a new style of behavior for men," he wrote. "They should no longer be *macho* and 'superior,' but instead should behave as supportive *equals*. Many men simply could not cope with the 'demotion' in status and power this change implied."

Myth of Impotent Men and Assertive Women

The theory that the new assertiveness of women would produce a lot of sexually impotent men was, for a time, a popular topic in the news media and even among some sex educators, counselors and therapists.[18] The belief that assertive, competent women discourage the male sex drive has persisted for generations. The fabled allure of the "dumb blonde" and the "vacuous Southern belle" are variations on this general theme.

Dr. Helen S. Kaplan, professor of psychiatry at Cornell University Medical College, believes that male attraction to non-aggressive women may be overstated. "I have always be-

---

[17] Zussman and Zilbergeld were quoted in *The New York Times*, May 1, 1978.
[18] See, for example, Dr. Theodore I. Rubin and David C. Berliner wrote in *Understanding Your Man: A Book for Women* (1977)

lieved that men found assertive, interesting women attractive,"
she said. "After all . . . long before [the current] liberated era,
men left passive dependent wives at home to care for children
and the house while they sought out active, independent women
as mistresses."[19]

Pornography and the Illusion of Control

Many sex entrepreneurs and business analysts say that the
changing social status of women is one factor accounting for
the recent upsurge in pornography and other forms of adult
entertainment.[20] Most adult business patrons are men. Psychi-
atrists believe that a large percentage of those turning to
"commercial outlets" for their sexual needs are seeking in fan-
tasy a sense of control over women that may be vanishing
from real life. "Sexual activity is inextricably entangled with
the rest of our lives," wrote social critic Michael Wood, who
associates pornography with wish fulfillment. The bulk of today's male-oriented sex entertainment, Wood observed, caters
to the fading "illusion" of masculine dominance.[21]

Traditional relationships between the sexes often put a special burden on men. The male frequently is expected to be
the aggressor, bravely facing down the possibility of rejection.
For the most part, the attraction of pornography, or any type
of "marketed sex," lies in the fact that the element of rejection
is virtually eliminated. But feminist groups complain that
pornography by its very nature is anti-female propaganda. "We
see pornographic material as encouraging a cultural climate
in which men feel that it is their masculine right to use violent
acts against women, to strike out against women in the name
of sexuality," said Susan Brownmiller, author of *Against Our
Will: Men, Women and Rape* (1975).[22]

Feminist leaders say there is an "obvious" connection between exposure to pornography and subsequent criminal behavior. But others see the agitation over pornography as excessive.
"Feminists are anti-modern and anti-individualist," wrote syn-
dicated columnist Joseph Sobran. "Men, to them, are the enemy — less a sex than a brutal conspiracy. The days of oppression are over, but these women can hardly afford to admit
that. Hence the harping on the worst male behavior as if it
were the norm, the loose charges of things like 'anti-woman
propaganda' as if porn were a phase in the War Between the
Sexes."[23]

---

[19] Quoted in "The Myth of the Assertive Woman and the Impotent Male: An Interview
with Dr. Helen Singer Kaplan," *Savvy*, January 1980, p. 87.
[20] See "Pornography Business Upsurge," *E.R.R.*, 1979 Vol. II, pp. 765-780.
[21] Michael Wood, writing in *The New York Review of Books*, May 31, 1979, p. 10.
[22] Quoted in *The Christian Science Monitor*, Oct. 2, 1979.
[23] Joseph Sobran, writing in *The Washington Post*, Sept. 24, 1979.

Problems for the Young and Aging

I N THE PAST few years, the term "mid-life crisis" has become familiar to millions of Americans as a description of what Gail Sheehy, in her book *Passages,* called the "treacherous footbridge between the ages of 37 and 43." After taking stock of their lives in this crucial period, Sheehy said, many people are struck by a sense of panic, a feeling of personal failure, of opportunities missed, things not done. The problem, however, can be particularly devastating for men, especially those who have devoted themselves to their jobs only to find that work alone has not provided them with what they need to be happy.

"The essence of mid-life crisis . . . comes down to two fundamental stresses which impinge on us when we are feeling most vulnerable," Sheehy wrote. "By the early to mid-forties, we have lived out the period in which we could convert the dream [of success] into a goal. Having reached that goal, or fallen short, or never having converted the dream at all, each of us now asks, 'Is there nothing more?' " The second stress, she said, is related to the passage of time, "the new sense of urgency and a very real deadline: the awareness of one's own personal death. It forces all of us to realize that we will never do, or be, all that we had hoped for."[24]

Sometimes the transitional period between being young and being middle aged can turn tragic. Michael E. McGill, author of *The 40 to 60 Year Old Man* (1980), pointed out that mid-life crisis in males usually is marked by "a rapid and substantial change in personality and behavior." In some cases, marriages end and careers are destroyed as men struggle to come to terms with suddenly feeling older. One key to avoiding the more destructive psychological effects of aging, McGill said, is for men to cultivate a "multi-dimensional" sense of self-worth, to have "lots of things that can make them feel worthwhile." Men in the throes of self-reappraisal, he added, "have to be careful to act without destroying the structures that have supported them all along. They should look at their lives as dispassionately as they can and try to separate the good from the bad. Before making decisions that may be irreversible, they should exhaust every possibility for meaning in what they are doing now."

---

[24] Gail Sheehy, "Why Mid-Life is a Time of Crisis for Couples," *New York,* May 1976, p. 107.

Special Problems Facing Black Men

Black men are surrounded by "a fog" of sexual and cultural mythology, Michele Wallace wrote in *Black Macho and the Myth of Super Woman* (1979). "Whether he is cast as America's latest sex object, king of virility and violence, master of ghetto cool, or a Mickey Mouse copy of a white capitalist ... what most people see when they look at the black man is ... myth," Wallace wrote. It is the "internalization" of this myth, she said, that has strained and distorted relationships between black men and black women.

Living in a white-dominated society, the black male frequently is forced to wear a mask of bravado to hide his true feelings about himself and others. This same mask has been an impediment in his dealings with women, according to Robert C. Tucker, assistant professor of psychology at Yale University. "If we permit women to take advantage of us, we are viewed as 'chumps'; if we're openly tender we're viewed as 'punks'; and if we openly show hurt, we're called 'turkeys,'" he said. "Behind all of this categorizing is a pervasive fear that openness will leave a man vulnerable to ridicule and scorn."

Burdens and Pleasures of Living Alone

No way of life has been made to seem more glamorous in recent years than that of the single male. In his most popular form he is glorified as a "swinger" endlessly occupied with seeking and finding good times. But in truth, unmarried men often live lives that differ significantly from that image. Psychologists tend to agree that bachelorhood for the great majority of men is characterized by "drifting" and lack of sustained commitment. Despite the spate of live-alone-and-love-it books, the single life for men can easily be a melancholy existence in which independence and freedom are poor substitutes for missing human connections.

The Census Bureau reports that increasing numbers of young Americans are choosing to stay single longer. The national average age for the first marriage, which was high in the early part of the century, declined steadily until it reached a low of 20.1 for women and 22.5 for men in 1956. Since then, it has risen steadily; by 1979, it was 22.1 for women and 24.4 for men. While both men and women are marrying later, the number of unmarried-couple households has more than doubled since 1970, to 1.3 million.

As more people in the population put off marriage, there inevitably will be a greater sanction given to aspects of the single lifestyle, including casual sexual relationships. Paradoxically, however, the liberalization of attitudes toward sex may only serve to emphasize the loneliness of many single males, who, more than their female counterparts, seem less able to cope effectively with the solitary life.[25] The tendency of divorced men to remarry more quickly than divorced women is pointed to by experts as evidence that women are better equipped than men to "survive" on their own.

Yet it is how they might better live together rather than apart that has always been, and probably will continue to be, the primary concern of both sexes. The simple fact is that men and women not only enjoy but need one another's company. In the end, it is the values they share in common that will determine whether society becomes a fabric of fully integrated sexual citizens or a collection of isolated individuals all in hot pursuit of whatever turns them on.

---

[25] See George Gilder, *Naked Nomad: Unmarried Men in America* (1974).

Selected Bibliography

Books

Friday, Nancy, *Men in Love,* Delacorte, 1980.
Fox, David and Anne Steinmann, *Male Dilemma: How to Survive the Sexual Revolution,* Aronson, 1974.
Goldberg, Herb, *The Hazards of Being Male: Surviving the Myth of Masculine Privilege,* New American Library, 1977.
Hefner, Hugh, M., ed., *Twelfth Anniversary Playboy Reader,* Trident Press, 1967.
Mailer, Norman, *The Prisoner of Sex,* New American Library, 1971.
Mayer, Nancy, *Male Mid-Life Crisis,* Doubleday, 1978.
McGill, Michael E., *The 40 to 60 Year Old Man,* Simon and Schuster, 1980.
Sheehy, Gail, *Passages,* Dutton, 1976.
Talese, Gay, *Thy Neighbor's Wife,* Doubleday, 1980.

Articles

Kaplan, Helen Singer, "The Myth of the Assertive Woman and Impotent Man," *Savvy,* January 1980.
"Male Fantasies," *Time,* Feb. 18, 1980.
Ms., selected issues.
Playboy, selected issues.
Psychology Today, selected issues.

Reports and Studies

Editorial Research Reports: "Single Parent Families," 1976 Vol. II, p. 661; "Changing American Family," 1977 Vol. I, p. 411.
Gordon, Robin, "The Ties That Bind: The Price of Pursuing the Male Mystique," *PEER Report* (a publication of the National Organization for Women), 1980.

Equal Rights Fight

by

Sandra Stencel

**Dec. 15
1 9 7 8**

Editor's Note: No state has ratified the Equal Rights Amendment since Indiana did so in January 1977. The list of states that have voted to rescind or nullify earlier ratifications now includes Kentucky and South Dakota, as well as Idaho, Nebraska and Tennessee. On June 30, 1981, the National Organization for Women and other feminist organizations kicked off a yearlong ERA ratification drive. The deadline for ratification is June 30, 1982.

An Associated Press-NBC Poll taken in May 1981 and published on June 4 found that the public continues to favor the proposed amendment by a wide margin. ERA was supported by 40 percent of those polled, while 25 percent opposed it. About a quarter of those surveyed said they had not heard or read enough about the amendment to have an opinion.

The U.S. Supreme Court, on Oct. 6, 1980, refused to review, thus letting stand, a ruling by the U.S. 8th Circuit Court of Appeals in St. Louis that the ERA economic boycott, mentioned on p. 185, did not violate the Sherman Antitrust Act.

EQUAL RIGHTS FIGHT

THE STRUGGLE to ratify the Equal Rights Amendment (ERA) is beginning to resemble the ordeal of Tantalus — the mythical Greek king who was condemned to perpetual hunger and thirst, with food and water lying just beyond reach. So far, 35 state legislatures have ratified the proposed amendment to prohibit discrimination on the basis of sex *(see box, p. 181)*. Only three more must do so before it becomes part of the Constitution. But it is entirely possible that the ERA will die inches short of its goal. Organized resistance remains strong in all 15 of the remaining states — some of which have defeated the amendment over and over — and no consensus exists on which three states, if any, might raise the total to the required 38.

Congress in October approved a resolution extending the deadline for ratification from March 22, 1979, to June 30, 1982. Passage of the resolution capped a year-long lobbying effort by backers of the amendment and marked the first time Congress had extended the ratification period for a constitutional amendment since it began setting time limits in 1917. Women's rights advocates hope the extension will give momentum to the stalled equal rights drive.

The last state to ratify the ERA was Indiana, which did so in January 1977. Since then the amendment has suffered a string of defeats. In the last two years resolutions to approve the amendment were defeated in Alabama, Arizona, Florida, Illinois, Missouri, Nevada, North Carolina, South Carolina and Virginia. In the other eight unratified states *(see map)*, ERA resolutions did not come up for a vote in 1977 or 1978. Furthermore, legislatures in three states — Tennessee, Nebraska and Idaho — voted to rescind earlier ratifications, although there is a legal question as to whether the rescissions will be permitted to stand *(see p. 193)*.

ERA supporters received a double setback in the November elections when voters in Florida and Nevada — two key states in the ratification drive — decisively rejected proposals which were viewed as test votes on the amendment. Florida voters rejected an amendment to the state Bill of Rights that would have forbidden discrimination against women. In Nevada, an advisory referendum asked voters if they favored passage of the amendment; over half of those going to the polls said no.

ERA proponents are by no means resigned to defeat. They point to public opinion polls which have consistently shown widespread support for the amendment. A poll conducted by the Gallup organization in June 1978 indicated that 58 percent of the respondents favored ratification. A Louis Harris poll conducted the same month found 55 percent in favor of the amendment. Support appears to have increased in the past year after a two-year period of decline. Earlier Harris polls indicated that between 1976 and 1977 the number of Americans favoring passage had dropped from 65 to 56 percent. By February 1978 the number supporting the ERA had dropped to 51 percent.

ERA supporters contend that the results of last month's elections bolstered their chances for winning approval of the amendment. "We are very, very pleased at the strong showing by candidates who support ratification," Mildred Jeffrey, head of the National Women's Political Caucus, said Nov. 9. She said that candidates which the caucus endorsed won 35 of 47 state senate races and 71 of 96 state house races. But opponents of the amendment also saw cause for optimism in the election results. "We feel we gained in every legislature," said Phyllis Schlafly, a leader of the anti-ERA forces.

Growing Resistance to Women's Movement

The extent of the opposition to the Equal Rights Amendment surprised many feminists. When Congress finally passed the amendment on March 22, 1972 — after a 50-year struggle *(see p. 186)* — it seemed like an idea whose time had come. Supporters predicted that it would be ratified well before the original 1979 deadline. Early reaction seemed to promise quick ratification. In the first two years after Congress approved it, 32 states ratified the amendment. But only three more have done so in the four years since then. "Success came too easily and we were not prepared," Dr. Jo Freeman, a political scientist, said recently. "There's always a backlash to social movements, and we were caught sleeping."[1]

Feminists believe that the struggle to ratify the Equal Rights Amendment provides further evidence that Americans remain deeply divided over the role of women in society. Over 50 percent of all adult American women now are in the labor force.[2] Yet a nationwide survey conducted in 1976[3] found that the overwhelming majority of American parents — including three-fourths of the working mothers interviewed — believed that

---

[1] Quoted in *The Christian Science Monitor,* Oct. 19, 1978.

[2] Figures, released by the Department of Labor in October 1978, include women looking for work as well as those actually working.

[3] By Yankelovich, Skelly and White for the General Mills Consumer Center. Results published in "The General Mills American Family Report 1976-77: Raising Children in a Changing Society," 1977.

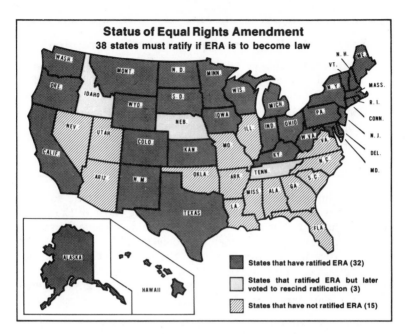

Status of Equal Rights Amendment
38 states must ratify if ERA is to become law

States that have ratified ERA (32)

States that ratified ERA but later voted to rescind ratification (3)

States that have not ratified ERA (15)

women with small children should not work outside the home unless the money is really needed. Nearly 70 percent of the parents said that children were better off when their mothers did not work.

Women's rights groups generally acknowledge that divisions within their ranks over tactics and priorities hampered the ratification effort. They also admit that at first they tended to underestimate the determination and political savvy of the opposition. But most believe that the chief obstacle to ratification has been what they consider unfair tactics on the part of ERA opponents. Legislators in unratified states have been flooded with literature linking the Equal Rights Amendment with lesbianism and the disruption of family life.

Anti-ERA groups argue that the amendment's passage would end alimony and child support, require military conscription of mothers, ban separate washrooms for men and women, and permit homosexual marriages. Feminists dismiss such arguments as ridiculous and charge opponents with deliberately misinterpreting the effects of the amendment. But they concede that such charges have put them on the defensive. "We've found ourselves arguing about women being drafted and losing custody of their children, instead of discussing discrimination in housing, insurance and credit," said New York lawyer Brenda Feigen Fasteau. "We cannot spend all our time telling our opponents how wrong they are and not go after the votes of grass-roots politicians."[4]

---

[4] Quoted in *Newsweek,* July 25, 1977, p. 35.

Text of the Proposed Equal Rights Amendment

Section 1. Equality of rights under the law shall not be denied or abridged by the United States or by any State on account of sex.

Section 2. The Congress shall have the power to enforce, by appropriate legislation, the provisions of this article.

Section 3. This amendment shall take effect two years after the date of ratification.

Those who oppose the Equal Rights Amendment do so for a variety of reasons. A common thread linking most of the opponents is the fear that the amendment would somehow overturn the traditional role of women in society. This, they believe, would be detrimental to the family, the church and the nation. In the minds of many opponents, the amendment is invariably linked with other issues they oppose — abortion, government-sponsored day care, sex education, gay rights.

Some opponents concede that women have been discriminated against. But they argue that specific legislation, such as equal-pay and equal-credit laws, are a better remedy than a sweeping constitutional amendment. Some admit that they personally have benefitted from improved opportunities for women in recent years. But they do not want to be associated with the "militant women-libbers" who, they say, are pushing the Equal Rights Amendment.

In most states conservative political groups and fundamentalist churches have led the opposition. Mormons, for example, have been instrumental in preventing ratification in Utah, Nevada and Arizona. The hierarchy of the Catholic Church has shown strong opposition to the amendment. A major committee of the National Conference of Catholic Bishops last May refused to endorse the amendment on the ground that it would, as one spokesman said, "pave the way for more abortions." On the other hand, many priests, nuns and lay members of the Church have indicated support for the amendment.

The nation's leading foe of the Equal Rights Amendment is Phyllis Schlafly of Alton, Ill. Long active in conservative Republican politics and a three-time unsuccessful candidate for Congress, Mrs. Schlafly publishes a monthly newsletter called the *Phyllis Schlafly Report* and has written eight books, the best known of which is *A Choice Not an Echo,* which boosted the 1964 presidential candidacy of Barry M. Goldwater. It was in the February 1972 issue of the *Phyllis Schlafly Report* that Mrs. Schlafly first publicly attacked the Equal Rights Amendment, then pending in Congress. To help in her anti-ERA campaign, she set up an organization called Stop-ERA, and it has chapters across the country. Later she established a second group, the Eagle Forum, which she called her answer to "women's lib" and it, too, joined the fight against the proposed amendment.

Since 1972 Schlafly has campaigned tirelessly against the ERA, which she calls the "extra responsibility amendment." In her view it would give women no new rights and it would take away some old ones while adding new responsibilities. "The claim that American women are downtrodden and unfairly treated is the fraud of the century," she once said. "The truth is that American women have never had it so good. Why should we lower ourselves to 'equal rights' when we already have the status of special privilege."[5]

Mrs. Schlafly has concentrated her opposition to the Equal Rights Amendment primarily around the issues of military service and financial support laws. In her latest book, *The Power of the Positive Woman* (1977), she contends that the amendment would "require mothers to be drafted" and "invalidate all the state laws that require the husband to support his wife and family and provide them with a home."[6]

Reaction of Supporters to Recent Setbacks

Women's rights activists have reacted to the backlash with a mixture of rage and frustration. But the success of the opposition has forced them to reassess their strategies. "ERA proponents, armed with what they regarded as the righteousness of their cause . . . neglected the political tactics by which any cause must be advanced," Roger M. Williams observed in 1977.[7] Williams also criticized ERA proponents for placing most of their state campaigns in the hands of feminist activists and female legislators.

"While [these women] may 'deserve' to direct the battle," he wrote, "they are seldom the best people for the job — the former because their ideological commitment is ill-suited to a political arena, the latter because they are vastly outnumbered, relatively inexperienced and, on this issue, seldom willing to make the routine trade-offs that would improve the chances of success." While some feminists might regard Williams' remarks as sexist, few could deny that in many of the unratified states ERA supporters were outmaneuvered by opponents who skillfully lobbied state legislators.

Feminists have made a concerted effort in recent years to broaden their appeal. The National Organization for Women, the largest of the women's rights groups, has doubled its mem-

[5] Quoted by Lisa Cronin Wohl in "Phyllis Schlafly: The Sweetheart of the Silent Majority," *Ms.*, March 1974, pp. 55-56.

[6] Phyllis Schlafly, *The Power of the Positive Woman* (1977), pp. 72, 99.

[7] Roger M. Williams, "Women Against Women," *Saturday Review*, June 25, 1977, p. 13.

bership in the past 18 months. Much of the credit is given to NOW's president, Eleanor Smeal, who identifies herself as a Pittsbugh housewife. "By assuring women that the movement is not trying to force them out of their homes, she has projected a new image of the organization and expanded its constituency," a recent article in the *Christian Science Monitor* noted.[8]

Concentration of Lobbying in Four States

Amendment backers are concentrating their lobbying efforts in four states — Florida, Illinois, North Carolina and Oklahoma. Florida long has been considered a must-win state by the amendment's supporters. They were stunned when the Florida Senate narrowly defeated the amendment in April 1977. State Sen. Lori Wilson, who sponsored the resolution, attributed that defeat to the "good ole boy" tradition in southern life.

So far this year the ERA resolution has not been brought up in the Florida legislature. The legislature is not scheduled to convene again until April 2, 1979. Gov. Reubin Askew, who is leaving office in January, had indicated that he might take up the issue at a special session of the legislature in December. But because proponents could not assure him that they had the votes for ratification, ERA was left off the agenda. ERA's prospects in Florida also were hurt when the state's voters in November rejected an amendment to the state's constitution that would have banned discrimination on the basis of sex.

Illinois, the only northern industrial state that has not ratified the amendment, has been a special source of frustration for ERA proponents. To pass in Illinois, the amendment must be approved by a three-fifths vote of each house. Last June the Illinois House of Representatives twice rejected the amendment, despite a personal appeal from President Carter, the support of Republican Gov. James R. Thompson and a massive lobbying effort by the League of Women Voters.[9]

ERA has been the subject of repeated votes in the Illinois legislature during the past six years. Before the two June ballots, the House had voted on the amendment six times and the Senate five times. In 1975 the amendment passed with 113 votes in the House, only to be bottled up in a Senate committee. ERA supporters still insist they can win in Illinois, but a spokesman for ERA-America, a coalition of some 200 groups supporting the amendment, recently said that the outlook was "quite iffy." In North Carolina, the amendment appears to have lost ground, ac-

---

[8] *Christian Science Monitor,* Oct. 19, 1978. At its annual meeting in Washington, D.C., on Oct. 8, NOW voted to focus most of its resources during the next year on the ERA ratification drive.

[9] The second vote, on June 22, was 105 to 71, just two votes short of the number needed for approval. The first vote, on June 7, fell six short of ratification; five black legislators who had been considered supporters of the amendment abstained because of a dispute with the House leadership.

cording to an analysis of the November election results by *The New York Times.*[10]

Supporters believe that there now are just 21 solid "yes" votes in the state Senate, five short of the 26 needed for ratification. They are afraid that anti-ERA forces will seek a Senate vote on the amendment shortly after the legislature convenes Jan. 10, in the hope that it will fail. ERA backers also face an uphill battle in Oklahoma, where the amendment has failed three times in the House but passed once in the Senate. The amendment has the support of Oklahoma Gov.-elect George Nigh.

Prospects for the amendment in the other 11 unratified states are not good, at least not next year. Many of the remaining states are in the South *(see map)*, where support for the amendment is lowest. Supporters thought they had a chance last year in Virginia, where the amendment had the support of the state's labor unions. But their efforts failed when the House Privilege and Elections Committee refused to bring the question to the floor for a vote.

Debate Over Impact of Economic Boycott

Virginia and the 14 other ERA holdouts are paying a price for their opposition. Over 50 business, political and professional associations have agreed not to hold their conventions in states that have not ratified the amendment. The list includes the Democratic National Committee, the League of Women Voters, the National Council of Churches, the National Education Association, the American Psychological Association and the United Auto Workers union.

The boycott, which is backed by the National Organization for Women, has had considerable impact on such big convention cities as Atlanta, New Orleans, Chicago and Miami Beach. There are no exact figures on overall losses incurred in these and other cities, but estimates run into the millions. The Chicago Convention and Tourism Bureau estimated that as of September 1977 the city had lost $15 million. As a result, the bureau passed a resolution supporting the ERA and urging state legislators to ratify it.

Missouri officials have estimated that the ERA boycott has caused the loss of at least $1.1 million in convention business in the Kansas City area alone. The estimate was included in an antitrust suit filed by the state against the National Organization for Women last February. The suit alleges that the boycott constitutes an illegal restraint of trade. Representatives of several national organizations testified in U.S. District Court in Kansas City Nov. 7 that NOW did not influence their decisions

---

[10] *The New York Times*, Nov. 27, 1978.

to move their conventions out of unratified states. U.S. District Court Judge Elmo B. Hunter indicated that he will not issue a ruling in the case until early next year.

Some persons worry that the boycott could intensify opposition to the amendment. The tactic has been criticized even by some ERA supporters. Morris B. Abram, a New York lawyer, wrote last year: "As long as the equal protection clause of the Constitution stands, as long as free speech lasts, as long as women have the right to vote...there is no dire emergency that requires or justifies the holding of the people of whole states hostages on a campaign to enact a constitutional amendment."[11] Despite such criticism, ERA proponents are pressing ahead with the boycott. In fact, some are convinced that the amendment already would be law if the boycott had been initiated sooner.

Long Struggle for ERA Passage

THE EQUAL RIGHTS AMENDMENT has been a source of controversy since it first was proposed in the early 1920s. Endorsed by one wing of the suffrage movement and opposed by the other, the amendment "embroiled the woman's movement in bitter strife and as much as anything else prevented the development of a united feminist appeal," William Henry Chafe wrote in 1972.[12]

The conflict over the Equal Rights Amendment can be traced back to the split between the more militant and conservative suffragettes. The militants, led by Alice Paul, founder of the National Woman's Party, turned to picketing, hunger strikes and other radical tactics when their lobbying efforts failed to persuade more congressmen to give woman the vote. The more conservative suffragettes, led by the National American Woman Suffrage Association (NAWSA), thought such actions would antagonize the people who would be needed for the suffrage movement to succeed.

The split between the two wings of the suffrage movement widened after the Nineteenth Amendment was ratified in 1920, giving women the right to vote. The conservatives felt their mission was accomplished, and turned their attention to an array of social reforms, including wage-hour laws, child-labor bans, social security and welfare measures, provisions for maternal-child health and other public health programs.

---

[11] Writing in *The New York Times*, Dec. 29, 1977.
[12] William Henry Chafe, *The American Woman: Her Changing Social, Economic and Political Roles, 1920-1970* (1972), p. 113.

The more radical suffragettes, on the other hand, viewed the vote as only an intermediate step on the road to full sexual equality. Only by inscribing the principle of female equality in the basic law of the land, they maintained, could women achieve true parity with men. The National Woman's Party in 1921 embarked on a campaign for an Equal Rights Amendment. Such a proposal first was introduced in Congress in 1923 by two Kansas Republicans, Sen. Charles Curtis and Rep. Daniel R. Anthony Jr. "The Woman's Party wished to eliminate in one blow all remaining laws which distinguished between men and women," William Henry Chafe wrote. "To campaign in each state for piecemeal reform, the feminists reasoned, would take years of effort. Consequently they relied on a blanket amendment which would outlaw all discriminatory legislation throughout the country."[13]

Continued Opposition to ERA During 1940s

Congress showed little interest in the Equal Rights Amendment from 1923 to 1940, safely burying the measure in committee year after year. The Woman's Party, the National Federation of Business and Professional Women and other early supporters continued to lobby for it, arguing that only a constitutional guarantee could eliminate continuing discrimination against women. In 1940, 11 states provided that a wife could not hold her own earnings without her husband's consent; 16 states denied a married woman the right to make contracts; seven states favored the father in custody cases; over 20 states prohibited women from serving on juries. Early supporters of the Equal Rights Amendment were particularly concerned about laws fixing the conditions under which women could be employed. In the mid-1940s, 43 states limited the daily and weekly hours a woman could work outside the home; 15 states prohibited night work for women.

Many states in the 1940s restricted the types of jobs women could hold. In Pennsylvania, for example, women were prohibited from working as crane operators, welders, truckers, meter readers, or on railroad tracks or in boiler rooms. At least 17 states prohibited women from working in the mines. Ohio had the longest list of occupational restrictions. Women were banned from bowling alleys, pool rooms and shoe-shine parlors; they could not handle freight or baggage, operate freight elevators, guard railroad crossings, or operate vehicles for hire.[14]

Opposition to the Equal Rights Amendment remained strong during the 1940s. Among the organizations which were prominent in the campaign against the amendment were the National

---

[13] *Ibid.*, p. 116.

[14] "Summary of State Labor Laws for Women," Women's Bureau, Department of Labor, August 1944.

League of Women Voters, the National Women's Trade Union League, and the American Association of University Women. In 1944 a "National Committee to Defeat the Un-Equal Rights Amendment" was organized. It included representatives from 42 organizations, among them the American Federation of Labor (AFL), the Congress of Industrial Organizations (CIO), American Civil Liberties Union, National Farmers Union, American Federation of Teachers, Young Women's Christian Association, and the National Councils of Catholic Women, of Jewish Women and of Negro Women.

The amendment was opposed by Frances Perkins, President Roosevelt's Secretary of Labor, and by the director of the Labor Department's Women's Bureau, Mary Anderson. Anderson denounced the amendment as "vicious," "doctrinaire"and "a kind of hysterial feminism with a slogan for a program." She also said it would be meaningless "because most of the real discriminations against women were a matter of custom and prejudice and would not be affected by a constitutional amendment."[15]

Attempt to Preserve Protective Legislation

What bothered Anderson and the other opponents of the amendment the most, especially organized labor, was its potentially destructive effect on protective legislation for women. The amendment, they feared, would endanger wage and hour laws for women, undermine support laws for wives and children, and terminate special penalties in the law for rape and sexual offenses against women. Secretary Perkins, testifying before the Senate Judiciary Committee in 1945, said that special labor laws for women represented a realistic recognition of biological differences which no constitutional amendment could alter. Their effect, she said, had been to lessen inequalities between men and women in industry.

ERA supporters argued that the position of working women could be improved by the removal of protective legislation based on sex. Many of the conditions originally cited to justify special laws, they pointed out, had improved by the 1940s. The only purpose of protective legislation, Maud Younger wrote in 1934, was "to lower women's economic status, keep them in the ranks with little chance for advancement...and perpetuate the psychology that they are cheap labor and inferior to other adult workers."[16]

Most ERA supporters insisted that they were not advocating the removal of all protective legislation, but merely the removal

---

[15] Mary Anderson, *Women at Work* (1951), pp. 163, 168.

[16] Maud Younger, "The NRA and Protective Laws for Women," *Literary Digest,* June 2, 1934, p. 27.

of the sex basis in most protective laws. "Protective legislation," said Alice Paul of the National Woman's Party, "should be made to apply to everyone alike so that industrial conditions may be definitely improved."[17]

Public and Congressional Support in 1970s

While women's groups argued among themselves about the ramifications of an Equal Rights Amendment, the fight for approval continued in Congress. From the late 1940s to 1970 the proposed amendment remained buried in the House, but it was favorably reported out of Senate committees or subcommittees at least ten times.[18] The first time the amendment was voted on by the full Senate was 1946 and it was defeated. The Senate in 1950 and 1953 passed resolutions to place the amendment before the states for ratification, but both times with a rider which supporters of the amendment said would have made it meaningless. The rider, introduced by Sen. Carl Hayden, D-Ariz., stated that the amendment "shall not be construed to impair any rights, benefits or exemptions now or hereafter conferred by law upon members of the female sex."

Support for the amendment picked up in the 1960s and early 1970s. Among its staunchest advocates during this period was the National Organization for Women, founded in 1966 by Betty Friedan, author of *The Feminine Mystique*.[19] Interest in the amendment also spread to civil libertarian groups, such as the American Civil Liberties Union (ACLU), and to government agencies. The Department of Labor, which for decades had opposed the ERA, switched its position in 1969 when Elizabeth Duncan Koontz became director of the department's Women's Bureau. The Citizens Advisory Council on the Status of Women[20] endorsed the amendment for the first time in February 1972. The council's Feb. 12 bulletin stated that "ratification. . . is the most effective and expeditous method of securing equal protection of the laws for women, who lag 40 years behind minority groups in achieving constitutional protection."

Among those who changed their position on the amendment during this period was Rep. Edith Green, D-Ore. She told her House colleagues on Oct. 12, 1971: "In the past I rejected the idea of an Equal Rights Amendment, arguing . . . that wrongs

---

[17] Quoted by June Sochen in *Movers and Shakers: American Women Thinkers and Activists, 1900-1970* (1973), pp. 118-119.

[18] See Mary A. Delsman, *Everything You Need to Know about ERA* (1975), p. 30, and "Equal Rights Amendment," *E.R.R.*, 1946 Vol. I, pp. 217-236.

[19] In *The Feminine Mystique* (1963), often referred to as the bible of feminism, Friedan denounced the forces in society that depicted women as sexpots or idealized them as perfect housewives and mothers.

[20] The council was established by executive order of the president in 1963 to advise government agencies on the status of women.

could be righted, and more quickly, through the legislative process and through the courts. But through the years I have watched the legislative actions on both the national and state levels and I have come to the conclusion that I was wrong . . . and that the groups who supported the Equal Rights Amendment were correct."

Increased public support for the amendment was translated into increased support in Congress. In July 1970, Rep. Martha W. Griffiths, D-Mich., succeeded in extracting the proposal from the House Judiciary Committee, a burial ground for the measure in years past, by getting the required 218 signatures of members on a discharge petition. The measure then went to the floor for debate. Less than a month later, on Aug. 10, 1970, the House approved the equal rights measure by a 350-15 vote.

The House-passed measure was placed directly on the Senate calendar, without approval by the Senate Judiciary Committee. After three days of debate in October, senators added two amendments to the ERA resolution — one upholding existing laws exempting women from the military draft and another guaranteeing the right of non-denominational prayers in public schools. Passage of the amendments was tantamount to defeat of the bill because it meant that a House-Senate conference would have been required to resolve differences between the two versions. The leader of the House conferees would have been Emanuel Celler, D-N.Y., chairman of the House Judiciary Committee, who for 20 years had refused to hold hearings on the Equal Rights Amendment in the House. The Senate adjourned without taking a final vote on the ERA resolution and the measure died at the end of the 91st Congress.[21]

The House approved the measure again in October 1971, after stripping it of a provision which the House Judiciary Committee had added, stating: "This article shall not impair the validity of any law of the United States which exempts a person from compulsory military service or any other law of the United States or of any state which reasonably promotes the health and safety of the people." Women's rights advocates argued that the effect of the additional language would be to undermine ERA's usefulness. In the Senate, a companion measure was introduced by Birch Bayh, D-Ind. But Senate action was postponed until 1972, partly due to the illness of Bayh's wife, Marvella, who was recovering from a cancer operation.

The chief Senate opponent of the Equal Rights Amendment was Sam J. Ervin Jr., D-N.C. Ervin asserted that the amendment, which he called the unisex amendment, would "have a

---

[21] See *1970 CQ Almanac*, p. 706.

most serious impact upon the social structure of America and for that reason, in my opinion, would constitute evil."[22] He said if the amendment were ratified, women would be conscripted into the armed services "and sent into battle to have their fair forms blasted into fragments by the bombs and shells of the enemy." He agreed that the "traditional customs and usages of society undoubtedly subject women to many discriminations." But he went on to say that since these discriminations "are not created by law, they cannot be abolished by law. They can be altered only by changed attitudes in the society which imposes them." Amending the Constituton to correct harm done by outmoded state laws, Ervin concluded, "would be about as wise as using an atomic bomb to exterminate a few mice."

Despite Ervin's opposition, the Senate finally approved the Equal Rights Amendment on March 22, 1972, and sent it to the states for ratification. Less than two hours later, Hawaii became the first state to ratify it. By the end of 1972, 21 other states had followed suit. But the problems which were to plague the ratification drive quickly became apparent. By January 1973, *The New York Times* was reporting that ratification of the Equal Rights Amendment no longer looked like a sure thing.

Future of the Ratification Drive

HAVING STRUGGLED so long and so hard to get the Equal Rights Amendment through Congress, many feminists find it difficult to accept the possibility that the amendment might not be ratified by the requisite 38 states. If the ERA is blocked, Betty Friedan said last spring, "it will be politically disastrous . . . . We will be set back 50 years." NOW President Eleanor Smeal concurred. Defeat of the amendment, she said, "might give a false message to the courts and state legislatures that the country does not want to have a policy against sex discrimination. The unthinkable risk is that we might go backward in the gains for women."[23]

Some feminists worry about the effect that defeat would have on the morale of the women's movement. But Gloria Steinem, the founder of *Ms.* magazine, insists that the feminist drive will persist even if the amendment fails to be ratified. "Some people would be very discouraged and bitter for six months, and I'm sure a few would never come back," she said. "But there's no

---

[22] Senate floor debate March 20, 1972.

[23] Both Friedan and Smeal were quoted in *The New York Times,* May 31, 1978.

turning back. No matter how discouraged we get, looking at where we've come from is more than enough to keep us moving ahead."[24]

Since The Equal Rights Amendment resolution was passed by Congress in 1972, new federal and state legislation and court decisions have provided women equal credit, educational and employment opportunities and moved to eliminate inequities in Social Security benefits.[25] But Steinem and other women's rights advocates stress that there still are thousands of laws on the books that discriminate against women. In a title by title review of the U.S. Code released in April 1977, the U.S. Commission on Civil Rights found hundreds of federal statutes that contained "unwarranted sex-based differentials."[26]

The cumulative effect of the sex-bias in the U.S. Code, the commission stated in a later report, "was to assign to women, solely on the basis of their sex, a subordinate or dependent role."[27] A report on the employment prospects of professional women and minorities released in November 1978 by the Department of Labor found that women with college degrees earned substantially less in 1976 than white male high school dropouts. According to Betty M. Vetter, co-author of the report, white men who dropped out of high school earned an average of $9,379 in 1976; white women with college degrees averaged $7,176.

Attempts to Determine Amendment's Effects

Whether or not the Equal Rights Amendment is ratified, there undoubtedly will be plenty of lawsuits over sex discrimination for years to come. If the amendment is adopted, the lack of specifics in its language leaves lots of room for interpretation by the courts. "The language of the ERA is written in the same grand manner in which many constitutional guarantees have been written," UCLA Law Professor Kenneth L. Karst said last year. "That's an advantage to courts in the long run. But in the near future . . . lots of litigation will be required."[28]

If the courts are called on to interpret the Equal Rights Amendment, they will rely to a large degree on its legislative history as contained in the Senate Judiciary Committee's 1972 report recommending its approval.[29] The report states, in part:

---

[24] Quoted in *The New York Times,* May 31, 1978.
[25] See "Reverse Discrimination," *E.R.R.,* 1976, Vol. II, pp. 561-580; "Women in the Work Force," *E.R.R.,* 1977 Vol. I, pp. 121-142; and "Burger Court's Tenth Year," *E.R.R.,* 1978 Vol. II, pp. 681-700.
[26] "Sex Bias in the U.S. Code," U.S. Commission on Civil Rights, April 1977.
[27] "The State of Civil Rights: 1977," U.S. Commission on Civil Rights, February 1978, p. 23.
[28] Quoted in the *Los Angeles Times,* Nov. 21, 1977.
[29] "Equal Rights for Men and Women," Senate Judiciary Committee, 92nd Congress, 2nd session (1972).

Essentially, the amendment requires that the federal government and all state and local governments treat each person, male and female, as an individual. It does not require that any level of government establish quotas for men or for women in any of its activities; rather, it simply prohibits discrimination on the basis of a person's sex. The amendment applies only to government action; it does not affect private action or the purely social relationships between men and women.

Most experts agree that the amendment would require that qualified women, as well as men, be subject to the draft and that the full range of military activities, including combat duty, be open to women. It would ban sexually segregated public schools and require that the obligations of spouses toward one another and of parents toward their children be defined in sexually neutral terms. But as the legislative history makes clear, there would be some key limitations to the general rule of sexual equality under the law. These exceptions occur for (1) situations which relate to the individual's constitutional right to personal privacy and (2) situations which relate to a unique physical characteristic of one sex. Thus the Equal Rights Amendment would not require both sexes to share restrooms or that colleges, prisons and the military services put men and women in the same barracks or dormitories.

Perhaps the best evidence of what the Equal Rights Amendment would mean comes from the 16 states that have written equal rights amendments into their own constitutions.[30] "The general trend, both in terms of common-law doctrines and statutory law, has been for courts in ERA jurisdictions to strike down outdated or unreasonable restrictions on one sex and to extend important rights, benefits and obligations to members of both sexes."[31] In Illinois, for example, a court ruled that under the state's equal rights amendment, a mother may not automatically be preferred over the father in deciding child custody after divorce. A state university in Texas was told that the state amendment required it to provide on-campus housing for men as well as women and to allow women as well as men to live off campus.

The state Supreme Court in Washington ruled that husbands as well as wives should not be denied unemployment benefits for leaving work to follow their spouses to a new location under

---

[30] In nine of the states — Colorado, Hawaii, Maryland, Massachusetts, New Hampshire, New Mexico, Pennsylvania, Texas and Washington —— the equal rights provisions closely resemble the federal amendment. In the other seven states — Alaska, Connecticut, Illinois, Montana, Utah, Virginia and Wyoming — the state provisions vary, but most are less inclusive than the federal proposal.

[31] Barbara A. Brown, Ann E. Freedman, Harriet N. Katz and Alice M. Price, *Women's Rights and the Law: The Impact of the ERA on State Laws* (1977), p. 32.

appropriate circumstances. The Pennsylvania Supreme Court ruled that a husband may no longer be presumed to be the sole owner of property acquired during the marriage, even if he paid for most of it.

Expected Challenges to Rescission Attempts

The future of the Equal Rights Amendment is clouded by several unresolved issues. Opponents of the measure, led by Phyllis Schlafly, have promised to challenge in the courts the resolution extending the ratification deadline to 1982. The courts will be asked to decide whether Congress had the power to extend the deadline and whether an extension would require a simple majority vote of the House and Senate, as was the case, or whether it would require a two-thirds vote.

Although Article V of the Constitution specifies how many states must ratify an amendment before it becomes law, it is silent on the question of how long the process may take. The Supreme Court ruled in 1921 *(Dillon v. Gloss)* that ratification should come "within some reasonable time after the proposal." On the question of what constitutes a "reasonable limit of time for ratification," the court held in 1939 *(Coleman v. Miller)* that it is a political matter which Congress is empowered to determine.

Until 1919 Congress set no time limits on the passage of constitutional amendments. The Eighteenth Amendment (Prohibition) was the first to specify a deadline for ratification. Three subsequent amendments contained a deadline in their texts. Since 1951, the time limitation has been included in resolutions proposing amendments rather than in the amendments. Traditionally, seven years has been the maximum time allowed.

Another unanswered question in ERA's future is whether the states can rescind ratification. In recent years the legislatures of four states — Nebraska, Tennessee, Idaho and Kentucky — have voted to rescind earlier approval of the Equal Rights Amendment. But in Kentucky, the rescission bill was vetoed by Lt. Gov. Thelma Stovall who was acting governor while Gov. Julian Carroll was out of the state. During the debate over extension of the ratification deadline, opponents argued that it would be unfair to allow the states more time to approve the Equal Rights Amendment without giving those states that had ratified it a chance to change their minds. In approving the extension bill, however, the Senate rejected a rescission amendment sponsored by Jake Garn, R-Utah.

The constitutionality of rescission never has been tested. The Department of Justice takes the position that once a state has

> ## Amending the Constitution
>
> Article V of the U.S. Constitution provides two methods for amending the Constitution — (1) via a convention called by Congress at the request of the legislatures of two-thirds of the states or (2) by a two-thirds majority vote of each house of Congress. Of the two methods only the latter has been used. An amendment that is proposed by Congress or by a Constitutional convention does not become part of the Constitution until after it is approved, or ratified, by the legislatures of three-fourths of the states or by constitutional conventions in three-fourths of the states. Congress determines which form of ratification will be employed. The president has no formal authority over constitutional amendments (his veto power does not extend to them); nor can governors veto legislative approval of amendments.

ratified a proposed amendment it cannot reverse the decision. Assistant Attorney General John M. Harmon told the House Judiciary Subcommittee on Civil and Constitutional Rights in November 1977 that Article V of the Constitution "gives the states the power to ratify a proposed amendment, but not the power to reject." ERA opponents disagree. They point out that although the Constitution only gives Congress the power to make laws, no one questions the authority of Congress to repeal laws.

Many legal experts, including Harvard Law Professor Laurence H. Tribe, contend that the final determination on rescission will rest with Congress. Before the amendment becomes law, Congress must certify that 38 states properly ratified it. At that time Congress will decide whether a state that rescinded its ratification should be included among the 38 ratifiers. The only historical precedent for this occurred when Congress ignored rescission attempts by Ohio and New Jersey in the ratification of the Fourteenth Amendment. Although the courts are likely to defer to Congress' judgment on rescission, Tribe added that "in a very close case, the courts might agree to review the congressional decision."[32]

Whatever the fate of the Equal Rights Amendment, the battle over ratification has had important side effects. It has prompted legislative reform aimed at eliminating sex discrimination from state and federal statutes. It has been at least partly responsible for the dramatic shift in judicial treatment of sex discrimination cases. And, according to Robert O'Leary of Common Cause, it "has served to pump people into the political process in the states more than any other issue."[33] But these achievements will be small comfort to women's rights advocates if the Equal Rights Amendment is not ratified.

[32] Quoted by Robert Shrum in "ERA Extension: All's Fair," *New Times,* Nov. 13, 1978, p. 7.

[33] Quoted by Jeff Mullican in "ERA: Beginning of the End?" *State Legislatures,* March-April 1978, p. 6.

Books

Alexander, Shana, *State-By-State Guide to Women's Legal Rights,* Wollstonecraft, Inc., 1975.

Brown, Barbara A., Ann E. Freedman, Harriet N. Katz, and Alice M. Price, *Women's Rights and the Law: The Impact of the ERA on State Laws,* Praeger, 1977.

Chafe, William Henry, *The American Woman: Her Changing Social, Economic, and Political Roles, 1920-1970,* Oxford University Press, 1972.

Delsman, Mary A., *Everything You Need to Know About ERA,* Meranza Press, 1975.

O'Neill, William L., *Everyone Was Brave: The Rise and Fall of Feminism in America,* Quadrangle Books, 1969.

Ross, Susan C., *The Rights of Women: The Basic ACLU Guide to a Woman's Rights,* Avon, 1973.

Schlafly, Phyllis, *The Power of the Positive Woman,* Arlington House, 1977.

Sochen, June, *Movers and Shakers: American Women Thinkers and Activists, 1900-1970,* Quadrangle, 1973.

Stimpson, Catherine, ed., *Women and the "Equal Rights" Amendment: Senate Subcommittee Hearings on the Constitutional Amendment, 91st Congress,* R.R. Bowker Co., 1972.

Articles

Congressional Digest, June-July 1977.

Ginsburg, Ruth Bader, "From No Rights, to Half Rights, to Confusing Rights," *Human Rights,* May 1978.

Miller, Judith, "ERA in Trouble," *The Progressive,* May 1977.

Mullican, Jeff, "ERA: Beginning of the End?" *State Legislatures,* March-April 1978.

O'Reilly, Jane, "The Bogus Fear of ERA," *The Nation,* July 8-15, 1978.

"The Unmaking of an Amendment," *Time,* April 25, 1977.

"What's Your ERA IQ?" *National Business Woman,* October 1978.

"Why Woman's Lib is in Trouble," *U.S. News & World Report,* Nov. 28, 1977.

Williams, Roger M., "Women Against Women: The Clamor Over Equal Rights," *Saturday Review,* June 25, 1977.

Wohl, Lisa Cronin, "Phyllis Schlafly: The Sweetheart of the Silent Majority," *Ms.,* March 1974.

Reports and Studies

Editorial Research Reports, "Equal Rights Amendment," 1946 Vol. I, p. 217; "Status of Women," 1970 Vol. II, p. 563; "Women's Consciousness Raising," 1973 Vol. II, p. 497; "Reverse Discrimination," 1976 Vol. II, p. 561; "Women in the Work Force," 1977 Vol. I, p. 121; "The Rights Revolution," 1978 Vol. I, p. 441.

United States Commission on Civil Rights, "Sex Bias in the U.S. Code," April 1977.

——"Social Indicators of Equality for Minorities and Women," August 1978.

——"The Federal Civil Rights Enforcement Effort-1977," December 1977.

——"The State of Civil Rights-1977," February 1978.

INDEX